Praise for *Dus*

"My first encounter with *Dungeons 'n' Durags* was with the podcast Ron produces for Ebony's Podcast Network. It's funny, clever, and full of surprises. But nothing prepared me for what he had in store in the book. Ron does a masterful job at tackling provocative topics in a way that often feels uncomfortably raw. It's a hilarious and biting commentary on not only white supremacy ideology, but also points a mirror at Black culture."

—Lavaille Lavette, president and publisher at *Ebony* magazine

"As someone who grew up in a blended family that was wall-to-wall identity struggle (my own included), I tend to love stories about reckoning with who we think we should be. Ron's profound and hilarious journey is like if *Conversations with God* had a baby with *Hollywood Shuffle*. And his love for cinema and popular culture makes it a great read for any cinephile and nerds everywhere. But Ron's voice is wholly his own, and fantastically entertaining, endearing, and truthful. This book is tailor-made for anyone who wants to spend a few hours with a really great storyteller."

—Mishna Wolf, author of *I'm Down: A Memoir*

"It's so important that we tell our stories, and Ron does a masterful job telling his. The same kind of passion and biting wit he's brought to *An Injustice!*, he expresses all throughout *Dungeons 'n' Durags*. He strikes a good balance of biting commentary on white supremacy ideology, as well as some aspects of the Black community, all while lacing it with a self-effacing humor that most people would find unable to share publicly."

—Zuva Seven, founder/editor-in-chief of *An Injustice!* Medium Publication

"It's not often you see Black men, or people in general, get this personal when sharing their stories. I appreciated the authenticity and vulnerability Ron shares in his experiences as a Black man and how a white-dominated world influenced him, as well as his complicated faith journey. Lastly, as a fan of film trivia, how could I not love all the hilarious cinematic homages?"

—**Nichelle Protho**, SVP Loud Sis Productions

"*Dungeons 'n' Durags* is a hilarious, masterfully written love letter to us 'Blerds' and so-called 'Oreos.' Dawson uses humor to seamlessly highlight and unpack his personal experiences and insights as a Black man in America. This book will make you laugh out loud and think deeply about racial identity and what it means to be Black."

—**Brandee Blocker Anderson**, CEO and founder of The Antiracism Academy

"Funny. Smart. Provocative. A hilarious page-turner that pulls no punches at addressing issues of white privilege and hypocrisy in the evangelical church."

—**Talicia Raggs**, writer/producer *The Equalizer*, *NCIS: New Orleans*, and *The Originals*

"I love everything about this book. The way Ron uses popular culture, his excruciating honesty, his humor, and especially the confessions (there's nothing an ex-Catholic likes more than a good confession). It's a timely work!"

—**Peter Crowe**, writer and editor of the humor and satirical collection *Dishonour the Right Thing*

"Witty, sarcastic, hilarious, and, well, blerd-y, this must-read story affirms the diversity within the Black diaspora and reminds us there is room for Durags, D&D, and even, maybe, Ron."

—Chrysta Wilson, racial justice and equity consultant, author of the award-winning cookbook *Kiss My Bundt*

"What is truly GREAT and sets Ron apart is his sincere and ongoing willingness and pursuit of self-examination and laying bare what some might deem his shortcomings, honestly to himself and for all to witness. That pursuit is always aimed at gaining a deeper understanding of the truths of his own humanity and behaving and interacting with others in accordance with that truth. If only there were more like him walking around in the world, it'd be a better place. But the book isn't just about Ron taking his medicine. It's actually spectacularly relatable and entertaining. In fact, as a producer, I know gold when I see it. I'm bound and determined to make it a hit TV show."

—Yolanda T. Cochran, Film & TV Producer/Academy member

"I wouldn't be surprised if there are Trump supporters reading this book who are gonna think, 'How the hell did this motherf*cker get me to read this thing?' Ron Dawson is Black Magic."

—Chris Spencer, handsome comedian, writer, director, producer

DUNGEONS 'N' DURAGS

DUNGEONS 'N' DURAGS

One Black Nerd's Comical
Quest of Racial Identity
and Crisis of Faith

Ron Dawson

CORAL GABLES

Cover Design & Art Direction: Elina Diaz
Cover Photo: dmLemattre Photography
Layout & Design: Katia Mena

For permission requests, please contact the publisher at:
Mango Publishing Group
2850 S Douglas Road, 4th Floor
Coral Gables, FL 33134 USA
info@mango.bz

For special orders, quantity sales, course adoptions and corporate sales, please email the publisher at sales@mango.bz. For trade and wholesale sales, please contact Ingram Publisher Services at customer.service@ingramcontent.com or +1.800.509.4887.

Dungeons 'n' Durags: One Black Nerd's Comical Quest of Racial Identity and Crisis of Faith

Library of Congress Cataloging-in-Publication number: 2022931108
ISBN: (print) 978-1-64250-875-8, (ebook) 978-1-64250-876-5
BISAC category code HUM006000, HUMOR / Topic / Politics

Printed in the United States of America

"You never really understand a person until you consider things from his point of view..."

—Atticus Finch, *To Kill a Mockingbird,*
by Harper Lee

Table of Contents

Definitions

Dungeons & Dragons: a fantasy role-playing game cocreated by Gary Gygax in the 1970s filled with dungeons and dragons (duh), paladins, fighters, wizards, orcs, elves, and a whole assortment of fantastic creatures and characters. Played by only the nerdiest of nerds.

Durag: a silk-like scarf with a tie and small flap hanging down in the rear worn by African Americans (usually men) as a fashion statement. Worn in the '80s to create some fly waves.

Foreword

What can be said about one of the kindest, charmingest, brightest human beings I've ever met? First, we must start from the beginning.

In the '80s, I had two sisters—one biological and one stepsister, who usually stayed with us two weekends a month. Even though I loved them immensely, I always wished I had a younger brother. That wish came true in 1984 in a double gift called the Dawson boys—Ron and Brandon. We had already been family friends, but their parents bought a new home in Hollywood Hills, and they didn't want to leave the South Pasadena school district where we attended school. So they came to live with us.

Elated was an understatement. Now I had two brothers to argue with, fight and get into trouble with, just like all my friends that had male siblings. *Wrong.* That would not be the case with the Dawsons. These two dudes arrived from Bethlehem. Arguing and fighting were something foreign to them. I said to myself, "Who are these perfect motherfuckers?!" They were mannerly, cleaned up after themselves, never backtalked to their parents, got good grades, and went above and beyond to please others. They made me and my sisters look like shit.

My brotherhood with Ron was closer because he and I were closer in age. Only a year apart. We share many stories, from being in youth and government together to breakdancing (which he will discuss in Chapter 14). As well as dungeons and dragons. That's a lie. That was some super-smart shit he and his white and Asian friends were into. I fall more in line with the "durags" portion.

He may not know this because he always said he looked up to me, but I looked up to him. I'm as charming as they come, but it's because I know how to charm. I'm handsome, funny, and try and be in control at all times. Ron's charm was different. He didn't have to put it on, at least, so I thought. From the outside it came naturally. In high school everyone loved him. He was carefree and he had an equal amount of guy friends as girl friends, from all walks of life. And he was smart as fuck. A's came easy to him. An A- would have him wondering what he did wrong and would want to meet with the teacher to see what he could do to get rid of the minus. Who does that?[1] And, he would charm the teacher into getting it done. To me, an A is an A even if the minus was in front of it. But it wasn't charm. I came to realize he had magic...Black Magic.

Ron never asked for anything, but he knew how to get what he wanted. Was he cunning or a manipulator? This is where that magic would come in. I would see him get things he wanted by not asking but getting you to give them to him. I remember we went shoe shopping with his mom and there were some sneakers he wanted. He said to his mom, who was one of the best-dressed women you would've ever met and always gushed when complimented for looking so beautiful, "Look at these." She said, "They are nice, Ronnie, but way too expensive." He then replied, "You're right. I wouldn't want to go to school and have the other kids envious of what I was wearing." He then walked away, as his mom stared, contemplated, and then bought the shoes. I remember thinking, *What the hell did he just do? This dude is incredible.* I then started to apply his Black Magic to get things I wanted in my life.

I remember once walking home from school and I was eating a Snickers and I watched him watch me eat it. I thought to myself, *Let's see what he's going to say to get me to give him a piece.* So I decided to eat it slowly and he stayed back and waited for his opportunity. Finally, after painstakingly being patient, he said to me, on my last bite, mind you, "Is that the kind with the nuts?" I was like, "If you don't get out of here with that bullshit... I know your tricks. I use them." He laughed and said, "Oh," and then he held his stomach, feigned being hungry, and walked off. I was like, "Goddamn, he got me." I ran back and bought him his own.

---

1   Ron here. For the record, I was fine with an A-. (Lol.) Okay. Carry on.

I didn't know there was another level of getting what you wanted. I wouldn't be surprised if Trump supporters reading this book are gonna think, *How the hell did this motherfucker get me to read this thing?* Ron Dawson is Black Magic.

—**Chris Spencer**,
*handsome comedian, writer,
director, producer*

Part 1

Chapter 1:

Bro Log: A "Perfect" Beginning

Guilty pleasures don't define a Black man

I'm currently in the middle of yet another one of my mind-numbingly frustrating and seemingly nonsensical debates with Samuel L. Jackson. Yes, *that* Samuel L. Jackson. Well, technically, it's not really Sam Jackson. It's his character Jules from Quentin Tarantino's *Pulp Fiction*. And to be honest, it's not even really Jules. He's something else (in more ways than one).

Supposedly he's some kind of angel. Or devil. He's conveniently vague about the details. He once quipped that one man's angel is another man's devil. Which, frankly, seems like a crock of shit if you ask me.

Some days he's more devil than angel. I'd say most days he's more devil than angel. He claims to be here to help me, but all he ever seems to do is be a pain in my ass. Like today.

> **Me:** I find it hard to believe I'm the *only* Black man in America that likes that movie.
>
> **Sam:** No. But I'm sure you're the only straight one that would openly admit that shit and broadcast it for the whole goddamn world like a flashing neon sign.

You see what I'm talking about? This is the kind of shit I've been taking from him. And he just kinda shows up whenever it suits his fancy.

It's usually when he has an unsolicited opinion or two about whether something I've said or done is "Black" enough. I don't think he would see it that way. In fact, he would probably find that description an insultingly oversimplified characterization of his purpose; he would most likely exhort me to dig deeper and find some other hidden meaning behind his rote manifestations.

But how else am I supposed to interpret the fact that his Soul Glo drippin' jheri curl ass is showing up now, all because I mentioned that one of my cinematic guilty pleasures is the movie *Pitch Perfect*? I mean, come on. Am I alone here? I know some of y'all be singing along during that riff-off. He's got me so riled up that I'm volleying expletives back at him like there's no tomorrow. Which is unlike me.

> **Me**: What the hell is so wrong with *Pitch Perfect*?
>
> **Sam**: It's not that I have a problem so much with the fact *that* you like that movie. With some bruthas, there's just no accounting for taste.
>
> **Me**: What the fuck does taste have to do with it? It's a *fun* movie! Geeze-us, Sam. Does every fucking movie I like have to be a fucking *Moonlight* to make you happy? Damn!

You see that? *Three* f-bombs in one exchange with no guilt or shame. This ain't good.

> **Sam**: The problem I have, Ronald, is that you seem to be tragically bereft of the slightest idea as to *why* you like it.
>
> **Me**: Um, maybe it's just because it has a bunch of fun and catchy cover tunes, a funny script with witty dialogue, and a nearly pitch-perfect ending. No pun intended.
>
> **Sam**: Of course, that's why you *think* you like it.
>
> **Me**: Not every reason a person likes a movie has to be steeped in significance, Sam.

Sam: And it doesn't bother you that in a movie about talented singers, singers who happen to be singing a whole bunch of songs made famous by Black folk, they barely got any Black people up in there?

Me: What are you talking about? They have Black people in that movie.

Sam starts rubbing his temples like he's got a headache. He tends to do that a lot around me.

Sam: Nigga! Did you just say what I think you said? You sound just like one of them Trump-supporting assholes you waste all your time on Facebook bitching about, who think just because that muthafucka took a picture with Muhammad Ali, he's not a racist. That fucking cast looks like it's right out of White People Central Casting. But they made sure to have just enough tokens so that ignorant muthafuckas like you can say dumb shit like, "They got Black people in it." They got the fat girl. They got the cute, quirky, skinny Asian chick (whose voice is conveniently too soft to be heard. What's *that* shit all about?). And they killed two intersectional birds with one stone by making the one sista gay. And not just gay, but like a straight-up *Orange Is the New Black* kinda butch.

Me: You have a problem with representing the LGBTQ+ community?

Sam: I don't have a problem with that shit at all. I think it's a beautiful thing. But I'm also not asleep as to what the fuckin' deal is. Could it have hurt them to drop in two or three other sistas for the rest of us? Some of us are not as fond of mayonnaise as others if you catch my drift.

I'm pretty sure that was a dig at me. Typical.

Sam: I have a list as long as my arm of fine sistas who can pass for college-aged a cappella singers they coulda got.

Me: *Oh. My. Gosh.* You are like a fucking walking caricature of an angry Black man. Tell me something—do you make it a point to go into local Italian-owned pizza joints and complain about them not having any bruthas up on the wall?

Sam: I bet you've been sitting on that joke for a long time, haven't you?

I can't help but chuckle at his continued uncanny ability to know me so well.

Me: Ha! I *have*, actually. You like it? How was my delivery?

Sam: You better keep workin' on that shit. Netflix ain't gonna be calling your Dave-Chapelle-wannabe ass anytime soon. Regardless, you calling *me* a caricature is like the muthafuckin' kettle calling the pot Black.

I proudly resisted the urge to correct the fact he reversed *kettle* and *pot*. But whatever. I'm sure he was just baiting me anyway.

Me: I'll just assume you're *not* talking about *me* being some kind of caricature of an "Oreo."

Sam: Assume away.

Me: *I'm* a caricature?

Sam: Yes.

Me: Me? You're talking about *me*?

Sam: Did I stutter?

And so it goes. Back and forth. But look at my manners. My momma brought me up better than this. I've been a terrible host. I have no doubt you're confused and disoriented about all of this. Here you thought you were getting an intellectually stimulating, nuanced, and engaging exploration of race relations in America—but instead, right out of the gate, you're getting a vapid tête-à-tête between me and a cinematic cliché. Allow me to start over.

I think the best thing to do is take Vizzini's advice and "go back to the beginning." And as Dame Julie Andrews beautifully sang, "It's a very good place to start."

> **Sam**: Leave it to you to reference two white-ass movies.
>
> **Me**: Are you eavesdropping on my conversations again? I told you that I don't appreciate that shit!
>
> **Sam**: And I told you this ain't a conversation. It's a book, muthafucka!

Lord, have mercy. Strap in. This could be a bumpy ride.

This page intentionally left blank.[2]

---

2 Which allows it to also serve as a metaphorical representation of the white background that is my life.

ROLL CAMERAS.
        SPEED.
                SETTLE.
                      AND...

                              ACTION.

Chapter 2:

Blackness Is My "Super Suit"

The evolution of a Black man

"When any white man in the world says, 'give me liberty, or give me death,' the entire white world applauds. When a Black man says exactly the same thing, word for word, he is judged a criminal and treated like one and everything possible is done to make an example of this bad nigger so there won't be any more like him."

—James Baldwin

How the hell did I get here? What path did I go down that led me to sit for hours on end, typing angrily away on my computer, debating with dumbasses on Facebook? This isn't me. Or, at least, it didn't used to be me.

I am not an "angry Black man." Although, I am angry and I am, well, Black. Don't think the irony of the nuanced distinction isn't lost on me. But I am somewhat of an anomaly—at once both one of the "whitest" Black men you'll meet, but also a proud, "woke," Black-fist-emoji-sharing Black man with a mission to stomp out racial prejudice and help white America recognize their privilege.

In a lot of ways, I feel like *The Greatest American Hero* of Blackness, a 1980s TV show about a mild-mannered, curly-haired teacher visited by an alien race and gifted a suit with superpowers, but he loses the instructions. What ensued was two and a half seasons of kitschy humor and bad writing. An ongoing joke was that he couldn't fly straight and was constantly crashing into things and landing badly as he tried to figure out the suit.

My "super suit" is my Blackness and my Black voice. And like the aforementioned superhero, I'm still figuring out how the suit works. I never attended an HBCU (historically Black college or university) or joined any Black fraternities where I would have gotten proper "training." And except for a short stint of my life when I attended an African American private school, and a few years of public school in the fifth and sixth grades, for most of my life, I've always been one of the few Black people in my circle of friends and coworkers.

So I'm still kinda figuring this stuff out. Or rather, I mean, I'm still kinda figuring this sh*t out.

See, I inherently want to say "stuff." It's that first part of me that doesn't want to perpetuate stereotypes of how Black folk talk.

But I feel like there's this little, itty-bitty version of Samuel L. Jackson sitting on my shoulder like the proverbial "devil," who starts saying, "Just say sh*t,[3] muthafucka!" And for other reasons that will become apparent later, I have a deeply ingrained issue with profanity that dates back to my childhood (my counselor would be so proud).

You see my quandary?

Anyway, so why am I angry? Well, I'm angry this day because I recently finished a rather unproductive (albeit extremely cathartic), five-day (yes, *five frakking[4] days*), back-and-forth senseless debate on Facebook (shocker) with a white man from the South who had all manner of notions as to the ailments of the Black community that he was all too willing to share. This dufus asshole had the caucacity, the unmitigated gall, to call *me* a racist—all because I shared a video of Black conservative commentator and right-wing propagandist Deneen

---

3   For the purposes of this book, I will undoubtedly bounce back and forth between stuff and shit. Consider them totally interchangeable.

4   You will also notice I love to use expletives from *Battlestar Galactica*. It doesn't feel like real cursing to me.

Borelli and called her a modern-day "house negro." (And trust me, she is! I mean, if you look up the definition, I'm sure her picture is there!)

The inane comments that vomited out of this dude's psyche will forever go down in Facebook lore as some of the most incomprehensible, circular logic and tone-deaf drivel ever to come from the mind of a privileged white man (from the South, no less). It wasn't just tone-deaf. It was tone-deaf, blind, and dumb! (But more on that whole ordeal later.)

Over two years ago, I was clean-shaven and wore my hair super short—like Will Smith and Jamie Foxx short. Today, I have a beard and mustache and my hair is more like Donald Glover in *Atlanta* (on a bad hair day, it's more like Childish Gambino in "This Is America.")

But my hirsute hygiene practices just scratch the surface of my racial evolution.

So how did I get here? How did I become "that guy"? That pissed-off Black man cussin' out stupid-ass wypipo on social media and using it (and now this book) to fight the good fight?

How did I go from mild-mannered, "white-people safe," conservative Black Christian raising my hands on Sunday morning to the tunes of Chris Tomlin and Hillsong, to spiritually conflicted, liberal-minded "follower of Jesus" (yet kinda diggin' Buddha too), Tommie Smith-fist-pumping "nigga," dropping f-bombs like it's nobody's bizness? What caused me to give up my fear of offending my white friends and say what's been on my mind? And be damned if Becky and Buford unfriend me.

You could say it was that orange-skinned disgrace of a POTUS who lived at 1600 Pennsylvania Avenue. But he was probably more of a catalyst. It is too easy to blame it all on "He who shall not be named." (Actually, he gets named a *lot* in this book. I just like comparing him to Voldemort.)

So how did it all happen? Well, as Guy Pearce's character Fernand said to Jim Caviezel's Desmond in 2002's *Count of Monte Cristo*, "It's complicated."

You are about to read the true story of how it happened. (Well, it's mostly true. But I have little doubt you'll have any trouble separating truth from, shall we say, creative license.)

And actually, what is "truth," anyway? As iconic filmmaker Akira Kurosawa so deftly illustrated in his film *Rashomon*, there are many sides to the same story. Despite my conservative, Christian upbringing, "truth," in some cases, can be very much relative.

But before we get to all of that, there are a few things you need to know and about three or four warnings I must share with you.

White people, proceed with caution.

Black folk, go easy on a brutha who's just comin' 'round.

Everybody else, pick a side 'cuz I have no doubt you'll relate too.

Chapter 3:

Wypipo Trigger Warning

Dear Caucasians, don't be scurred.

You might have gathered from the subtitle of this book that racial tension in America will play some part in the story that's about to unfold. And you can't have a memoir by an African American man that does not at some point (or lots of points) reference "white privilege."

Now, my experience and research about using that term have shown that many of you of Caucasoid descent in America have a visceral reaction to hearing it. As soon as you do, you shut down and shut out. Your defensiveness goes to "eleven" and you immediately start protesting about reverse racism or how you grew up poor in the Appalachians. You all usually fall into one of four camps.

Camp 1: The Poor White Trash Camp

Some of you will take offense at the remark because you grew up po' white trash and had no privileges. In fact, most Asians and Blacks you've come into contact with were smarter, richer, and/or had way more advantages than you. So the very notion that you somehow have benefited from some kind of leftist, liberal, fairytale notion of white privilege is insulting.

To you, I say, "Congratulations!" I'm happy that you have lived a life where your circumstances have yielded a level of empathy to the plight of people of color that many wypipo can never understand.

And believe me when I say, I sincerely appreciate your stance. I do not take for granted one second that I grew up in the household of a doctor inherently gave me a certain level of economic privilege you did not have.

I hope that you channel that empathy, be patient, and—for at least the time it takes you to read this book—you just give me the benefit of the doubt and accept that there does indeed exist a level of privilege afforded you that transcends economic status.

In the world of *Dungeons & Dragons*, your alignment[5] would most likely be *Chaotic Neutral*.

Camp 2: The "Hey, I'm On Your Side, But..." Camp

A certain segment of white people will read this and recognize white privilege exists, but still kinda feel uncomfortable inside when it's used to describe them. There's that part of you that understands history and the long-term effects of hundreds of years of subjugation and disenfranchisement of an entire race of people can have on society, even when some of the descendants of said subjugated people live a relatively successful, even "privileged" life.

But there's still that tiny voice in you that says, "But really? I mean, we had a Black president. And I do kinda think some of it is overblown." At the end of the day, you sympathize with your fellow people of color who deal with racial injustice, but a part of you still squirms when "white privilege" is brought up.

To you, I say, "Thank you." Seriously. Thank you for standing by and supporting people of color, even when maybe there's a part of you that's

---

5 For the uninitiated, in *Dungeons & Dragons*, "alignment" was one of nine traits your character could have that dictated their ethics and actions and even what disciplines they could practice. They're on a spectrum of *good to evil*, graded as lawful, neutral, or chaotic. Using politicians as examples: President Obama would be Lawful Good, and Bernie Sanders would be Chaotic Good. Trump is most definitely Chaotic Evil, but someone like Steve Bannon would be Lawful Evil. Capeesh?

uncertain. That term may make you uncomfortable for any number of reasons. One of which may be that it's a term that requires all white people to hold up a mirror, and I get that that's uncomfortable.

> **Over time I've learned to hold up that proverbial mirror, and in that learning, I have seen where I have not always been the best ally or have simply just said stupid shit.**

As a man, regardless of my race, I recognize I have benefited from male privilege that may from time to time even trump (no pun intended) some of the privilege white *women* have. But over time I've learned to hold up that proverbial mirror, and in that learning, have seen where I have not always been the best ally, or have simply said stupid shit. I have learned to listen, and in turn, have broadened my appreciation for the plight of women. So I thank you for doing the same.[6]

Alignment: Neutral Good or Chaotic Good

Camp 3: "F*ck You! I No Longer Need to Feel Guilty for Being White"…

(or, the "I didn't enslave you or make you sit in the back of the bus" Camp)

Next is that group of you sick and tired of being made the villain all the time. You're sick and tired of Black people always pulling the race card. You're sick and tired of Affirmative Action. And you're sick and tired of self-righteous liberals (white and Black) who refuse to see that this is [insert whatever year it is because any year after 1968 is a year they think racism is over]. We're not living in the '60s anymore.

The election of Donald Trump has emboldened you. The words of Ben Shapiro and Jordan Peterson inspire you. Black people have just as much privilege as whites—maybe more! (Did I already mention your disdain for Affirmative Action?)

---

6   I can appreciate the fact that even though Gwyneth Paltrow has millions of dollars and has seen more of the world, *my* privilege as a man has allowed me to avoid some horrible circumstances in life she has undergone. I offer that perspective as a possible argument to those of you in Camp #1. Just sayin'.

But trust me on this: if you think you're tired of hearing us complain, we're exponentially more tired of the experiences about which we're complaining. So you have a way to go.

To y'all wypipo, all I can say is if you're reading this book, I commend you. You're most likely not the kind of wypipo who would pick up a book like this (if you're standing in some local bookstore or reading this page on the Amazon.com preview, then this doesn't apply to you; even now I'm sure you're rolling your eyes). For purposes that will be revealed later, I am not yet prepared to call you out or say anything I really want to say. So, suffice to say, if you're at all interested in learning what I really want to say, you're gonna have to grin and bear it. Just have fun with it. Even if you think everything here is total bullshit, I bet you'll still enjoy the ride.

Alignment: Straight-up Chaotic Evil son (some of you are probably smart enough to be *Lawful* Evil. I'm talkin' a very select few).

Camp 4: Woke White Knights

The fourth and final camp of white people are those of you who are not just woke but you're genuinely interested in knowing how you can help fight the good fight. You recognize your privilege, and like the Force, you want to use it for the powers of good. You're smart and self-aware enough to know that the term "white privilege" isn't in and of itself a bad thing. Some of you even walk through life with a metaphorical cat-o-nine tails, whipping yourselves for the guilt and shame you feel for the hundreds, nay, thousands, of years your kind has wrought death and destruction on the world.

To you I say, there, there now. Don't be so hard on yourselves. Me and my kind "see you" (and by "see" you, I mean in a Na'vi, *oel ngati kameie* sort of way). We appreciate your wisdom, compassion, empathy, and desire to help unify the races of this world and make so many wrongs right. You will no doubt have the most fun reading this book.

You are the white knights of the world, and as the only good part of season 8 of *Game of Thrones* showed us, both men and women can bear the term "knight," take up their Valyrian swords of justice, and help join me and others in fighting the onslaught of white walkers making their way 'cross these good lands.

Alignment: Neutral Good, Lawful Good, or Chaotic Good

If you're a white person who's reading this book, whichever camp you fall into, I appreciate you taking this journey with me. I genuinely mean that.

If you're a white person who happens to be a Trump supporter and you're reading this, don't take the next chapter title too personally. It might not even apply to you.

Chapter 4:

Stupid Shit Trump Supporters Say

This is all your fault, Mark Zuckerberg

It's no secret that the evil, sadistic, Russian-hackable algorithms that make up Facebook are designed to optimize engagement.

Or as I like to put it: stir up shit.

Every now and then I see other people post photos and stories about their trips to the French Riviera, or their beautiful grandchildren, or the comical antics of their cats, dogs, and hamsters. And those posts are accompanied by so many comments and likes.

If I post a fun, light-hearted meme or photo, I usually get crickets.

But let me post some provocative commentary about Trump or a critique of the church, and within seconds, I start getting likes; within a few minutes, the comments start rolling in. I'm not joking. I've timed it.

And I know I have only myself to blame. I've fed this monster with every complaint and political critique. I've trained the Facebook algorithms to ignore *my* cute cat video posts or inspirational *Successories* memes.

I guess it's no surprise then that so much of my ire, and really, the fuel for this book, has come out of my frustrations with the dolts and idiots who roam the social media cesspool that is my Facebook feed. I can honestly say without them, this book would not be what it is.

You can't make this shit up

The following statements you are about to read are 100 percent real comments by various Trump supporters. This book is partly dedicated to these, and many others like them, who have lost their Vulcan minds. Thank you for giving me the kick in the ass I needed to tell this story.

And if any of you are reading this and recognize your comment, I hope there are no hard feelings. Consider it like your fifteen minutes of fame—albeit anonymous fame. I hope instead of being insulted you're proud that you made it into a book. It's like winning a major award!

And now, the quotes.

Stupid is as stupid does

In response to a discussion I had with one Trump supporter, the aforementioned stupid guy chimed in and called me stupid, when the first Trump supporter (the one I was having the discussion with), remarkably referred to me as a "nice guy." Mr. Stupid Buttinsky then offered this ironic contribution to the conversation:

> "Good, reasonable people continually bend over backwards to accommodate childish, unreasonable, petulant, deceitful behavior and after awhile you have to call it what it is."

Let that sink in. A Trump supporter described me like this.[7] Hmmm... Who does this description particularly sound like to you?

Apparently "rape culture" is a myth

Remember all the fun we had on social media when Dr. Christine Blasey Ford had to testify before the Senate during Brett Kavanaugh's

---

7   I am big enough to admit that sometimes I *can* be petulant. But the times when I am are few and far between. I can barely remember the last time I was pet...no, wait. Now I remember.

Supreme Court confirmation hearings? You know, the "job interview" for the highest court in the land where BK lost his collective shit in front of the Senate, displaying the judicial prudence and decorum of a spoiled and privileged teenager? Ah, those were good times.

If you recall, Dr. Ford had accused Brett of sexual assault during the summer of 1982 when they were in high school. According to Brett's supporters, Dr. Ford made the whole thing up, forever changing her life and enduring sheer hell, perhaps ruining her career, all so that she could someday write a book or some such nonsense. One astute TSer on my feed made this profound sociological observation:

> "Dr Ford's testimony, full of pertinent things she can't remember and inconsistencies, does not promote RAPE CULTURE. There is no rape culture in America. If a woman on this planet wants to be safe from rape, America is where she would want to be or anywhere with an Anglo-Saxon Christian Judeo culture and social mores."

There is no rape culture in America? This is the kind of stupid shit privileged white men say all the frakking time. Let's forget or ignore whatever problems this country does have just because when graded on a curve, we're not as bad as Saudi Arabia or Somalia. Google the top ten safest countries for a woman to live, and the US rarely, if ever, even makes the top ten; on the few in which it does, it's always toward the bottom of that list.

Trump's non-racism

This is by far one of my favorite Trump supporter stupid sayings.

> "Trump can't be a racist; he used to pal around with Al Sharpton."

I love it when Trump supporters use a person's interaction with any person of color to prove not being racist.

Profound political commentary

One TSer, while complaining about the kind of laws that Democrats pass and propose vs. the ones conservative Republicans champion, wrote this:

> *"In fact, the entire retinue of Democrat laws, both real & imagined, centers on telling people what they must, or must not do."*

Hmmm? Last time I checked, *all* laws do this.

Oh, and I would be remiss if I did not include at least *one* of the *many* comments I've received from *white* conservatives (usually from the South) about the idiocy and foolhardiness of Black people to follow the Democratic agenda:

> *"Blacks are waking up to the realization they have been lied to by Democrats in huge numbers."*

Few things are more humorous than Trump supporters commenting on other people believing lies.

A Trump-supporting woman

This next statement was in response to my question to a white (naturally) Christian (of course) woman (sadly) who is a vehement supporter of Trump. I asked her how she, a woman, could support such an openly misogynistic person as Trump. This was her response, verbatim:

> *"I do not give Trump a pass on his treatment of women. However, he has never been accused of rape."*

Well, that right there is technically untrue. His first wife did (although she later re-characterized it as something else). Anyway, she continues...

> *"The majority of his romps were consensual and therefore, not an issue. I think pretty much every high-powered man in office, in some*

shape or form, has treated women like objects. I can't tell you the amount of time I spent as a Certified Legal Videographer getting patted or swatted on the bottom. I was always confused for being a court reporter instead of the videographer too. Attorneys were always making comments to me and/or asking me out knowing full well I was married. It didn't make me mad or hinder my career, but it was irritating after a while. But, that really is just the nature of male to female relationships and anyone who says it isn't is kidding themselves. Those events didn't make any of those men less capable of doing their jobs, nor did it make those men evil or incompetent in any other sense. So, just because a man can act, what people now see as inappropriate, doesn't mean he can't perform his job well. Hell, I was even hit on by my old dentist, but I still let him fix the cavity in my tooth."

I swear. You can't make this stuff up. She first said she didn't give Trump a pass; she then spent an entire paragraph doing just that. Her outlook and complicity with the white, patriarchal society was no doubt shaped by treatment over the years. I didn't know whether to be pissed at her or feel sorry for her. She then brings it all home...

"Nobody is saying Trump is perfect or a Saint. He is far from that, but he does know business and finances and how to make great deals, and he has proved that he loves this country. THAT is why we support him and why he will be elected again in 2020."

Dear Lord, Heaven help us if that man is ever elected again.

Chapter 5:

All I Need Are Dreadlocks and a Sword

When my friend became a Trump zombie

One of the most profound (and dare I say, saddest) turning points came when a good friend and colleague unfriended me on Facebook—all because I dared suggest that some cops may be bad.

This friend was a fellow filmmaker. A well-respected and world-renowned one at that. He wasn't a Hollywood filmmaker. He was a wedding filmmaker, and among other wedding filmmakers, he was da bomb! Unless you're in the wedding event business (or one of his celebrity clients), you've probably never heard of him.

He had been one of the most popular guests on my various podcasts over the years. Funny. Successful. And wicked talented. He also happened to be an ex-police officer of all things. An ex-police officer turned world-famous wedding filmmaker. (I often suggested that his life would make a great sitcom: a tough SWAT captain leaves the force to go shoot weddings instead of perps, and the fellas make fun of him.)

As an ex-cop, he still held a sense of brotherhood for his fellow brothers and sisters in blue. I once interviewed him for two hours where we discussed a few video recordings of cops who had fatally wounded suspects in situations that empirically seemed didn't warrant killing the individuals. I found a site with over two dozen such videos, including all the "famous" ones you undoubtedly know (e.g., Philando Castile, Michael Brown, Oscar Grant, etc.).

But there were a bunch of examples that never made mainstream media. And for every one, this friend had a legitimate reason why the use of fatal force was needed.

Now, I like to think I'm a reasonable guy. Many of his points made sense. Cops have one of the hardest jobs in the world. Every interaction with a perp, suspect, or traffic stop could mean life or death. I have good friends who are cops, and I hold the highest amount of respect for them and the duties they perform.

But you get to a point where you say, "Come on. Look at that case. The guy is on the ground, face down, hands behind his back, and the cop shoots him?" There were several examples like this, and I just got the feeling that there was no situation where my friend would say a killing was unjust and/or unavoidable.

Then I saw some of his posts on Facebook and I was blown away.

A while back, I saw him post a video of a gay wedding he shot, and he said something along the lines of supporting gay marriage. So I had assumed that he had a more liberal bent. But on November 9, 2016, I saw him post a photo of Obama getting on the presidential helicopter for the last time, and my friend said something like, "Good riddance! This guy can't leave fast enough!"

Now, that's no big deal. So he didn't like Obama, primarily because of Obama's comments about the police. Fine. I get it. But then I saw him post all these Trump-train posts and praise for Trump and I was like, "What the hell! Is he really a full-blown Trump supporter?"

The fateful parting and unfriending happened when a college student (who apparently, he had helped or mentored about filmmaking in the past) was respectfully questioning him about the latest news of an officer killing someone. My friend ripped into her. It seemed so uncharacteristic of how I thought of him. (Sadly, uncharacteristic comments from Trump-supporting friends are a common occurrence for me now.) I came to her defense, at first thanking my friend and all officers for their service, but raising the question that "maybe, just maybe, some of them might be bad."

Well, that was enough for him. No one would be disrespecting his "family." And just like that, I was unfriended.

By now, we're all used to the record numbers of unfriends and unfollows that have happened among friends and even family members since Don the Wannabe Dictator took office. But this happened shortly after the election. So it was fresh and new.

I liken it to *The Walking Dead*. In the first season, every zombie encounter was freaky, weird, and riveting. But by season six, you were like, "Eh. I'm used to it."

These Trump supporters were like *The Walking Dead*, slowly making their way through the social media landscape, drawn to political posts and memes like zombies to a car horn. As you made your way through your social media world, you would become terrified to find who was "bitten" by Trump-mania.

My friend was bitten. No leg amputation would save his life. He was too far gone.

From time to time, I would see him post yet another obnoxious post. Many had the same level of racial insensitivity that is so common among Trump supporters. And again (don't get me started on his toxic drivel about the evil "Marxist" Black Lives Matter movement). It was kind of like *The Walking Dead* when one of the main characters would come across an old friend or relative, meandering around the Georgia countryside, looking for flesh to eat.

That was my friend. A racially insensitive, social media-wandering, Trump-supporting zombie. It was too painful to continue to see his ongoing outlandish posts. I eventually had to block him outright. (The social media equivalent of putting a knife through a zombie's head.)

"Cats and dogs living together. *Mass hysteria!*"

The world was not what it used to be. Truths I thought I knew turned out to be lies. I was in a world where fellow Christians said horrible and hateful things to me, and atheists were showing me the kind of love Christ talked about. *Christian* friends and colleagues I broke bread with, laughed with, or whose houses I used to spend the night at were posting memes depicting survivors of the Stoneman Douglas school shootings as "Hitler" or accusing them of being crisis actors.

I just couldn't take it all anymore. I had to speak out. And as I did, I began to rub some people the wrong way. People who used to see me being an apolitical person that normally blogged and posted inspirational stories about filmmaking and creativity now saw me posting more and more about the injustices I saw.

Feather-ruffler turned social justice warrior

I was always the sort who ruffled feathers in my industry. But it was usually when I said something like why Final Cut Pro X was the editing software of the future; or why a mediocre photographer with a consumer camera, a $99 photography seminar under his belt, and a slick website could be more successful than a graduate of Brooks Institute shooting with a Hasselblad. I had a knack and talent for throwing professional photographers and filmmakers into tailspins with my blog posts and podcasts.

But this time, I was calling out racism and injustice. I questioned fellow Christians on how they could possibly support a man like Trump. And I started calling out "white privilege." I was like Michonne, the bold and brave Samurai-sword-wielding survivor in *The Walking Dead*, fighting the "Walkers" one by one.

And the grand irony in all of this is that none of these people have the slightest idea of the life I've had. Many would assume that I was a die-hard Obama supporter whose blood has run "blue" my whole adult life.

Oh, if they only knew.

Chapter 6:

Wonder Woman Was Black

Questionable parenting decisions notwithstanding

I don't know what you were like when you were twenty-four, but when I was twenty-four, I was young, excited about life, starting my filmmaking education, and interested in living the bachelor life. The last thing I could ever imagine doing would be having children. Let alone two!

But at the age of twenty-four, that's exactly what my mom had. Two rambunctious little, nappy-headed Black boys.

As a single mom and registered nurse, she longed for a better life for those boys. So she packed up her yellow Volkswagen bug with whatever she could fit in that little front trunk, threw us in the back seat, and headed west—from Philly, Pennsylvania, to the big lights and glitz of Hollywood, where she got a job at Cedars-Sinai Medical Center, the hospital to the stars.

I've often tried to imagine just what it must've been like for a single mother in the early '70s to parent two boys and drive cross-country with them. I'm guessing my brother and I were loud and obnoxious, rolling around, and wrestling in the backseat. And seat belts? Pfft! Fuhgeddaboutit! Remember, this was almost two decades before seat-belt laws.

And how did she feel about her prospects of meeting a man? Did she long for a man who could help her shepherd these two into God-fearing, respectful young men? How often did she sit in her bed at night, sad, alone, and tired from working all day then dealing with two rowdy and ashy little boys at night?

Can I take this moment to give a shout-out to all you single moms out there? I can unequivocally say that I am the person I am today because of the sacrifices my mom made. When I think about her choices, I can see so many different paths our lives could have gone. What if she'd moved to South Central instead of Hollywood? What if she'd dated dogs instead of doctors? And what if she'd just said, "F*ck it, go live with your father"—or worse, given us up to foster care? Is there some multiverse variant of me out there writing about how I led a life as a Crip or Blood gang leader?

We don't realize things about the sacrifices our parents made until we're parents ourselves.

Yeah...my mom was pretty special.

That being said, I gotta say, there were some choices Mom made that were, um, shall we say, questionable.

The Best Darn Babysitter in Town

There's only so much a single mom can do in the process of raising two boys. And if you work seventeen-hour shifts three to four days a week and only have the weekend to catch up on sleep, hell yeah, you're gonna use the TV as your weekend babysitter. And boy, she worked that sitter to death.

This was our typical weekend schedule, starting with Saturday morning[8]:

- 6:00 a.m. to 7:00 a.m. – *The Little Rascals* hour

- 7:00 a.m. to 7:30 a.m. – *Scooby Doo* (and Frosted Flakes)

---

8   Now, before you go Googling what the TV show line-up was for the greater Los Angeles area in the mid-to-late '70s, let me just say I did not bother to make sure these were the exact times. Trust me when I say these were the shows of my youth and the general times I watched them. The whole point is... we watched a lot of f-ing TV.

- 7:30 a.m. to 8:00 a.m. – *Electra Woman and Dyna Girl*

- 8:00 a.m. to 9:00 a.m. – *Super Friends*

- 9:00 a.m. to 9:30 a.m. – *Sigmund and the Sea Monster* (get more Frosted Flakes)

- 9:30 a.m. to 9:32 a.m. – *Schoolhouse Rock* - History Rock

- 9:32 a.m. to 11:00 a.m. – *Bugs Bunny and Friends* (Fruit Loops for breakfast "dessert")

- 11:00 a.m. to 11:02 a.m. – *Schoolhouse Rock* - Math Rock

- 11:02 a.m. to 12 noon – the *Tom and Jerry Hour*

- 12:00 p.m. to 12:05 p.m. – Run like hell for the kitchen to make peanut butter and jelly sandwich and get back to TV

- 12:05 p.m. to 12:30 p.m. – *Jabber-Jaw*

- 12:30 p.m. to 1:00 p.m. – *Sid and Marty Kroft*

- 1:00 p.m. to 2:00 p.m. – Two back-to-back episodes of *Gilligan's Island* (Ginger vs. Mary Ann? Hello? Mary Ann. How was this ever even a debate?)

- 2:00 p.m. to 3:00 p.m. – Two back-to-back episodes of *The Munsters*

- 3:00 p.m. to 5:00 p.m. – Saturday afternoon movie special

- 5:00 p.m. to 5:30 p.m. – See Mom. Grab dinner. We ate at the table together. And you know how praying grace went. C'mon now. Say it with me. "God is great. God is good. Let us thank Him for our food. *Amen!*"

- 5:30 p.m. to 7:00 p.m. – Saturday evening movie special (usually a badass monster movie like *Godzilla, Gamera, Rodan*, etc. Man, oh man. We *loved* us some Godzilla movies!)

- 7:00 p.m. to 8:00 p.m. – *Love Boat*

- 8:00 p.m. to 9:00 p.m. – "Da plane! Da plane!" You guessed it. *Fantasy Island*

- 9:00 p.m. – Bedtime

Then Sunday came around. I'm a little fuzzier on Sunday's activities. But it was generally something like:

- Get up early and watch a slew of "Bible" cartoons like *Davey and Goliath*

- Go to "Black" church

- Still at church

- Still at church

- Still...At...Church! (This was inhumane)

- Come home in time to catch...

- Two back-to-back episodes of *Gilligan's Island*

- Two back-to-back episodes of *F-Troop*

- Sunday Afternoon movie special

- Dinner

- *Battlestar Galactica*! Yeah boyeee! That was my show! It was like getting to watch *Star Wars* every week! I don't remember what we watched Sunday evenings before BSG came on the air. Maybe *All in the Family*?

- Bedtime

The weekday line-up (in no particular order) usually involved after school specials, *H.R. Pufnstuf*, *Lidsville*, *Lost in Space* (more on this later), more Japanese superheroes, Batman and Robin, *The Electric Company* (starring one Morgan Freeman), *Sesame Street*, *321 Contact* (Trini! Oooooh!), *Dr. Who* (the curly-haired one with the long scarf), *The New Zoo Revue*, *Speed Racer*, *The Bugaloos*, and *Gomer Pyle*.

You then had your weekly evening shows like *Sanford and Son*, *Good Times*, *What's Happening*, *Alice*, *Give Me a Break*, *Chico and the Man*, *All in the Family*, *The Jeffersons*, *Different Strokes*, *Buck Rogers*, *Logan's Run*, *Facts of Life*, *I Love Lucy*, *Candid Camera*, and of course *The Brady Bunch*. (I'm running out of breath just reading all the TV I watched when

all we had were thirteen channels and TV went off the air at 2:00 a.m.
Today's never-ending overload of content is beyond mind-boggling.)

Half-naked white women, great white sharks, and other questionable parenting decisions

But perhaps the one that stands out the most to me was *Wonder
Woman*. First, because of well, you know, Linda Carter in a bathing suit
running around, kicking ass. I mean, c'mon! What little, prepubescent,
heterosexual Black boy didn't love seeing a gorgeous white woman
running around in her underwear and beating up bad guys?

But even more than that, I remember that this was the show we'd watch
in the middle of the week right before our mother would take us to
work with her to do her night shift. Either she didn't have money for a
babysitter, babysitters didn't exist in the '70s, or she didn't trust anyone.
But during her night shifts, she'd take my brother and me to the hospital
with her and we'd sleep under her office desk. It was a blast! Kind of like
camping. The next morning when she was off her shift, she'd take us to
the International House of Pancakes for breakfast. Life was good.

The amount of television my mother let us watch is not the only
questionable parental media-related decisions she made. Again, I don't
know what the babysitting situation was for her in the '70s, but there
are a few movies I remember her taking us to that no parent should ever
take six, seven, eight, or nine-year-olds.

I remember going to a drive-in to see *Super Fly* and her covering my eyes
during some part of the movie. I've never seen the film as an adult, so I
have no idea what she was shielding me from. My guess was it was most
likely something sexual. She didn't have any problem with us seeing
violence. How do I know that? Because...

She also took us to see *Jaws* when it came out. Yeah. *Jaws*. The story of
how a shark terrorized the small, fictional seaside town of Amity Island
with a taste for fat white men and skinny white female skinny dippers.
(You see, this is one reason why Black people don't like to go swimming.
I'm sure wypipo were scurred too, but let's be real—how many bruthas

do you see out hanging "ten" off the coast of shark-infested waters? Exactly.) Do you know how disturbing it is to see a man get chewed in half by a great white shark when you're only seven or nine? Trust me. It's *very* disturbing. I don't recommend it at all.

She took us to see other R-rated movies like *Earthquake* and *Mommie Dearest*. Again, I haven't ever seen *Mommie Dearest* as an adult, and I barely remember the famous "No wire hangers ever" scene. So in writing this chapter, I Googled the movie to see a few scenes, and let me just say...

What the fuck!

Have you seen this movie?

The scene where she attacks and chokes her daughter. The scene where she gets in a shower with her boyfriend. And of course, the aforementioned wire hangers scene. Having seen that scene now as an adult, both of those are as equally disturbing as Robert Shaw being chewed in half by a great white. I was disturbed now at fifty watching those.

But without a doubt, my mother's piece de resistance of poor movie decisions was when she took us to see *The Amityville Horror*. Keep in mind that by this time, my brother and I were good little Christian boys with a healthy belief in God and the devil. And given the broad and diverse television viewing habits we had, you can only imagine where our minds could go. This is one of those movies where certain parts linger with you (most notably, the famous "get out" scene). I didn't even bother Googling this movie. Uh-uh. Hell no! (No pun intended). All I remember from seeing that movie at the tender age of about ten was that I could not leave my mother's side for an entire weekend. Coming out of that movie, my whole body felt different. It was like being in a different dimension. It was beyond disturbing what watching that movie was like.

What. Was. She. Thinking?

Now, before you go off judging my mother's parenting decisions, remember—single mom, in the '70s, two sugared-up little boys. (And one with ADHD, based on the diagnosis he got when he was forty, but I ain't sayin' which one of us... it was me.)

Now, add to all of that, she bought her first two homes *by herself*. She enrolled us in private schools for a few grades and kept us off the streets and out of trouble. (Do y'all know the statistics of Black men who get into trouble who were raised by single moms? Actually, I don't either. But I'm guessing it's not good.)

And at the end of the day, I think I turned out all right. Relatively speaking. So I probably watched a little too much TV as a kid. Everyone was doing it. You know good and well, that if you're in your mid-forties or older, unless you grew up Amish, you recognized all those same shows I referenced earlier.

I have nothin' but love and respect for my mom and how she raised us.

I love you, Mom. And I miss you. (But really. What *were* you thinking? I look forward to the day you can one day tell me yourself.)

I can't help but wonder if the shows I watched as a kid had any effect on who I loved and liked in the real world?

Nah. Probably not.

Chapter 7:

To All the White Girls on TV I've Loved Before

Forget Marcia. I had a thing for Jan.

"In this country, what we call education is actually indoctrination, and it takes us from the age of five to the age of eighteen to thoroughly indoctrinate people so that they will believe in the myth of white superiority."

—Jane Elliott, *Red Table Talk*

Are there any memories more profound for a teen boy or a man (or an even older man writing his story) than the memories of the girls or women he saw on television for whom he pined and had crushes as a child? For many young boys, those will be their first "loves."

Too young to realize that the paragons of beauty they see on screen are not real, we are at an early age taught about what society says is beauty, perfection, and the standards by which every girl (or woman) is judged in real life.

As someone who engaged in a copious amount of television viewing at an early age, I have a long list of "manic pixie dream girls" who captured my heart from behind the red, green, and blue pixels of my CRT TVs. (CRT in this context is cathode ray tube, *not* "critical race theory."

Given the topics addressed in this book, I just wanted to make sure you weren't confused. Lol.)

My earliest memory was Darla from the *Little Rascals*. As Alfalfa and Porky battled for her affection, my young six- or seven-year-old heart knew I could write a better poem.

The first time I remember seeing Jan Brady was when I was at the dinner table. *The Brady Bunch* was on and when I saw her long, golden hair, my heart skipped a beat. Yes, Marcia had long hair too. But there was something about that younger Jan's innocence and "girl next door" vibe that appealed to my sensitive soul.

I had a thing for that "girl next door." I used to dream about rescuing Dorothy from the Wicked Witch of the West.

I also had a thing for girls in space—or from space. Little Tia Malone from *Escape to Witch Mountain* made the harmonica in my heart play a jig. But it was Penny Robinson who stands out as one of the most memorable crushes from my youth.

In fact, *The Sound of Music* is one of my favorite movies,[9] and the only reason I let my mother talk me into watching what looked at the time like a boring movie about kids having a picnic on a grassy mountain was that I immediately recognized that "Penny" was in it. By this time in my life, I was old enough to separate actors from their characters and I knew that really wasn't "Penny." (For the uninitiated, it was American-British actress Angela Cartwright, little sister to Veronica Cartwright.) But she was still just as captivating.

The rest of the people who make up the "Hall of Flame" from my youth:

- Trini from *321 Contact*: Technically, she was of Latin American descent, so you could make the argument that she was one of the few women of color I fawned over in my youth.

- Electra Woman from *Electra Woman and Dyna Girl*: Imagine my excitement when I discovered that Deirdre Hall, the woman

9 I distinctly remember a joke from Arsenio Hall in the '90s where he said something along the lines of, "You never see bruthas walking down the street singing show tunes." I can neither confirm nor deny if that is not entirely a true statement where I am concerned.

who played her, was a star on my mom's favorite daytime soap opera, *Days of Our Lives*. So guess who started watching soap operas as a kid?

- Karen from the original *Mickey Mouse Club*: How disappointed I was when I was old enough to understand that what I was watching were syndicated reruns that were about twenty years old. Both she and Darla were probably old hags by the time I was falling "in love" with them (well, Karen was probably only in her early thirties by the time I started watching the show, so not quite an "old hag." Darla, on the other hand...)

- Joy from *The Bugaloos*: This was yet another Sid and Marty Kroft creation that captured the imagination of an already imaginative little Black boy. And Joy not only had the cute short skirt and "girl next door haircut," but she had a British accent to boot!

I also can't forget...

Sam: Well, well, well, my nigga. That is quite a list you have there.

And with that, *he* made his first appearance in my life. The devil (or angel) disguised as Sam "Jules" Jackson. My life would never be the same after that.

Shit is about to get weird up in here.

Chapter 8:

Origin of a Blaxistential Crisis

A Black man digs up his white roots

Throughout history are stories of heroes being visited by supernatural beings who provide wisdom, sage advice, guidance, or warnings. Scrooge got the ghosts of Christmas Past, Present, and Future. Moses got a talking burning bush. Luke got the Force ghost of his friend and mentor Obi-wan Kenobi.

I got Sam Jackson. *The* Samuel L. Jackson! In all his glory as the hitman Jules Winnfield from *Pulp Fiction*—jheri curl, goatee, Black suit, and all.

Remember that reference I made earlier about a little "Sam Jackson" on my shoulder telling me to just say "shit"? Well, like a clichéd plot from an '80s B-movie, somehow or another, I actually conjured him.

Now, I know what you're thinking. "How cool! Sam Jackson is a badass!" Yes, he's a badass. But it is *not* cool. And while I'm pretty sure he wasn't sent to shoot me as his character does in the movie, I am not entirely convinced his presence in my life isn't to make me wish I were dead.

I have documented my encounters with him in this book.

I try to get the words in my brain to connect to my mouth, but all I can get out is...

Me: You...you...you're...

Sam: Yes. Yes, I am.

Me: But how is this possible? Where did you come from? What are you doing here?

Sam: I'm here to help keep you on your path of enlightenment, Ronald. Or in *your* case, endarkenment. Think of me as your guardian angel.

Me: That's funny. Earlier in my book, I referred to you as a metaphor for the little devil that sits on a person's shoulders.

Sam: Angel. Devil. Spirit animal. Different cultures call us different things, but we all kinda do the same thing.

Me: Hmmm? I'm not quite sure I would classify an angel and devil as doing the same thing.

Sam: Really? One man's devil is another man's angel? What I am to *you* is gonna depend on a lot of muthafuckin' things, my brutha.

Me: Okay. So what exactly is it you do?

Sam: Mind if I have a seat to rest my weary feet?

Me: Sure. By all means.

I move my papers aside and Sam makes himself at home. He kicks his feet up on my desk and crosses them. He then pulls a boiled egg out of his inner pocket, peels it, salts it, then tosses the whole thing into his mouth.

Sam: Well, Ronald. I'm here...

Me: Excuse me. But my middle name is actually Ronaldo. There's an "o" at the end. That's where Ron comes from—Ronaldo.

He raises his left eyebrow and gives me a sort of side-eye smirk. He swallows the egg, wipes his mouth, then proceeds.

Sam: Well, Cleve...

The fact that he switched to my legal first name immediately tells me
that he 1) already knew my name and didn't care, and 2) wasn't amused
with the correction.

> **Sam:** I see that you are on a sort of personal—and dare I say,
> spiritual—journey. You're going through what we in the biz like to call
> a blaxistential crisis.
>
> **Me:** A blaxistential crisis?

He responds in the emblematic way of the perfect, hard-ass Sam
Jackson caricature.

> **Sam:** Yessir. You see, you're struggling with what it means to be
> really "Black" in America, and are reflecting on the many Black
> sins you've committed in the past, with a hope of reaching Negro
> salvation here in the present by becoming a real, down-home, woke
> brutha ready to fight the racial oppression of our people and those
> that look like us—all living under the thumb of one orange mother
> fucker with a fucked-up hairdo.

He smiles, reaches into his inner pocket, and pulls out a blunt.

> **Me:** What makes you think I need a lesson on how to be "really" Black?
>
> **Sam:** Have you read your book, Ronald? Goddamn, man. Like, let's
> start with that list of bitches you just rattled off as all the girls you
> had the hots for.
>
> **Me:** Whoa! Sam! Is that kind of language really necessary?
>
> **Sam:** Nigga. I haven't even gotten started. Now, what's up with all
> the white girls?
>
> **Me:** Excuse me?
>
> **Sam:** You heard me, nigga. You didn't like no sistas on TV when you
> was a kid?

Me: Oh, yeah. Of course, I did.

There's an uncomfortable pause between us as he looks at me. I then look at him. He looks at me. He then takes a puff from a joint. Then responds.

Sam: Who, muthafucka?! Shit! Do I have to drag it out of you?

Me: Oh. Yeah. Sorry. Well, um, Tootie from *Facts of Life.*

He starts to laugh that stilted laugh that comes when smoking a joint.

Sam: Ah yeah. She was kinda fine in those later years. She had some real curves on her. Not bad, Ronald. Go on. Who else?

Me: Well, actually, I had a crush on her in season one. When she was on those skates.

I smile and chuckle a bit as I recall some fond memories.

Me: Actually, it was so funny. My brother and I used to fight to see who could kiss the TV first when she was on screen.

My chuckling kinda dies off as Sam frowns and gives me a cross look.

Sam: That's fucking adorable, Ronald. Anyone else?

Me: Ummmm? Let me see.

I rack my brain, trying to remember. For the life of me, I can't think of any other Black girls on TV I had crushes on.

Sam: What about Thelma from *Good Times*? I'm sure you had a crush on that fine sista.

Me: Huh? No, not really. Maybe because she was so much older.

Sam: Older? Nigga, didn't you write earlier that you had a thing for Wonder Woman *and* fuckin' Electra Woman?

Me: Yeah?

Sam: Well. They're like whole, old-ass women.

Me: Oh yeah, right. I guess I did. I don't know. I just never had a thing for Thelma. I don't know.

Sam: What about Penny from *Good Times*?

Me: Oh. Wow. Yeah. Janet Jackson! I totally forgot about her!

Sam: So you *did* like her?

Me: Oh. No. I just meant I had forgotten Janet Jackson was on that show. But I don't ever remember having a crush on her.

Sam: Okay, how about Dee from *What's Happening*?

Me: Ummm? I don't know? I guess not.

Sam shakes his head.

Sam: Man, oh man. This is going to be harder than I thought. You didn't like Janet from *Good Times*, but you liked Jan Brady? You didn't like Dee from *What's Happening*, but you liked Darla from *Little Rascals*?

Me: I didn't like Penny from *Good Times*, but I liked Penny from *Lost in Space*?

I chuckle at my attempt at humor.

Sam: Was that an attempt at humor, Ronald?

Me: Just trying to keep the mood light. Haha...

Sam rubs his temples.

Sam: What about when you were in high school or college? You still watched TV then, right?

Me: Yes. Of course.

Sam: Okay. How about then? Did you even go for the light-skinned sistas like Lisa Bonet or Jasmine Guy?

Me: Well, by high school and college, I sorta grew out of having crushes on TV characters.

Sam: Oh, I get it. Too busy having crushes on white women in real life, huh?

I just roll my eyes and say the best comeback I can think of...

Me: Whatever.

Sam: "Whatever"? Is that your fuckin' come back?

He laughs.

Sam: Ahh shit. This *is* going to be harder than I thought.

Me: What's your point in all of this?

Sam's laugh dies and his face turns into a scowl. For the first time, I am genuinely afraid of what he's going to do. I finally know how Brett must have felt in that chair in *Pulp Fiction* right before hearing Ezekiel 25:17.

I don't feel any better when he gets up, puts his joint out on his tongue, sticks it back in his pocket, and gets up in my face.

Sam: My point, Ro-nal-*doh*, is origin stories.

I cock my head, confused.

Me: Origin stories?

Sam: Yeah. You like superheroes and shit, right?

Me: Yeah, of course. Who doesn't?

Sam: Millions of people, actually. But don't change the fucking subject. As I was saying, this is like your origin story.

Me: My origin story?

Sam: Yes. The origin of your disconnection from your people.

He backs away and walks toward my computer on the desk. As he does so, he pulls another egg out of his pocket, peels it, tosses some pepper on it this time, and swallows it whole. With a full mouth, chewing and spitting bits of egg here and there, he continues.

Sam: Since man first walked da ert, women have been the soul and heart of every civilization and community. It is from the woman that man is born. From the breast of a woman, man gains his first bit of strength. And men have been chasing titties ever since.

He starts to laugh.

Sam: No, but seriously. I laugh but my words are straight up the real deal. Your connection to women in a community will be your connection to that community.

Me: Huh? Wow. That sounds very PC and pro-woman, coming from a man who, just a few minutes ago, referred to a whole group of women as "bitches."

Sam: Nigga! You think I give a shit about a bunch of stank-ass white girls you had a hard-on for when you were ten? Open your eyes, muthafucka! I'm trying to help you here.

Me: How is this helping me, exactly?

Sam: Because unless you recognize, acknowledge, and make amends for your sins, you can't move forward. And right now, you need to confess.

Me: I need to confess?

Sam: Yes. This is your "Step 5," muthafucka, and I'm your sponsor.

I'm not quite sure how I feel about Sam's reference to the 12-Step Program. I don't really see how having a string of crushes on TV stars as a kid, who all happen to have been white, equates me with being an alcoholic.

He pulls out his joint again, lights it, and takes a puff.

> **Sam:** You're going to have the opportunity to admit your sins, Ronald. As you do, I want you to just keep one thing in mind.
>
> **Me:** And what's that?
>
> **Sam:** If you remember nothing else, I tell you, remember this. There are two people in this world you can never fool: yourself...
>
> **Me:** And God?
>
> **Sam:** No. *Me*, muthafucka!

And with that, he vanishes a la *Alice in Wonderland*'s Cheshire cat. His whole body goes, leaving just his mouth. He takes one more puff on his joint, blows out the smoke, and as the smoke disappears, so does the rest of Sam.

I take a seat and marvel in awe at the unusual and supernatural encounter I experienced. Was it real or imagined? Was Sam an angel or a devil, and how would I know? And what did he mean, I'd have to answer for my "sins"?

I was about to find out, all too soon.

Chapter 9:

My First Times All Have One Thing in Common

From crushes to kisses to you-know-what

Few things are more memorable to a person than the various first romantic encounters you have in life. Mine all have one thing in common. No doubt you may already know what it is.

My First Crush (IRL)

The first girl I ever remember having a crush on (in real life) was Jennifer in the second grade. (Yes, that was her real name. The fact that I remember it so many decades later illustrates its impact.)

She was a brown-haired little girl with dimples and ruby-red lips. It was a small private elementary school in Southern California. My class was located down the hall from the bathroom. Halfway down the hall was Jennifer's class.

Whenever I'd go to the bathroom, I'd have to pass her class. She'd get up from her seat, then blow me a kiss right before I got to the bathroom. I reacted the way any boy that age would. I'd wipe the air kiss from off my cheek, exclaim, "Ewww! Blech!" then slam the bathroom door behind me.

Gross, I would think to myself.

But I started to notice that I was going to the bathroom a lot that school year.

"Mrs. Crabtree, may I go to the bathroom?" (For the record, I don't think my teacher's name was Mrs. Crabtree. So if you're gonna make one up, Spanky and Alfafa's teacher seems as good as any.)

"Again, Ronny? You've been twice already."

"I know, but I really gotta go."

"Very well. But hurry back."

I'd then take a leisurely stroll down the hall, slowing down just as I approached Jennifer's class. As I passed the door, I'd casually look over my shoulder toward her desk, adjusting the length of my gait so as not to pass the door too quickly. But still walking fast enough so it wouldn't look like I was lollygagging around. (In *Star Wars* parlance, this would be known as "flying casual.")

As soon as she saw me, I'd feign panic, then run to the end of the hall and patiently wait for her to come to the class doorway, turn the corner, and blow me a kiss.

"Ewww! Blech!" Wipe face. Slam door. Then sit on a closed toilet seat, smiling ear to ear.

My First Kiss

My first kiss came relatively late in life. I was a senior in high school at a YMCA retreat held at an abandoned army base in San Luis Obispo, California. I was hanging out alone in my cabin with Helen (not her real name). Helen and I were flirtatious friends all semester. She had a cute blonde bob haircut and a bright smile.

For some reason I don't recall, we had been at odds for several weeks, and this evening we talked it out. One thing led to another and kissing ensued. Things got a little more heated than I had expected. I think we were both surprised by how far we went. It wasn't "all the way," as they say, but it was far enough.

Shortly after, as I walked her back to her cabin, I got another first—my first lesson on what *not* to say to a woman after an intimate encounter.

Referring to the fact that we had been at odds for a while, I said to her, "So are we better friends now?"

I could see the pain and disappointment in her eyes after those words left my lips.

"Better *friends*?" she exclaimed.

I could tell by the tone in her voice and the emphasis on the word "friends" she probably thought we were way more than "friends."

She was visibly upset and wanted to walk the rest of the way back by herself. Confused, I said, "Okay." (Lesson #2: When a woman whose heart you just broke says she wants to walk back to her place at night in the dark, you accompany her, even if it's an awkward, silent stroll that seems to last forever.)

More than twenty-five years later, I would learn in a counseling session that I have what's called a low EQ, or emotional quotient. It's not like autism or anything. Sometimes I don't pick up on emotional cues that people give, or I'm oblivious to how certain things I say may emotionally land on people. There was no clearer example of this than that evening when I told a starry-eyed sophomore, hopelessly infatuated with a clueless senior, that after such an intimate encounter, all she was to me was a "friend."

Later that night, I had a pie thrown in my face by Helen's best friend. Me. The nice guy that everybody liked. I felt mortally guilty after that. I tend to feel guilty easily. (This quality will play a role in our story later.)

My First, Well, You Know

I was nineteen, and she was twenty-nine. We met at a dance club in Los Angeles during my winter break. We had spent a few days together hanging out. She was a great kisser. (In college, I made up for a lot of lost kissing time I didn't get in high school.)

She was also the first time I ever got a case of blue balls. We spent an entire day hanging out and holding hands. She wore a loose blouse and "Daisy Duke" shorts. All day I kept thinking exactly what you'd think a nineteen-year-old heterosexual boy would be thinking hanging out with a hot twenty-nine-year-old MILF. (Yes, she was a single mom of two. Or was it three? I forget. And frankly, at the time, I didn't care.)

Nothing happened that evening because she said she had the Clap (or something like that). In retrospect, it was probably sweet of her to show restraint. (Although, it was kinda messed up to dress like that and be rubbin' up against me all day. WTF!)

The big night happened in a car in front of my cousin's house after going to a dance club together. As we made out in the car, she gave me that look. You know the one. The one a cougar gets right before pouncing on its prey.

I was the prey. She pounced. (Cue fireworks!)

Those are pretty much all the details I want to share about that (use your imagination for the rest).

Oh dear. I hope my aunt isn't reading this. She's a nice Christian lady who would not be too fond of the fact that I lost my virginity in a car in front of her house.

Anyway, yes, she was white. (The person I lost my virginity to, not my aunt. Just to be clear.)

My First Girlfriend

The first serious girlfriend I ever had was in my junior year at Cal Berkeley. You guessed it. White.

Little did I know that this string of pale-skinned love interests would come back to haunt me in a way I could never imagine.

Chapter 10:

The Second Most Embarrassing Confession in this Book

Of all the iconic spaghetti western adobe churches in the world, why'd she have to walk into mine?

What you are about to read is another supernatural encounter I had in the writing of this book. One of many I had on this journey.

It was time for me to confess. And Jesus, Mary, and Joseph, this is a hard one.

One of the aspects of the Protestant division of the Christian faith is the idea that we don't have to "confess" to anyone but God. We don't have to go into a confessional and tell some priest all the sins we've committed. My sins are between God and me (and maybe my counselor).

Apparently, that is not the case in the Church of Blackness. Just as Sam said, I have come to confess my Black "sins." I'm standing in the middle of a deserted road, in front of a small adobe church. I can't quite place my finger on it, but something about it looks vaguely familiar.

I walk in and head down the center of the church, then take a seat in the front pew. As I scan the interior, it hits me. This is the frakking church from Quentin Tarantino's *Kill Bill Vol. 2*. Considering what happened in that movie, this can't be good at all.

To my right is the organ where Sam Jackson's character Rufus sat. Was he going to show up as that mysterious musician?

I would soon have my answer.

In a few minutes, the front door opens, and I hear footsteps coming toward me. The unmistakable sound of high heels draws closer. The owner of those heels takes a seat at the organ, and my mouth drops in awe. There, seated facing me, makeup perfectly intact and not a hair out of place, is none other than Miss Viola Davis.

> **Me:** Dear Lord.
>
> **Viola:** No. I'm not the Lord. But I do believe you're here for a confession. Am I right?
>
> **Me:** Ummm. Yeah. I believe so.
>
> **Viola:** How long has it been since your last confession?
>
> **Me:** Actually, this is my first time. I guess.
>
> **Viola:** What? You're not sure?
>
> **Me:** Oh, yes. Yes. I'm sure. This is the first time.
>
> **Viola:** So. What did you do?
>
> **Me:** Well. You see. I gotta admit. It's a little unnerving cuz I'm not sure how you're gonna take it.
>
> **Viola:** It's like taking medicine. Just down it and get it over with.

I sit there and look into Miss Davis's eyes, and I think about all the pain and heartache Black men like me (and including me) have caused Black women. Whether intentional or not. How would I tell her this thing? How could I let myself do to her what so many other bruthas have done?

I must be strong and resolved. So I proceed.

Me: *Okay.* Here goes. Man. I can't believe I'm telling you this. Anyway, I've never had a long-term relationship, or even been with, a Black woman. You know, a sista.

There. I said it. I pray that I have not too terribly crushed her spirit. I know you, Viola. I know what you have endured. Please, please forgive me. You and your sisters have not deserved what Black men have wrought upon you.

She looks at me for what seems like an eternity. Staring back at me with those piercing eyes. What a life they must have seen.

She speaks.

Viola: Excuse me. I'll be right back.

Me: Yes. Of course. Please. Take all the time you need. I understand.

Viola gets up and walks toward the back of the church and out the door. Then from out of nowhere she starts laughing hysterically. I'm talking one of those keel-over-cuz-your-side-aches-from-laughing-so-hard kinds of laughs. I sit and wait for her to finish as she continues laughing.

And laughing.

And laughing.

After what feels like forever, Viola walks back to the stool, sits down, wipes the smile off her face, and re-composes herself.

Viola: Sorry about that. So tell me, why is this my problem?

Me: Well, it's not really *your* problem per se. It's more like, you know, the plight of the Black woman.

Viola looks at me. Pauses. And just like that, she starts cracking up again. I'm not sure how I feel about this.

Me: Excuse me. But is this really protocol? I mean, I don't get what's so funny.

> **Viola:** You really think *you* not dating a Black woman is our plight? Or some kind of sin to the African American community?

Only a little taken aback by the question (and wondering if she just insulted me), I regroup my thoughts.

> **Me:** Didn't you see *Jungle Fever*?

> **Viola:** Sure. What about it?

> **Me:** Well, do you remember that scene where all the sistas are gathered in a living room, complaining about how all the good Black men end up with white women?

> **Viola:** Oh, so are you saying you're one of the "good" ones?

> **Me:** No! I'm not saying that. Look, you're twisting my words around.

> **Viola:** No, I'm not. What I'm doing is asking for clarification about what is a clear implication you gave based on words you *actually* said.

I fidget in my seat, adjust my collar, and try to get more comfortable.

> **Me:** Is it warm in here to you? It's feeling a little bit warm.

> **Viola:** I'm quite comfortable. Thank you.

> **Me:** Look. Let me start over.

> **Viola:** Please do.

> **Me:** Let's see. What I said when I meant the plight of the Black woman... I mean, what I *meant* when I *said* "the plight of Black woman" was...

> **Viola:** Yes.

> **Me:** Okay. You see. Statistics show that—wait. If you look at the historical...

You know that look that a mother gives a child she knows is trying to squirm out of something he said that he shouldn't have said? Yeah, that's the look I was getting.

> **Me:** I mean. C'mon, Viola. I mean, Miss Davis. Vi? Surely *you* know what I'm talking about?
>
> **Viola:** Oh, really? And why is that, pray tell?

Foot, meet mouth.

> **Me:** I don't know. This isn't really what...are you *sure* there isn't a thermostat or something around here we can adjust?
>
> **Viola:** Like a lot of bruthas, seems to me your sin isn't *not* dating a sista, but rather an over-inflated sense of self-importance.
>
> **Me:** Now. Wait just a minute. I don't think I'm self-important.
>
> **Viola:** Really? So what makes you think I care who you have or haven't dated?
>
> **Me:** You don't. I mean, you shouldn't. Look, I'm just trying to come clean on things that I have done or even haven't done that may have, you know, damaged the Black community.

Viola starts laughing again.

> **Me:** I'm failing to find the humor in this situation. Why do you keep laughing?
>
> **Viola:** Again, you think you're *that* important? Do you really think there are any Black women out here worth their weight in salt worried about whether Ron Dawson has dated any of them or not?
>
> **Me:** No, not exactly.
>
> **Viola:** So again, why are you here?
>
> **Me:** I was told that this was something I had to do.

Viola: Oh, you were told?

Me: Yes, that's what I said.

Viola: Oh, yeah. Who gave you this information?

Me: You wouldn't believe me if I told you.

Viola: Is it any less believable than you sitting in an old spaghetti western adobe church talking to me?

Me: That's an excellent point. Okay. Samuel L. Jackson. But dressed as his character, Jules, from *Pulp Fiction*.

Viola lets out a few more guffaws.

Viola: So let me get this right. Sam Jackson from *Pulp Fiction* told you that you need to come and confess to me that you never dated a Black woman?

Me: Well, when you put it that way, it sounds a little silly.

Viola: Is there a way to put it where it wouldn't?

Me: Wait. I'm getting all confused.

Viola: Yes. That's apparent.

Me: You see...it's just—

I can't quite find the words. I put my head in my hands and close my eyes as I try to come up with a sane explanation for what's happening.

Viola: Do you want to know what I think?

Without lifting my head, I answer.

Me: Sure.

Viola: I think this is just a way for you to get a lot of crap off your chest so you can relieve some guilt complex you must have.

I snap back up and answer indignantly.

> **Me:** Wait. No, it's not. That's not it at all.
>
> **Viola:** Oh, no?
>
> **Me:** No.
>
> **Viola:** Why? Because the truth is Sam Jackson told you to confess to me?
>
> **Me:** No! He didn't say I had to confess to you specifically. He just said that I would have to confess my sins. I had no idea to whom I would be confessing. And to be quite frank, you are not being very priestly or pastoral, if I may be so bold.
>
> **Viola:** What, you think this whole situation is some kind of allegory for the Catholic Church?
>
> **Me:** I actually think this is probably more like a metaphorical device to explore issues of racial identity than an allegorical one that—

Viola gives me a look of daggers as if to say, "Shut the fuck up!"

> **Me:** Or, it could be an allegory. Allegories are good. I mean, they're both so similar, it's really hard to—
>
> **Viola:** Shut up!
>
> **Me:** Okay. Shutting up.
>
> **Viola:** Look. You seem like a nice guy. And if you need me to absolve you of your guilt for never having been with or dated a Black woman, sure. You're absolved.
>
> **Me:** I really don't think that's what I need or what I'm looking for. I can honestly tell you that I don't feel guilty about it.
>
> **Viola:** Oh. So you're *proud* of the fact that you've discounted and disregarded your own kind. Wow. That's pretty messed up.

Me: Hey! Wait. I didn't say that either. Damn! It's complicated, I guess. I...I... I don't really know what to say.

Viola: Let me ask you something.

Me: Okay.

Viola: Why?

Me: Why what?

Viola: Why have you never dated a sista?

Me: I don't know. It's not like I've never liked Black women or anything. And I've gone out with them. Just never anything long term. I just like who I like, and there never seems to be any Black women in my circle of friends, I guess.

Viola: Well, that's bullshit.

Me: Excuse me. I think I know my life a little bit better than you.

Viola: Actually, Ronald, you don't.

She leans down by her feet and pulls out a lawyerly satchel. Hmm? I didn't notice that there before. Anyway, from within the satchel, she starts taking out reams of paper and starts flicking through them.

Me: Wow. That's a lot of paper. Is that like my dossier or something?

Viola: Yeah. Sure. It's your dossier.

I'm not certain, but I think I'm picking up just a wee tinge of Viola Davis-infused sarcasm. As she continues to flick through the papers, she finds what she's looking for.

Viola: Tell me. Do you like coffee?

Me: Sure. Of course. Doesn't everyone?

Viola: I don't.

Me: Really? You don't like coffee?

Viola: No. What makes you assume everyone does?

Me: I don't know. Just seems like kinda an obvious thing, I guess.

Viola: You like to make a lot of assumptions about people, don't you?

Me: No more than anyone else. I mean, doesn't everyone, to some extent, make assumptions about people?

She rolls her eyes, shakes her head, chuckles, and looks down at the paperwork.

Viola: You are indeed a piece of work, Mr. Dawson. Anyway. It says here that on long drives when you lived in the South, you and your family would often drive miles and miles off the main highway to find a Starbucks. Is that correct?

Me: Excuse me, but what does any of this have to do with dating Black women? I'm not following your logic.

Viola: Just answer the question.

Me: Yes. We would, on occasion, take lengthy detours in more rural areas to find the closest Starbucks.

Viola: Seems like a lot of energy to take to get a cup o' Joe that any rest stop or McDonald's would have.

Me: Well, I would get the Frappuccinos, not the traditional coffees.

Viola: Really? What was so special about those?

Me: Well, at the time, I wasn't yet drinking coffee. I didn't really get into drinking coffee until we moved to Seattle. Ha! It sort of becomes mandatory to be a coffee drinker when you live there.

She wasn't amused.

Viola: Oh, so for a considerable amount of time in your life, you didn't like coffee?

Me: I guess not.

Viola: Huh? Interesting.

She chuckles and shakes her head again.

Viola: A piece of work indeed. <sigh> So, Mr. Dawson, have you ever gone out of your way to get a Five Guys hamburger?

Me: Uh, yeah. Have you tasted them?

Viola: Again, didn't find McDonald's, Burger King, or Wendy's to your liking?

Me: Well, apparently, you've never had a Five Guys burger if you have to ask that question.

Viola: And Mr. Dawson, is it not true that when you lived in Atlanta, you'd drive your family as far as forty-five minutes to go to your church?

Me: I'm really not getting where you're going with all of this.

Viola: Yes, I see that you are slow on the uptake here. But humor me.

Me: Yes. We would drive that far to go to church.

Viola: You'd drive forty-five minutes on the godforsaken freeways of Atlanta, Georgia, just to go to church when there is literally a church on every other block in the South? That must have been some church.

Me: It was one of Andy Stanley's churches. I really dig his theological views on life and the Bible.

Viola: Yes, I'm sure he's a very nice white pastor.

Me: Again. Where are you going with this?

She puts the paperwork away, sets the satchel back to her side, then leans back in her stool and gives me a stern look.

> **Viola:** My point is this: you'll add up to a half-hour or more to an already long drive between Atlanta and Nawlins, wasting more gas, to spend $5 on blended ice mixed with chocolate syrup and coffee. You'll drive an extra three to five miles, passing up Golden Arches and red-headed little girls in pigtails selling ninety-nine-cent burgers so you can pay $5.95 for a cheeseburger, and that's *without* the fries. And you'll suffer in the insane traffic inside of Atlanta's Perimeter to go to a church, where parking is ridiculous, passing literally dozens of other perfectly fine churches, all praying to and preaching about the same white Jesus. And I want to know...Why?

> **Me:** Because, well, you know. I guess it was worth the effort.

Viola Davis sits up from her reclining position then leans toward me.

> **Viola:** That's right. It was worth the effort. When there is something you *want*, you Mr. Dawson, will go out of your way to get it. And *that's* my problem with your having never dated a sista. We were not worth the effort to you. When you found yourself in a situation with little to no Black people in general, it was not worth the effort to you to find them. Despite the fact you lived in one of the Blackest metropolitan areas in this country for nearly six years. Despite the fact you went to UC Berkeley, a hop, skip, and a double-jump from Oakland. I and women who look like me were not worth it to you. And that's sad. It's sad because I meant it when I said you really *are* a nice guy. You're not one of these tired bruthas purposefully knocking Black women as being "too much work" to deal with. We don't want a man like that anyway. But what do we do when the good ones, even the ones who *would* otherwise be with us, don't see it worth their effort to seek us out when they find themselves stranded in mainly white enclaves of corporate and collegiate America?

I gulp.

Viola: Listen closely to what I'm about to tell you. And make sure it sinks in real deep.

Me: O...kaaay.

Viola: The Black woman is the mother of the human race. We were queens of nations when Europeans were still living in caves. We've conquered kingdoms. We've wooed men pale and dark. White women secretly want to be us. Black men fear us. White men used rape and fear to keep us down, yet, in the beautiful and immortal words of our dear mother Maya, "*Still we rise!*" We're the glue for communities. We're the force that empowers and emboldens political parties. We are the fathers when our children are fatherless. We breastfed, cared for, and raised generations of little Black *and* white babies. Our blood runs through the veins of every man, woman, and child on this planet. We are the yin and the yang of human existence. We are the greatest women in the Bible, and we are the face of the new sexy. There is nothing you can say, nothing you can do, and nothing you can keep from us that will prevent us from being what we have always been from the dawn of woman. *Strength personified.* And while it's sad and hurts my heart that so many good men of any color don't see us as being "worth the effort," frankly, in a lot of ways, it's sadder for you. Because at the end of the day, I say you're the one who missed out.

She leans back in her seat again to deliver the final "blow."

Viola: And with regard to your confession, while I admire your concern over the well-being of the African, African American, African European, Afro Hispanic, and Afro Asian woman, rest your little heart and put your small mind to rest. Despite the bruthas too stupid, too ignorant, or too *lazy* to seek us out, we still gonna be right as rain.

With that, she folds her arms, raises her right brow, and purses her lips.

Me: Allll-righty then. Um. I guess that just about wraps it up.

Viola: I guess it does.

Me: Okay. I guess I'll be leaving now?

Viola: Are you asking for my permission?

Me: Oh. No. Just wanted to make sure there wasn't anything else you needed to say.

Viola: Nope. I'm good. You have yourself a fine day.

With that, I tip my head in a nod to say goodbye, then head to the church entrance. Just before leaving, I look back one more time. Viola Davis— dark, bold, and beautiful Viola Davis—sits with her legs crossed and waves goodbye. I wave back then walk out the door.

As I turn around, right there in front of me is Sam. Smiling ear to ear.

Sam: Man. Now *that* was some muthafuckin' shit! You still got your balls intact? I think you may have left them inside. Want me to go get them for you?

Me: Is *this* what I'm going to have to go through? You never said I would have to confess to like huge movie stars or anything.

Sam: Look, Ronald. I don't control how this shit works. I'm just a messenger. But in answer to your query. Yes. This is what you have to go through. So just man up and take it, muthafucka.

And with that, he was gone.

Chapter 11:

Black People Aren't a Monolith

The most iconic voice in cinema teaches me a valuable lesson

"I've listened to this nonsense quite a bit. This concept only serves to create a divide where none exists, provides some people with an excuse, and serves to silence dissenting viewpoints. And those who perpetuate it are little more than useful idiots for the extreme left."

—Yet another Jackass on Facebook

"White people denying the existence of white privilege is kinda like a fish denying the existence of water."

—Me

That first quote from Mr. Jackass (again, not his real name, but more of a descriptor of his personality) was the inspiration for that second quote by me. It genuinely baffles me that people can be so dense about something blatantly obvious to so many other people.

I can appreciate that some white people are ignorant of their privilege and are genuinely good, so they feel needlessly attacked when that term is thrown at them. But they at least have open minds and soft hearts willing to listen and change.

And then you have Jackass, who wrote this to me after I shared a post giving examples of white privilege.

"Victimhood. Yay!"

Now, if he disagreed with my views on this issue, he could have easily rolled his eyes and scrolled down his feed. But no. He just had to throw in his two cents and invalidate everything I had written.

So I call him on it, and he responds with the quote above, then continued:

"How much actual racism have you been subjected to? Rather than engaging in racism yourself by blaming white men, maybe you should just live your life. I've found over the years that people tend to find what they're looking for. If you look for racism everywhere, guess what, you're going to find it. Or at the very least you'll believe any injustice, insult, or boorish behavior is based on race...whether it is or not. Quit worrying about what other people think and live your life."

A part of me didn't want to engage with or reply to this dude. I had been on that ride way too many times (remember our friend Dufus Asshole?) But on the off-chance others were reading who may have similar questions, I addressed his comments and each one of his questions.

We go back and forth in typical Facebook fashion. I offer a long, well-thought-out, vulnerable, and passionate expression of what it's like living in this country as a person of color. I remind him that I'm not creating a divide where none exists. It exists! The fact he doesn't see it is, all together now, "privilege."

I tell him about the importance of empathy. And most importantly, I admit that even though I personally have never had a cross burned on my lawn or been in a church that was bombed, that doesn't mean I can't empathize with those who have. The amount of overt racism I have or haven't experienced should have no bearing on whether I stand up for racial justice.

Lastly, I remind JA that my acknowledging his privilege is *not* the same as calling him a racist.

This issue of white privilege has its own meta element. Those white people who deny its existence, or call it nonsense, or bullshit, or an excuse, are by that very act participating in the thing they so vehemently deny. How do you convince a fish who denies the existence of water that he is swimming in it if he refuses to believe it?

Or, could it be that squirmy little fellow knows full well it exists but is afraid of contaminating it with the crap, scales, and activity of other fish and amphibians who dare to swim in his pond or breathe his same water?

We had some more of the usual unproductive back and forth. I said that what I'm telling him is apparently falling on deaf ears, then he accused me of the same. I promptly corrected his false equivalency with this analogy:

> *"If you tell me my experiences are NOT real, and I disagree with you, that is NOT your words falling on deaf ears. That is a man passing another man who is being mugged, and while the guy being mugged is yelling for help, the passerby tells him, 'Stop complaining. You're not being mugged.'"*

More back and forth. And then he said something that really struck me.

> *"I love the interview with Morgan Freeman where he said we could eliminate racism if we'd quit talking about it all the time and if people would refer to him simply as a man instead of a Black man."*

He's referring to a 2005 interview on *60 Minutes* with Mike Wallace. And I must admit, I was taken aback when I read that. How could Morgan Freeman ever say such a thing? How could any African American older than fifty (who isn't Clarence Thomas or some right-wing political commentator sell-out) ever say such a thing? It seems like an infuriatingly stupid comment to make.

Why do you say that, Ron?

From out of nowhere I hear the unmistakable voice of Morgan Freeman. What the hell—or, er, heaven—is going on!

Easy did it

Growing up in the early '70s (especially as a kid who watched a lot of TV), a few shows were must-see TV. *Sesame Street* (of course). *321 Contact*. And the third was none other than *The Electric Company*. I'm guessing many of you reading this will be old enough to have seen it (or at least would have seen old videos on YouTube). But on the off chance you don't know what I'm talking about, *The Electric Company* was a children's show contemporary to *Sesame Street*. But it had a cool, '60s, flower child, hippie kinda vibe. And it was one of the earliest acting gigs for such stars as Bill Cosby, Rita Moreno, and the man whose voice was now echoing in my room—Morgan Freeman.

Morgan played several characters on the sketch education show, but perhaps his most famous was Easy Reader. (Get it? Like *Easy Rider*.)

Easy was an afro-having, bell bottom-wearing, walking cliché of a '70s, jive-talkin' hippie. He was sorta like a reject from a Gordon Parks blaxploitation casting call. His whole gig was reading things: from menus to matchbooks to bottles—if it had words, Easy Reader would read it real coooooool.

He also played a few roles in the Spider-Man skits on the show. (If you think the earliest TV incarnation of the wise-cracking web-slinger was that corny early '80s cartoon, just Google "Electric Company Spider-Man.")

Then, of course, after that, you have all the other film appearances of Morgan that have made him an indelible part of our collective consciousness. Without a doubt, two of my favorites are Red from Frank Darabont's adaptation of *The Shawshank Redemption* and Principal Joe Clark in *Lean on Me*, the 1989 film about the real-life principal that turned around the New Jersey inner-city school of East Side High.

With all of these iconic and strong African American characters (his *Driving Miss Daisy* character notwithstanding), I couldn't understand how such a comment would come out of his mouth. But I Googled it, and there it was. The video interview with Mike Wallace where he not only said Black History Month was ridiculous (because "Black history is American history"), but he said racism would end when we "stop talking about it." Oh, why, Morgan! *Why*?!

> **Voice of Morgan Freeman:** Son, don't you think you're being a little melodramatic?

There again, was the voice of Morgan Freeman. Just his voice. Booming down from heaven.

> **Me:** No. No, I don't think I'm being melodramatic. I am seriously at a loss for words.

I must have looked like a crazy man talking to my ceiling. Morgan replied.

> **VOMF:** Why?
>
> **Me:** Because suggesting we don't need Black History Month because Black history is American history is just so, so...
>
> **VOMF:** So what?
>
> **Me:** I don't know. Stupid? Ignorant? Naive? If African American history was as an ingrained part of what is taught in school as white history, we wouldn't need a Black History Month.
>
> **VOMF:** And what is "white" history?
>
> **Me:** C'mon, Voice of Morgan Freeman. You know what I mean. The history of people, events, and places in this country largely favors those topics as they pertain to white people.
>
> **VOMF:** And it apparently upsets you that you didn't learn more about Black people?
>
> **Me:** Well. It's not that it's a matter of upsetting me.
>
> **VOMF:** Well, obviously it has.

Me: No. What was upsetting was hearing you offer such a ridiculous sentiment. "Racism will end if we stop talking about it"? That comment right there is a classic case of the proverbial ostrich sticking its head in the sand.

VOMF: Tell me something, son; how old are you?

Me: I'm old enough to know that racism won't disappear by ignoring it.

VOMF: Okay. Fine. But humor me. How old are you?

Me: Five-oh. As in Hawaii.

VOMF: So basically, you were in diapers when MLK was shot?

Me: Well, technically, he was shot almost exactly six months before I was born.

VOMF: Proves my point even more. Who do you think has a stronger leg to stand on when addressing the evils of racism? A "kid" like you? Or someone who was in the prime of his life, early thirties, living in the thick of the American Civil Rights era?

Me: Well, I obviously...

VOMF: That's right. You obviously have neither the experience, wisdom, nor right to tell any man or woman from that era what they can or can't say about what they lived and breathed every day while you were sitting and sleepin' in your own crap and piss.

If I didn't know any better, I would say Morgan is channeling his role as Joe, the principal from *Lean on Me*. I kinda wish I'd be getting the *Driving Miss Daisy* Morgan Freeman.

Me: So no part of you sees that statement as problematic?

VOMF: That interview was nearly fifteen years ago. Imagine if you were to be held accountable for some of the things you did or said ten, fifteen, or twenty years ago? Can you tell me you have a great leg to stand on when it comes to your outlook on race relations? If you were in some court of law where you had to prove your Blackness, and we were to peel back the curtain and reveal the history of a one Ron Dawson, you mean to tell me you could win an award for "Most down brutha of the century"?

Considering my experience with Samuel L. Jackson, I think it's safe to say that the Voice of Morgan Freeman "has laid my shit bare." And he's right. I don't have shit to say to him or any person. Given my shameful history, I am probably the last person to be holding any Black person in judgment for their past deeds. Least of which, the Voice of Morgan Freeman.

Me: I see your point. And it makes sense. It does. I shouldn't have come at you sideways like that. I'm sorry.

VOMF: Apology accepted.

Me: But can you at least tell me how you feel now? Is that a belief you still have?

VOMF: Let's just say that in life, not everything is black and white. Some things aren't always as they seem. And rather than trying to determine where you think mine or anybody else's beliefs stand, I think you have a lot more soul-searching of your own to do. And when the time is right, I promise you'll understand, and you'll realize you won't even need to ask me that question.

Me: Okay. If you say so.

VOMF: In the meantime, I'll be around, and I'll drop in every now and then to see how you're progressing.

Me: Sort of like your God character in *Bruce Almighty*.

VOMF: No, son. Not like that at all. This isn't a movie. It's a book. I'll be seeing you.

Me: I'll be seeing you too. Or rather, hearing you?

The Voice of Morgan Freeman was gone. In the immortal words of Alice, this shit is getting "curiouser and curiouser."

Chapter 12:

Babysitters, Bad Words, and F-Bombs

Sometimes you just have to say "shit"

"To be a Negro in this country and to be relatively conscious is to be in a rage almost all the time."

—James Baldwin

I mentioned earlier how my mother must have had trouble finding babysitters because of all the crazy movies she took us to. I wondered if they even had babysitters in the '70s.

But then I totally remembered that when we first arrived in Hollywood from Philadelphia, my mother dropped us off at a babysitter daycare. I don't remember her name. But I have vague memories of a large, Craftsman-style home that backed to the Hollywood freeway and had a large sleeper camper out front.

I would peg my age around six. It was definitely before first grade. Mom would drop us off, go to work, then pick us up later.

And I only have three vivid memories from my time going to that babysitter's house.

- Sleeping from time to time in that cool camper.

- Walking to preschool with the other kids unaccompanied (it was a totally different time).

- And the time I had my mouth washed out with soap (yes, parents really did that). Not only do I remember it happening, but I also remember how it happened.

I had recently arrived back from walking home. For some reason I don't remember, the kids told me to say "shit." I had never even heard that word before. My mother was a nice Christian woman who grew up in the South with strict Southern Baptist parents. You know for damn sure she never let us say, or even know about, words like that.

So the kids told me to say "shit," and I said it. Just as the daycare lady was coming outside. She heard me and immediately took me inside, got out whatever was the most popular brand of soap in the early '70s, and proceeded to wash my mouth out with it.

After the punishment was executed, I remember slowly and solemnly walking onto the back porch. There I sat, sad and pathetic, with the piquant aftertaste of Palmolive (or whatever) burning my tastebuds.

The other kids stood there, looking at me. No one said sorry. No one went to the sitter and said they told me to say it. No one came next to me and put a reassuring hand on me. These little pricks stood looking at me the way you'd look at a bug dying in the sun. You're kind of intrigued at the pain it's suffering, with almost a research scientist level of interest.

I wouldn't say another bad word again for another four years. It was another one of those distinct memories that stand out. The first time I would purposefully say a bad word was in the fourth grade. While climbing a fence, I got my shirt caught and ripped it. Without thinking, I said "it." The granddaddy of all bad words. The "f dash dash dash" word.

> **Sam:** Did you just say "the F dash dash dash" word? Nigga, how old are you?

From out of nowhere (as usual), it was Sam.

> **Me:** Must you always be eavesdropping on my conversations?
>
> **Sam:** This isn't a conversation, Ronald. It's a book. Conversations involve audible words between two or more parties.
>
> **Me:** So do you have a new lesson in Blackness to share with me?
>
> **Sam:** As a matter of fact, I do. And based on that "F dash dash dash" shit you just said, I'm here none too soon. So here is what I want you to do. Every time you have an urge to say "stuff," I want you to say "shit." Every time you want to say "Frak" or "freak," I want you to say "fuck."

I look a little concerned.

> **Me:** I don't know, Sam; do I really have to curse?
>
> **Sam:** Damn, nigga. You like a fuckin' Black George McFly! Yeah muthafucka, cuss!
>
> **Me:** Is it your contention that profane language is somehow a necessary component of the authentic Black experience?
>
> **Sam:** Despite your *Leave it to Beaver* childhood, I understand you actually have Black friends?
>
> **Me:** First off, my childhood was actually quite Black, thank you very much. But in answer to your question, yes, I have Black friends.
>
> **Sam:** Have you ever been around a group of them for an extended period of time? You know, like at a party, card game, barbeque, game of bones (that would be dominos in case you're wondering), or some other kind of social exchange with Caucasian attendance of 5 percent or less.
>
> **Me:** Sure. Of course, I have.

Sam: And in these social exchanges, have you paid attention to how they address one another?

Me: I suppose so. Why?

Sam: And how often do you hear them say "frak," "freak," "stuff," "darn," "dang," "golly," "gee whiz," or any of those other nerdy euphemisms you're so fond of saying?

Me: Excuse me, but I don't say "darn," "dang," or "golly." But again, in answer to your query, no, it's not a common occurrence that my Black friends will talk like that.

Sam: Exactly.

Me: I just don't see how dropping f-bombs every other word or using the n-word interchangeably with "dude" will make me more Black.

Sam: It's not about making you more Black. Trust me on this. You saying "fuck" and "shit" every other sentence is just a drop in the bucket of the work I need to do with yo' ass.

Me: So then, what's it about?

Sam: It's an exercise in releasing your inhibitions. It's a way for you to get used to making yourself (and the people around you) uncomfortable. To push the envelope. Walk on the edge. For whatever reason, you have a bugaboo up your ass about saying shit that's got to be said, especially if "shit" is what's got to be said. And at the end of the day, Ronald, "Frak da Police" just doesn't carry the same weight, if you catch my drift.

Me: First of all, I don't want to "frak" or "fuck" da police. We need police, and most of them in this country do good work and are good people.

Sam rubs his temples as if he's got a headache. He says softly under his breath:

Sam: Lord, Jesus in heaven, help me with this muthafucka.

Me: Besides, I don't have a problem saying those words.

Sam: Oh yeah. What words?

Me: The ones to which you were just referring.

Sam: Which are...?

Me: The "F" word and the like.

Sam: Do you mean to tell me that even now you can't say them?

Me: I just said "Fuck da police" not thirty seconds ago. I have no problem saying it. I can say them just fine. It's just that I like to use them when it feels more natural.

Sam: Really. So when is that?

Me: Hmmm. I guess when I'm angry mostly. I can drop an f-bomb like it's nobody's business when I'm mad.

Sam: Wow! Really? Like it's nobody's business, huh? That must be a sight to behold!

Me: Make fun of me all you want, but I don't think whether I curse has any bearing on my connection to the issues confronting the Black man today.

Sam: It absolutely does. And you know why?

Me: No. Please, educate me.

Sam: Because you said that you could drop f-bombs like it's nobody's business when you're mad. Well, Ronald, if you ain't in a constant state of anger as a Black man in this fucked up shit, then brutha, we gotta address that!

Me: Oh, I'm angry. That's for damn sure. I'm just not always at a nine or ten, that's all.

Sam: Well, you need to dial that shit up to eleven, muthafucka.

Me: Actually, I just make my "ten" angrier.

I chuckle at my comedic allusion to *This Is Spinal Tap*. As usual, Sam stands motionless and unamused.

Sam: I'm going to leave you for now, Mr. Dawson. I think I've taken just about as much as I can today. But I'm fucking serious. You need to dial that shit up a lot more than you are.

And he was gone again.

I take a seat, sit back, and stare out the window, pondering Sam's comments. I can't help but think that some of what he said makes frakking sense.

Chapter 13:

Me and Mr. T

The first time my Blackness earned me a standing ovation at my predominantly white high school

Few things caused a rush of adrenaline to course at two times the speed through my thirteen-year-old veins than the anticipation of breaking out a new *Dungeons & Dragons* campaign to play. I could spend hours at the bookstore reading through all the different pre-packaged campaigns sold by TSR for the worldwide phenomena. I'd then go home and spend more hours creating my dungeon campaigns for my brother and me to play. (Yes, I had to play both Dungeon Master *and* player character. It's odd, I know. Kinda like managing an election for a state gubernatorial race *and* running in the race yourself. But I digress.)

Dungeons & Dragons wasn't just a game. It was a way of life. It opened up a world of imagination and wonder. And I always played the same character, Darthenswain the Paladin.

Anyway, when I wasn't playing one-on-one with my little brother at home, I'd play during lunch with my Asian friends at school. You know that opening scene in the first episode of season one of *Stranger Things* when the boys are all playing *Dungeons & Dragons* in the basement? Yep. I was basically the Black kid in that scenario. (I was not at all surprised that his first girlfriend ended up being white.)

And in that scene, the main character slams the small metal figure of a Demogorgon down on the table. This is clearly a foreshadowing of the real monster the boys will all face later in the series.

The equivalent scene in my story might be me slamming down a small, three-headed, Ghidorah-looking monster with an orange-colored Trump caricature as the center head, flanked on either side by a Steve Bannon head and a Michael Flynn head. (Or maybe Bannon and Sessions? Pence and Stephen Miller? Sarah Sanders and Ann Coulter? Frak it. I need a seven-headed hydra!)

But I digress, again (I digress a lot). The reason I'm venturing down this memory lane is to set the stage for how my Blackness earned me my first standing ovation. And no, D&D has nothing to do with it. My love for D&D and the fact that I played it at school set the stage for what you are about to learn.

The first Black president

The school where I played D&D at lunch with my friends was South Pasadena Junior High School. In the early '80s, South Pasadena was a small, suburban community of middle-, upper-middle-, and upper-class families, primarily white and Asian. The few times I've visited or seen the school (and the high school) since I graduated, I believe it has become significantly more diverse. But when I attended, you could count on two hands the number of Black kids in my class.

This was quite a difference from the schools I attended before. In fact, the school I attended right before South Pas was Marshall Junior/Senior High School in Pasadena, California. From what I recall, Marshall was a diverse school. Lots of Black kids, white kids, brown kids, Asian kids, you name it. I also remember that it had somewhat of a danger element. Like this one time, on the bus, I saw this kid showing another kid a knife, and I was like, "I'm not sure you're supposed to bring knives to school. Especially ones that big!" It was pretty frakking big. (Side note: right when you read that section, what color were you assuming the kid with the knife was? I bet you a *million* dollars you were thinking Black.)

Weren't you? Don't lie. Now, the fact that he *was* Black doesn't matter. Why did you think that? Just something to think about.)

I attended Marshall my first semester of the seventh grade, and it was the first time I ventured into the world of school politics. I ran for class president, and by some miracle, I won. It's funny because I have no recollection of how the process worked. I don't remember giving a speech. I don't remember having a day of voting. I just know that I was the seventh-grade class president in the first semester of the 1980–81 school year. I remember my friend Juanita would call me "Mr. President." I liked the sound of it.

But alas, my presidency would be short-lived. My mom had met a new fella. Someone who was going to stick (I remember her dating a few men during my elementary school years). This new guy was head of anesthesiology at the hospital where she worked. And they were going to get married. And with that marriage, we would be "movin' on up," as it were. From my mom's modest, three-bedroom, two-bath home in the Black part of Altadena to a large, Spanish-style home in the white-ass hills of South Pasadena.

Moving to South Pas meant leaving my friends at Marshall, my constituents, my teachers, and, of course, my current crush. (Hey, at least this time she was Filipino!)

Unfortunately, my longing for the good life I had back at Marshall made me miss out on opportunities in my new school.

Novelties last only so long

The first time we drove up to South Pasadena Junior High, I thought it was a private school. The architecture has a Spanish feel, and the building looked like the kind of buildings I'd seen in college movies. The principal drove a Mercedes. There were patches of green throughout the campus called grass. It was a far cry from the concrete jungle and spartan architectural design that was Marshall.

And what I immediately noticed as I went from class to class: I was usually the only Black kid in the class (or one of two or three, tops).

As I think about it, South Pas is where my journey of having predominantly white or Asian friends all started. Marshall had all kinds of ethnicities. As did my sixth-grade school, fifth-grade school, and fourth-grade school (which were all-Black).

Naming all these schools reminds me that there was something else I soon learned. All these kids had known each other since *kindergarten*! Apparently, you could go to the same school all throughout your elementary school years. *What the hell! Really?!*

My mom moved about every year to year and a half, so I went to a different school every grade from first through seventh. (I went to two schools in both sixth and seventh grades.) It was only after she married my stepdad that we settled down more permanently in South Pasadena. Up to that point, I thought you were *supposed* to change schools after every year. Go figure.

When I arrived at the new school, I sensed that there was this interest in me as the "new kid on the block." Lots of kids talking to me, asking me about where I came from, etc. I vaguely remember some of the girls seeming to have a crush on me. (Or maybe it was just the novelty of another Black kid.)

Had I been more up on the social ladder-climbing abilities, I might have taken advantage of that novelty. Unfortunately, I was too "homesick" for Marshall, and I probably came off as cold and distant.

That would ultimately land me in a spot where I had never been before: unpopular, hardly seen, and playing *Dungeons & Dragons* with my Asian friends outside the science class (no, I'm not making that up).

At Marshall I was class president, loved by many, and a rising star. At South Pas, I joined the cast of freaks and geeks. (No offense to my old South Pas Jr. High friends. But dudes, come on. We were nerds.)

I tried my darndest to recapture my past glory and ran for eighth-grade class president. And lost. Then I ran for ninth-grade class president. And lost. I gave tenth-grade politics a shot too. You guessed it. The big "L."

I probably never would have ever been noticed by the kids at my school if it weren't for two other Black people in my life. The second, you'll learn about in the next chapter. But the first one was our vice principal.

Me and Mr. T.

Do you remember that John Hughes comedy where the tough, military-trained, hard-as-nails Black vice principal shakes things up at the predominantly white junior high school? You don't? Oh, that's right. Of course, you don't. John Hughes didn't put Black people in his movies. What I remember is my freshman year at South Pas.

His name was Mr. Tripplett, and he was just as I described. A tall, dark, bad-ass brother you did *not* want to fuck with. Man, I wish I could have been on a fly on the wall of the school administration meeting that decided to bring *him* to South Pas. There is no way of ignoring the ramifications of bringing such a starkly *Black* Black man to be the harbinger of death and destruction on all the white class clowns and cut-ups at that school.

Mr. Tripplett patrolled the school halls with a confident walk, finely pressed suit, and dark shades. And boy, did he have the walk. It wasn't a clichéd, JJ Walker, arms-swinging-like-a-jigaboo kind of walk. It was the walk of a tall, proud, ain't-gonna-take-no-shit-from-no-privileged-ass-white-kids kind of walk. Imagine if Shaft were Ferris Bueller's principal instead of Principal Rooney. That was Mr. Tripplett. And he did not take no shit from any kids. As such, my memory of the kids' reception of him was that he wasn't particularly liked. (Most school disciplinarians aren't liked. But him being such a dark Black man in a white school only added to the complexity of the situation. Hmmm? I should pitch a TV show about this. But I digress.)

So how does he end up helping to raise my social status, even just a tad? Serf Day.

I can dig this kind of "slavery"

Serf Day was a fundraising event the ninth-grade class held every year. If I recall, the money raised was saved and put toward what would eventually be our prom. Now, for some odd reason, the junior high at South Pas went from seventh to ninth grade (typically, ninth grade was the start of high school, not the end of junior high). So the ninth graders were like "seniors" at the school. (But chances are, many of you reading this went to a *middle* school and don't even know what the fuck a "junior high" is. So just forget about all that shit.)

Serf Day was an opportunity for the lower classes to "buy" a ninth-grader for the day and have them be their serf. The older students would have to carry their books around, walk behind them, serve them lunch, etc. And the tradition was to dress the ninth-grader up, usually in a ridiculous outfit. At the end of the day was an assembly for the school where all the serfs would parade on stage and a winning outfit was chosen.

And for my costume, I came as, you guessed it, Mr. Tripplett.

I had his shit down, man. The look. The walk. The kids in school absolutely loved it. I got handshakes and high-fives all day. Boy, was I ever intoxicated by the newfound attention. And when I strutted my stuff across that stage, I got my first ever standing ovation.

Alas, stardom only lasts so long. Serf Day came and went, and I was back to rolling twenty-sided die and mastering dungeon campaigns. My fifteen minutes of fame were up.

The following year I would move up the street to the high school. Still nerdy. Still mostly alone in the quad.

Until I met the kid that would help change my life forever.

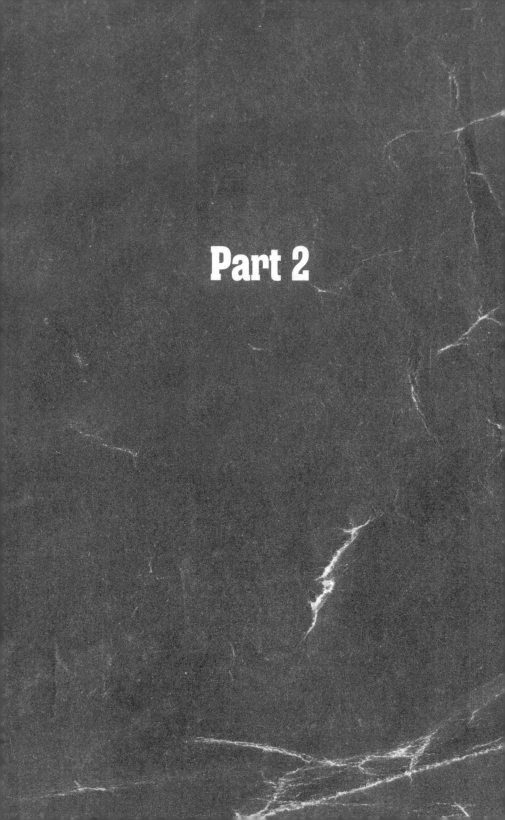

Part 2

Chapter 14:

Breakdancing and Breakthroughs

The second time my Blackness earned me a standing ovation at my predominantly white high school

Did you ever see the John Hughes teen comedy about the Black kid from "da hood" that goes to a predominantly white school and becomes the equivalent of the "Black Ferris Bueller"? No? Oh, that's right. John Hughes didn't cast Black people in his movies.

What I remember, again, is my childhood. And no, I wasn't referring to myself as the Black kid from da hood. I was referring to one Chris Spencer.

Chris is a successful comedian, award-winning writer, executive TV producer, comedy show host, and now feature film director. His Instagram feed (@therealchrisspencer) is chock full of snaps rubbin' elbows, playing golf, and hanging out with the veritable royalty of Black Hollywood.

But back in the mid-'80s, he was the wise-crackin', dashing, and infinitely charming junior from Inglewood, California, newly transplanted to the wide white world of South Pasadena. And his presence was instantly felt.

It's hard to capture the essence that was (even still is) Chris. When I described him as a Black Ferris, I wasn't joking. Everyone loved this dude: the sportos, the motorheads, geeks, bloods, waistoids, dweebes, dickheads—they all adored Chris. The best way I can describe him is, think Eddie Murphy in *Beverly Hills Cop*, except instead of a police force, it was a high school (and I was his "Billy Rosewood").

Chris was a laugh a minute. And he was one of those dudes that was just as comfortable hanging with his homeboys from Inglewood as he was with the preps from South Pas.

And as luck would have it, his Jamaican mother was old friends with my Jamaican stepdad. That meant that I got a chance to hang out with him during lunches from time to time. (In retrospect, I have to believe his mom told him to let the poor, goofy, nerdy kid hang with him. I can think of no other reason he'd give me the time of day). And the first lesson he taught me was this:

"Dude. If you're gonna hang with me, you gotta put away your backpack. Put that shit in your locker."

I *loved* my backpack. My favorite part of the yearly back-to-school shopping experience was picking a new backpack. Putting it away in my locker was hard. I know how Dany must have felt in season four of *Game of Thrones* when she locked up her dragons after they killed that kid. That's how I felt putting my backpack in my locker during lunch. But it was a price worth paying to hang out with Chris.

Hanging with Chris taught me so much. I studied his suaveness. His way of charming everyone, from students to faculty. There is perhaps no stronger aphrodisiac in a white school than a tall, charming, good lookin', funny Black kid with a killer smile and joke for every occasion. I learned up-close what a ladies' man looked like. (Note: learning it and pulling it off are two completely different things.)

Slowly but surely, the nerd-like husk that was my backpack, oversized corduroys, and Buster Brown shoes, shed and transformed into Izod shirts, Members Only sports jackets, and penny loafers (sans socks, of course). But the real breakthrough, the event that is probably the single most profound turning point in my young life, was the talent show that school year.

Despite my affinity for elf culture and *Star Wars* lore, I did have one thing going for me—I could dance. (I know. It's somewhat cliché and even ironic that in a book about breaking Black stereotypes, it was the number one Black stereotype that shaped my future.)

Dancing has always played a role in breaking me out of my shell and endearing me to friends. From breakdancing in high school to club dancing in college to swing dancing and Lindy Hop in my late twenties and early thirties.

If you recall, breakdancing was that dance craze that blew up in the '80s and remarkably still has staying power. Not too long ago I saw a documentary about the top breakdancers in the world. While it's cool seeing how the dance has held its own over the past three decades, its popularity is nothing like it was back in the early to mid-'80s.

Movies like *Breakin'* and *Beat Street* were blockbuster juggernauts. They were like the West Coast/East Coast battle of the breakdancing movies. And in this retired breakdancer's opinion, *Breakin'* was cartoonish, and the dancing, while not bad, paled in comparison to what you got from *Beat Street*. (And I kinda had the hots for the character of Kelly in *Breakin'*. And in case you're wonderin', no, I didn't have a thing for Rae Dawn Chong in *Beat Street*. But I *did* have a thing for her in *Soul Man*. Which, in retrospect, given the themes and controversy of *that* movie, is tragically ironic.)

And despite my nerdy exterior, I *could* breakdance. Well, sorta. Chris was a pretty good pop-locker, so we decided to perform together for the school talent show (for me, this was like that scene in the Bradley Cooper/Lady Gaga version of *A Star Is Born* where Bradley invites Gaga's character to sing with him on stage for the first time).

Chris and I made up a loose routine that we threw together in his family room. We would do a mime routine of a baseball game. He'd throw me the "ball" by passing a wave to me (as in the pop-locking move where you move your arms in such a way that they look like rubber). I'd pretend to hit it, then moonwalk around the bases (I hope I don't need to describe the Moonwalk).

The talent show would take place during the Friday morning assembly. One by one, the routines went down. Not including mine, all but one were totally forgettable. (I hope no one from my alma mater in one of those is reading this now. If so, sorry.) Anyway, the only other act I remember was the dual drummers. They were pretty amazing. I was kind of nervous.

Chris and I were up next. For outfits, I got green doctor scrubs from my stepdad. We also wore jeans, white gloves, and shades.

The MC approached the mic.

"And now, for our final act, we have Chris Spencer and Ron Dawson as 'Freak and Zoid.' Let's hear it for them."

Do you remember your high school dance days? Nerdy kids sitting on the bleachers ogling over the cute cheerleaders and jocks leaning against the wall, checking out the dance floor like cheetahs on the prowl? And there would be those popular songs that whenever they came on, everyone would excitedly rush the dance floor—jocks, nerds, babes, and all! Well, in the fall of 1983, at South Pasadena High School, that song for us was "Freak-a-Zoid" by Midnight Star. Whenever that song came on, everyone would go crazy—the white kids, the Asian kids, the Hispanic kids, the half dozen or so of us Black kids. We all went wild. (I jest. There were more Black kids than that. I'm sure. I think.)

So there were Chris and I, backstage at the assembly. Waiting for our cue. Then the lights came down. The audience quieted. And from the ceiling speakers, you could hear...

Freak-a-zoid robots, please report. Freak-a-zoid robots, please report to the dance floor.

At the sound of that song coming on, the crowd erupted in a thunderous roar. Then Chris pop-locked onto the stage and I Moonwalked. And oh...

my...God! Everyone lost their collective shit. They immediately rose to their feet.

I did every breakdance trick I knew in the book (it was a short book, I might say). And the piece-de-resistance was when I spun on my back. I must have done at least, oh, I don't know, two or three revolutions. The crowd lost even more shit.

By the time the song and our act ended, we stood and bowed on stage to applause that must have lasted five minutes. (It is entirely possible that my ADHD brain is remembering this whole affair a tad more exuberantly than it actually happened. But they stood for what seemed like a long freaking time.)

No one would ever look at me the same again. In the immortal words of another Dawson—Jack Dawson, to be exact—I was "King of the world!"

And that, my friends, was the second time my Blackness earned me a standing ovation at my white high school.

Reality check is a beyatch!

There's nothing like getting a standing ovation for doing a breakdance routine in a predominantly white high school to give a young Black youth an inflated sense of ego and confidence in what truly was only mediocre breakdancing ability (I could never do a helicopter). That became abundantly clear later that afternoon at my wrestling match.

When my wrestling team traveled to an inner-city tournament later that day, I was ready to bring on my A-game during the breaks between matches. I was Freak (or was I Zoid? I forget). Anyway, a bunch of us all went out to the quad at the high school where the tourney was held, boomboxes and cardboard mats in hand. I was ready for some serious b-boy battling.

It's the same for every breakdance dance-off. A bunch of kids gather in a circle as one by one, tough-looking dudes in parachute pants, Fila sweatjackets, and Kangols take turns to show their stuff. That is where reality gave me a real kick in the ass.

While the ability to do two or three revolutions spinning on my back at my high school was enough to garner a standing ovation, once I went out against b-boys from, um, shall we say, a more culturally diverse (<cough> Black) environment, I saw what real breakdancing was.

My abilities paled in comparison (no pun intended) to the dudes I saw at the wrestling tournament. Coin drops. Windmills. Head spins. These cats were the real deal. I was just a squirrel trying to get a nut.

Sam: Now that is some funny shit.

What the hell? Why the freak-a-zoid does this ass-wipe always show up at the most inopportune times?

Chapter 15:

A Faker's Dozens

My ability to throw shade is about on par with my breakdancing

Why does it seem like whenever I'm having a special memory moment, Sam shows up to make fun of me?

Me: Geeze. You startled me.

Sam: Sorry, brutha. Or should I say, "Boogaloo Shrimp." Tell me, did you honestly think you were that good?

Me: Yes, Sam. I did. It's not like I had a lot of competition to compare.

Sam: Yeah, but you could watch TV and movies and shit. You mean to tell me, you looked at those cats in *Beat Street* and thought to yourself, *Oh gee, gollywillickers, I can do that too. Garsh darn.*

Me: Ha. Ha. Very funny. I don't sound like that.

Sam: Oh, really?

Me: Well, what's your point?

Sam: My point is this is some Steve Jobs–like reality distortion field shit you created for yourself about your relative breakdance abilities. The fact that you could look at the dudes in that movie, who seemed to literally defy gravity and physics, and come away thinking you were just as good.

Me: It's not that I thought I was just as good. I knew I wasn't that good. The movie inspired me. The same way *Wall Street* inspired me to one day be a New York investment banking tycoon.

Sam: As Dr. Phil would say, "How did that work out for ya?" I don't see you buying 2-million-dollar paintings, ballin' in a penthouse in Dumbo, or working in two-thousand-square-foot offices. How many more dreams as a kid did you have that fell utterly to the wayside?

Me: You are just a veritable Tony Robbins, aren't you? I had the impression you were here to help me better come in contact with my inner Black man.

Sam laughs.

Sam: What do you think this is, muthafucka? Are you just gonna stand there and let me disrespect you like that? Ain't you got no kind of comeback and shit?

Me: Excuse me?

Sam: Jesus, man. Do I have to spell it out for you? You never heard of the dozens?

Me: Oh yes. Of course. I was never particularly good at it though.

Sam: No shit.

At this moment, I hear the Voice of Morgan Freeman again.

VOMF: Ron. How you doin', son?

Sam: Ahh, shit. Not this fool again.

Me: Hey there, Morgan. Good to hear from you again. I take it that your presence suggests I'm at another blaxsistential crisis point.

VOMF: I'm here just to provide another voice, son. Another possibility to consider.

Sam looks to the sky to address the Voice of Morgan Freeman.

Sam: No, actually, you're not here at all. Why don't you come down instead of playing "God"? This is like some Sauron-level voodoo shit where we never see you but always hear your ass.

Me: I think it's kinda cool we can't see him. It's like my life is narrated by Morgan Freeman. Who wouldn't want that?

Sam: Nigga. What? You think this is a movie? Life is not a movie, Ronald.

Me: Ronaldo.

Sam: Excuse me?

Me: I've told you a few times now, my middle name is actually Ronaldo, with an "O."

Sam: Do I look like the kind of person who gives a fuck?! As I was saying, *Ronald*. Life is not a movie. There is some real shit going down in this country that's not going to have some Hollywood, John Hughes ending where Black folk and other people of color revolt against the racial injustices of this country with some witty dialog, a rebel yell, and a fist pump as we walk into the fucking sunset. We need bruthas and sistas who are down for the cause, focused, and don't have their fucking heads in the clouds. And here you are, fucking reminiscing about the day you put on a lame-ass b-boy routine.

I don't know what it is—maybe it was the smirk on his face, or the way he cocked his head when he said it. But something in me just snapped.

Me: You're the last person to be talkin' about witty dialogue and fist-pumping, you Tarantino lovin', saying Nigga every other word, jive-ass, full of shit, think he's the coolest brutha on the planet, one-eye patch wearing, lightsaber-wielding, gun-toting, frost-blast blowing, motherfucker. Why don't you take that fake ass, outdated, Soul Glo drippin', wannabe Michael Jackson in "Thriller" looking jheri curl and go fucking walk da ert?! Bitch ass, judgmental asshole.

Sam laughs and starts to applaud.

Sam: My nigga! Now *that's* what I'm fuckin' talking about! You got some fire in your belly, after all. You might not be so hopeless as I thought.

Me: Huh? What? Wow. Did you just fucking Miyagi me?

Sam smiles and gives me a wink.

Sam: Correctomundo.

VOMF: Actually, Ron. I think a better analogy would be the Emperor in *Return of the Jedi* when he got Luke to go off on Vader, then starts to clap right when Luke cuts off Vader's hand.

Sam: Shut the fuck up! No one asked you a goddamn thing Voice of Morgan Freeman!

Sam turns back to me.

Sam: Now listen. I've got some business to attend to. I think we've made some real progress here, Ronald. I'll catch you later.

And with that, he's gone.

VOMF: How did you feel when you went off on him like that?

Me: Oh. I didn't know you were still there, Morgan.

VOMF: Yep. I'm still here. That was quite a performance you put on.

Me: Yeah. I don't know what got into me. I fucking *love* Sam Jackson. His are some of my favorite roles in cinema. It's weird that I would say those things. I'm glad he took it in stride. I hope I didn't hurt his feelings.

VOMF: I'm pretty sure you could not hurt Samuel L. Jackson's feelings, son. He'll be okay. But how are *you* doing?

Me: I don't know. I'm not quite sure how I feel about what I did. It did feel sort of freeing saying those things. And it was kind of fun. I never could go off like that when I was a kid. It did make me feel more, I hate to say it, but...Black.

VOMF: That's interesting. What makes you say that?

Me: Well, you know. Playing the dozens is like a significant part of the African American experience. I never used to do anything like that growing up. Mainly because I never hung out with Black people that much, and that kind of thing is not what goes down during junior high school lunches playing *Dungeons & Dragons* with your three Asian friends in school hallways. It also wasn't on the agenda of any of the business fraternity meetings at Berkeley. I liked the fact that I could hold my own, you know what I mean?

VOMF: I think I may have some idea. So do you think if you play the dozens, at your current age, that other Black people will somehow respect you more?

Me: No. Yes. I don't know. I think if they know I can do it, then like I'll have some street cred or something.

VOMF: Is there something happening in the streets where your "cred" is needed?

Me: You know what I mean. I just think that I will be taken more seriously and respected by my people if...

VOMF: If what?

Me: If I can throw shade with the best of them.

VOMF: So let me get this straight. If you excel at insulting and throwing shade at Black folk, they'll respect you more?

Me: Well, when you put it like that, it sounds ridiculous. But I think it's a kind of Black paradox, you know?

VOMF: I can't say that I do. What I can say is that it would seem to me that the real measure of a man, any man, is his ability to earn respect and love for his fellow man through integrity and being his true self.

Me: I don't know that I can honestly argue with that. I'm really confused now.

VOMF: Well, just think about it. Let it sit with you for a while. Marinate on it.

Me: Okay. I will, Morgan.

VOMF: In the meantime, if I'm not mistaken, you were going somewhere with your breakdance story, correct?

Me: Oh shoot. Yes! Yes, I was. Thank you for reminding me.

VOMF: My pleasure, son. I'll be seeing you again soon.

Me: Yeah. And I'll be, um, hearing you soon, I guess.

VOMF: Heh, heh, heh. Yes, you will.

And with that, the Voice of Morgan Freeman faded into the distance.

My personal after-school special

Despite my utter failure at the break-off at the wrestling tournament at the urban high school, back in the land of South Pas suburbia, my performance at the talent show created somewhat of a name for myself. Kids were talking about it. I was being noticed in a way I never thought of. The "cool" kids were talking to me. I know how cliché that sounds, but I'm totally serious. I by no means metamorphosed into a Black Jake Ryan or anything, but my climb up that proverbial high school caste system was put into overdrive with that one performance.

I was now ready to capitalize on my tag-along status with Chris. Whereas before I was more like an Oxpecker to his rhino, with the freak-a-zoids performance under my belt, I could now kinda morph into a full-blown rhino myself (or at least a baby one).

We'd go to football games and all the girls would hug Chris. Then I'd hug all the girls that just hugged Chris. "Oh, this is that cute little sophomore that did that cool dance with you. Nice." Hey, I'd take any excuse for a hug from a junior girl.

At the after-game dances, I'd strut my mediocre breakdance stuff and bring the house down. During lunches on "the quad," I was seen by fellow sophomores hangin' with the older juniors. (More cred.)

This newfound confidence and subsequent "fame" led me to run for junior class president. And after losing every class presidency I ran for at South Pasadena from the eighth to the tenth grades, I finally won. And I would go on to become senior class president as well.

The end of my high school days was very much like an after-school special highlighting the possibilities of every young boy or girl to gain friends and become popular, with just a little bit of charm, the ability to walk backward while looking like you're stepping forward, and making two to three and a half revolutions spinning on your back.

I share my high school experience with you because I believe it sets the stage for the rest of my life in a way whose effects I feel (both negative and positive) today.

I was loved, appreciated, and in some cases, adored by white people (and a fair amount of Asian people). I had garnered this level of affection from them in a way I never quite did from Black people. Is there any wonder then why I wouldn't naturally gravitate toward them? In the music I listened to, the movies I watched, the restaurants I frequented, and naturally, the women I dated? In my mind and heart, I was just as good and worthy as a white or Asian person. And in some ways, that's a good thing. I never had any issues navigating the white world in which I predominantly lived.

But there was a downside, too. One that became heartbreakingly painful once I went to college.

Chapter 16:

My George Costanza Moment

Oh, the things I would've said in college had I been a hard-ass brutha instead of a sensitive Black man

Remember that episode of *Seinfeld* ("The Comeback") when one of George Costanza's workmates zinged him with a funny one-liner, and only later did George come up with a perfect retort (that he obsessed over wanting to use with the guy in another meeting)? I'm sure at some point you've had the same experience.

In the process of writing this, I've had a few. One is directly tied to my racial identity crisis. It dates to my days at UC Berkeley when I was part of the professional coed business fraternity Delta Sigma Pi, Rho Chapter.

My reputation as a consummate dancer followed me to college. My fellow fraternity brothers (yes, even the women were called "brothers") all knew that I could cut it up and could always be relied upon to provide my group of white and Asian friends copious amounts of dancing entertainment.

So with that information as context, let me tell you about this traumatizing experience.

We were all discussing the activities and schedule for that semester's initiation banquet, including the fact that the DJ would be playing music during dinner. Now, when I heard this, I couldn't help but think to myself, *I hope they don't play all the fun dance songs during dinner.*

I think this is a reasonable concern, don't you? I mean, come on; no one wants to be sitting in their seat stuffing their face when the DJ puts on the cool dance jams like "Blue Monday" or "Bizarre Love Triangle" by New Order or "People Are People" by Depeche Mode, and I sure as hell didn't want to be sitting in my seat if the B-52s "Love Shack" came on (am I right?)

So I raised my hand and asked the question. "Excuse me. But will the DJ be playing the same songs during dinner as during the actual dance time?"

And that's when the social chair, Loretta LuLu (not her real name), responded...

"Not everyone wants to listen to rap music, Ron!"

What the actual fuck! Did this...this...person...just make the racially ignorant and stupid-ass assumption that just because I was the only Black person in the chapter, that I wanted to listen to rap music?! What made her comment even more frustrating (and ignorant) was the fact that she was woefully ignorant of the kind of music I *actually* liked to dance to (hello? "Bizarre Love Triangle"?).

Now, had I evolved into the hardened, Shaft-like, angry-Black-man persona I am today, I would have most definitely had some *very* choice words to say to Miss Looney Lucy and her f-ed up remark. Something like...

"WHAT THE F**K DID YOU JUST SAY TO ME! WHO THE HELL DO YOU F**KIN' THINK YOU ARE? YOU DON'T KNOW ME! YOU BETTER STEP OFF WITH YOUR IGNORANT, FAKE EYELASH WEARING, CHIPPED FINGERNAIL WEARING, COULDN'T PASS ACCOUNTING 101 WITH AN HP CALCULATOR HAVING ASS! JUST ANSWER THE MOTHERF**KIN'

QUESTION AND DON'T WORRY ABOUT WHAT KIND OF MUSIC I'M
CONCERNED ABOUT HEARING YOU STUPID-ASS B***!"[10]

As it turns out, I was a little more, um, sensitive during this time of
my life. I was the guy who used to write poems to girls I liked, despite
the fact I was constantly relegated to the "friend zone." (But that's a
deleted chapter or a whole other book.) This week I was especially sullen
because I was feeling caught between two worlds—not Black enough for
Black people and feeling like it was being Black that kept the girls I liked
from liking me back (in "that way").

So instead of the hard-ass brutha response, what I actually said was...

"Just because I'm Black you think I want to listen to rap music?"

I then started to tear up, and I ran out of the room. (Yes, yes, I know.)

> **Sam:** WHAT THE ACTUAL FUCK INDEED!

What a surprise. Sam is back.

> **Me:** I had a feeling you'd show up.
>
> **Sam:** Man. I don't even have the time or patience to deal with *this*!
> You go back to telling your little story. I...Just...Can't. Not today!

And as soon as he appeared, he was gone in an indo-clouded
poof of smoke.

> **Me:** Wow. That was easy. I gotta remember that strategy next time
> he shows up.

Okay, where was I? Oh yes.

So I went out into the corridor of Barrows Hall, sobbing and feeling more
lost than ever. Now, I know what you're thinking. But believe me when I
say, I wouldn't normally have been this emotional and dramatic. But for

---

10 I tried to refrain from using the b-word in this, but if I'm being intellectually honest, if I was a hardened
    brutha back then, I almost certainly would have used that word. Please don't let it reflect what you think
    of me today.

weeks, I had been in this terrible slump. Heartbroken over some girl. Discouraged. Feeling like I didn't belong. Not to mention that I was on the verge of flunking Calculus 1B.[11] So don't you go judgin' a sensitive Black man.

I sat on the floor in the hall outside, wiping the tears from my face and asking "God, why me?" like David in the hills and desert of biblical Jerusalem. My friend Jenny came out to try and console me. A few other of my white and Asian friends came out too.

Through sobs, I tried to explain what I was going through. I knew they cared. I knew they wanted to help. But it was difficult trying to express to them the depth of my pain. (I guess the gap between races understanding one another still hasn't closed now thirty years later.)

Eventually, it all worked out. The rest of the brothers in the chapter gave Looney Loretta a good talking to, the party was a smashing success, I cut up the dance floor, and just like the voice of Morgan Freeman will tell me later, those times also passed, and my identity crisis issues at Berkeley eventually faded. I would go on to have all the various romantic firsts I alluded to earlier during my college years. My world was white, right, and my self-esteem and character became that much stronger.

But if my love life in college was like a bastardized Frankenstein combo of a John Hughes/Hudlin Brothers rom-com, not even *that* compares to the Coen Brothers-esque road trip romp that was my drive cross country from Berkeley to Miami, Florida, the summer of '87.

Because, you know, racism was over by the '80s. Right?

---

11 I *had* to go and enroll in the hard calculus class designed for f-ing engineers! It would eventually take two semesters of getting an "incomplete" and two additional semesters breaking up the four-unit semester class into two two-unit classes over fall and spring before I got through the damn thing. And I'm so glad I took it because I probably use differential calculus and conversions every day in my job as a managing editor and content marketer! WTF!

Chapter 17:

Newsflash—America Was/Is Still Racist

I was shocked to learn there was still racism in America…in 1987!

The summer of 1987, between my freshman and sophomore years at UC Berkeley. My best bud at the time was a white dude named Sean. Sean was slightly older and had enrolled in college late. He was a professional photographer and had a successful photography business. He and I lived in the same dorm, Davidson Hall.

That summer, Sean was hired by some newspaper to do some photojournalism work, so he was going to drive cross country in his cherry-apple-red BMW (which he lovingly named "Ma Cherie") and asked me if I'd like to tag along. We were going to be like Crockett and Tubbs from *Miami Vice*, hitting the streets of 'Murica (the '80s smash hit was our mutually favorite show at the time).

Anyway, when he invited me along, I was like, "Hell yeah! Let's do it, Crockett!"

So we packed up his car and headed east.

As you may know, Berkeley is famous for being a rather liberal town in what is already a pretty progressive state. And that became clear the minute we left the border.

In Denver, Colorado, when at a gas station, Sean overheard one guy say to his wife, "Honey, look at that white guy in that car with that nigger." This was in Denver. I had no idea Denver had racists.

In Dallas, Texas, when Sean went to pay for the gas (remember, this was way before the days you could pay at the pump), the attendant asked him in a deep, Texas drawl, "Where are y'all from?"

Sean answered, "Oh, we're driving from California to Miami."

This guy was an older gentleman, messy gray hair, some kind of baseball cap, and gray stubble. The guy looked over at me in the cherry-red BMW, then looked over at Sean and said, "Yep, it figures."

Oh, it gets better.

After a seventeen-hour nonstop drive from Flagstaff, Arizona, to Memphis, Tennessee, we booked a room at a Stuckey's. Those of you down South probably know what Stuckey's is. It's kind of like the illegitimate union of Denny's and Motel 6, with a dash of 7-11.

I was chillin' out in our room when Sean went to buy some food and supplies from the convenience store. The clerk was this college-aged coed, probably twenty or so. He asked her for her opinion about directions to Florida.

"Hello there, miss," he said. "My friend and I are driving down to Florida, and we're trying to decide if we should go down through Louisiana and cross over, or take the more direct route through Georgia."

Mind you, she had not seen me yet. I was still back in the room, trying to grab some zzzzzs. So she answered...

"Oh, I think you'd like it much better if you go down through Georgia."

Intrigued, Sean asked, "Really. Huh? Why do you say that? I'm a photographer and I hear the swamps and trees down in Louisiana are beautiful."

She replied, "Yeah, they are, but trust me, you're gonna wanna go through Georgia."

"But why?" Sean insisted.

She leaned in, looked around, and whispered to him, "Truth is, ain't too many of them damn Blacks through Georgia. Way too many of them in Louisiana. So you'll like that much better."

How does a white man traveling cross country with his Black friend (who's kickin' back in the room) respond to an answer like that from Little Miss "Daisy Duke"? He said all he could say.

"Oooo-kaaaay then. Thank you, Daisy. I appreciate that warning. Wow. Lots of damn Blacks, you say?"

"Lots and lots of them."

"Well, um, I will certainly keep that very fine warning in mind when planning my route."

"White power!"

"Yes, er, white power indeed."

(Okay, honestly, I don't think she said, "white power." That was added for effect. But I gotta believe that she was thinking it!)

Sean came back to the room and started cracking up, saying, "You are not going to believe this. This one takes the cake."

He proceeded to tell me this story and I was dumbfounded. Shocked to learn that there was still this kind of racism in America. This was 1987, after all!

Well, I certainly wasn't going to let Miss Daisy Duke get away with this. So I promptly put on my favorite *Miami Vice* outfit: a bright yellow baggy suit, pink shirt, pastel-colored sweater vest, gray dress shoes with pink socks, and white shades. I then went into the convenience store and pretended to be a Hollywood location scout on a mission to find a location for a cross-country buddy picture we were filming.

I let her know that she and this fine establishment were *just* what we were looking for, and I would be so honored if she would agree to be in our movie. She enthusiastically said yes and I replied, "Great," then handed her a business card of a real producer I got at some networking event a few weeks earlier. That producer's name was also Ron, which made me feel better because then I could tell her my real name, give her that card, and not feel guilty for lying about my name. (Under the circumstances I know that makes no frakking sense, but that's how my eighteen-year-old brain processed it.)

A small part of me likes to think that some thirty-three years later, a fifty-year-old, down and out Miss Duke is still slinging cigarettes and donuts at that podunk Stuckey's, waiting for her fifteen minutes of fame!

But the crazy racism didn't stop there. Later during our time in that city, Sean wanted to visit some girl he had met on a cruise the summer before who happened to live in Memphis. When we got to her house, I had to wait in the car to prepare her parents for the idea of a Black guy coming into their home. I kid you not. (I will say, for a racist-ass couple, they were just as pleasant as you wanna be. I could see going back there and having dinner.)

I swear, that cross-country trip was like traveling back in time thirty years.

And here's the thing—I was legitimately shocked at this amount of racism. I kept thinking to myself, *What the hell is going on?* This was 1987, for crying out loud! It was such a huge eye-opener for me. I never experienced anything like that growing up where I did. I thought that kind of racism only existed in the movies. It was shameful in many ways.

Sadly, you could make the argument that even today, this is still an issue. The difference is that "Miss Daisy Duke" and "Gary the racist gas station attendant" now have the internet, Twitter, Facebook, and Instagram to hop online, read a politically provocative post from someone like me, look at my avatar and reply, "Yep. It figures."

And I was about to meet the Facebook equivalent of that gas station attendant.

Chapter 18:

My Relationship with Facebook Is...Complicated

How a house negro and a Dufus Asshole on Facebook helped me find the secret of life

It was August 3, 2018. The day of my sixteenth wedding anniversary and two days before my daughter's wedding. My wife, daughter, and mother-in-law were all out shopping and celebrating the pending nuptials of my daughter. For a whole host of complicated reasons that go beyond the scope of this book, I was spending it at home alone.

So here I was. Frustrated. A little salty. And missing my wife. Then I see a BlazeTV video by African American talk-piece for the Republican party, Daneen Borelli. Borelli was a Fox News political columnist and author of *Blacklash: How Obama and the Left are Driving Americans to the Government Plantation*. She was laying into LeBron James for his statements against Donald Trump.

I fucking lost it, and I called her something I have never, ever called another Black person in my entire life. Here's what I wrote on Facebook that fateful day.

MODERN DAY HOUSE NEGRO

Straight up, African-Americans like Daneen who so publicly support #45 and denounce those making a stand to raise awareness of social injustice are examples of modern-day house negroes! There I said it. They put the "Uncle" in Uncle Tom. She (and those like her) are to African-Americans what tax collectors were to the Jews.

And let me be clear. I am NOT talking about African-Americans with conservative values. Having conservative values is not mutually exclusive to recognizing social injustice and making a stand against it.

At the end of her total sell-out tirade on her now-canceled "Here's the Deal" segment on BlazeTV, she says:

"...only in America can a person earn nearly ½ billion dollars and criticize the president, and that freedom of speech is something he should respect."

I finished my tirade as thus:

WHAT THE HELL LADY! That's what this is all about. In the same video, you criticized Kaepernick and the other NFL players for exercising THEIR freedom of speech, and you ironically are attacking LeBron's because he chooses to criticize the president?

I called Mrs. Borelli a house negro because here was a Black man, LeBron James, using his wealth to uplift the Black community by creating the *I Promise School* for at-risk youth in Akron, Ohio. Did Mrs. Borelli make a point to talk about the benefits of education in at-risk communities? No. In acknowledging her political difference from LeBron did she at least also acknowledge that he was doing something that has always been a foundation of the Black conservative movement—reinvesting in the Black community to help its inhabitants rise above the crime, drugs, and violence that plague so many Black communities? Nope.

What she *did* do in that video was spout off a deluge of anger, vindictiveness, and judgment on LeBron. Why? Was it because he committed some form of white-collar crime? Did he misuse the funds or cheat the school (like President Trump had been accused of doing, which led to him paying millions in court-ordered damages)? Did he commit some form of sexual harassment or assault against any of the women he worked with? (Yet another set of accusations made against Trump, and even something he's bragged about.) No. The terrible and awful deed LeBron James did was highly criticize President Trump. And that didn't sit too well with Mrs. Borelli.

One of the tell-tale signs of a house negro back in the days of slavery was the speed and passion with which they would defend their white masters should a field negro get out of hand.

LeBron James = Field Negro

Daneen Borelli = House Negro

A turning point

I can easily say that this post was a turning point for me in my evolution as a Black man recognizing, speaking out against, and fighting injustices in this country. I couldn't take listening to her ridiculous drivel.

In that same post, I then wrote how Martin Luther King, Jr. was as hated by white people in his day as Colin Kaepernick is today. And it was this post that introduced me to that Dufus Asshole from Atlanta I referenced way back in Chapter 2. Allow me to share with you how we met. In response to my description of MLK, he wrote:

> **Dufus Asshole:** *Simply not true, Ron. I grew up in Atlanta. I know about Dr. King. I remember him. I heard people speak of him as I grew up. He was a Christian minister and no one could ever accuse him of being disrespectful. Did he ever advocate disrespecting the Anthem? No. Yes, protesting the Anthem is a good tactic. It gets attention. So would throwing a handful of feces in the face of the Prez. Would you defend that? Lastly, I have to say, your comments about "holding onto privilege" – THAT is racism. White people shall not be allowed an opinion. Sad.*

> **Me:** *Dufus Asshole 1) It's obviously apparent you know little about what was happening around the time King died. You remember him? Really? Dude, you're barely older than I am? What exactly do you remember?*

2) Nowhere in the world did I say a white person can't have an opinion. You are grasping for straws now.

3) I no longer have time to educate you. I appreciate the civil discussion, but this is going nowhere.

Go do some research on King. Read a book that really looks at his life. Or read any of the multitudes of articles about what this country thought of him at the time he was killed. Then, after doing that, I'm happy to have a discussion with you.

Oh, I probably should make it clear, Dufus Asshole is not his real name (although I can neither confirm nor deny he has the same initials). I mean, you probably figured that out already, but just in case. (Trust me when I say this made-up name suits him.) As I wrote back in Chapter 2:

> **"The inane comments that vomited out of this dude's psyche will forever go down in Facebook lore as some of the most incomprehensible, circular logic and tone-deaf drivel ever to come from the mind of a privileged white man in the South."**

Stop. Cut. Slow your roll.

(Cue audio sound of a record scratch)

I have a problem

I can't keep telling you this story. Dufus Asshole doesn't deserve the time, and frankly, my need to talk about it is part of my problem. I think I'm addicted to Facebook attention. There. I said it.

My name is Ron Dawson, and I'm a social media-holic.

There's a part of me that thinks I'm making a difference. You know what I mean? I am by no means even close to an Instagram "influencer" with millions or even hundreds of thousands of followers. Between all my various social media channels, as of this writing, I have around 10,000 followers. It's nothing to sneeze at, but let's be honest. It's not going to make a dent in changing the mind of the political zeitgeist.

So why. Why the bloody hell do I insist on continuing to use it to scream into the void of social media? Trump supporters aren't going to change their minds. As I once wrote on Medium, debating with a Trump supporter is like debating a Flat Earther. No amount of video or audio you show them—one where any other sane human can see Trump is a narcissistic, racist, misogynistic, baby-man-child—will convince them he's not the second coming of Jesus.

Likewise, those who are against him are already against him. I'm therefore preaching to the choir. Right?

So why? Why, as of this writing, have I continued? I have given it a lot of thought, and like most profound revelations in my life, the answer can be found in a movie.

One

I'm a huge fan of Billy Crystal. I can think of very few (if any) cinematic moves he's made that I do not like. From Miracle Max in *The Princess Bride* ("Have fun stormin' the castle!"), to Harry Burns in the paragon of all rom-coms, *When Harry Met Sally* ("Men and women can never be friends because the sex part always gets in the way"), to his history-making stint as host of the Oscars throughout most of the '90s. BC is funny, charming, loveable, and his presence in a film increases its watchability exponentially.

One film that can easily be classified as a Crystal classic is the 1991 film *City Slickers*. In it, Crystal stars along with Daniel Stern and Bruno Kirby as three best buds who go to a cattle farm to re-find their manhood. Once there, they meet the chief cowboy, Curly, played to Oscar-winning perfection by Jack Palance.

Curly scares the shit out of them for most of the film. His rugged exterior, quiet demeanor, and give-zero-fucks attitude make him a formidable "opponent" to the pansy-like antics of Crystal and company.

In one of the most touching and poignant scenes in the film, Curly teaches Crystal's character the secret of life. He holds up his index finger to indicate the number one. He tells Crystal that the secret to life is "one thing. You figure that out, and everything else don't mean shit!"

The reason I continue to pontificate on social media, Medium, and in this book, screaming into the proverbial "void," is one. "One thing." Or in this case, one person. It's that one person who reaches out to me now and then in a private message to tell me, "Thank you. Thank you, Ron, for sharing your stories and helping me better understand where you're coming from and the issues that face Black people."

That one person who privately reaches out to me to say, "Thank you for so eloquently expressing exactly what I've been feeling but unable to express myself."

The one person who, although disagrees with me, decides to engage with me civilly, privately, without thousands of potential commenters. And in that engagement, their hearts, minds, and sometimes even their "eyes," are opened.

For every one hundred futile and frustrating comments, there's one—one individual who I was able to reach through the noise. One individual whose life was changed or whose heart was touched.

Perhaps that one person is reading these words right now. Perhaps that one person is *you*. And if it is, let me say thank *you*. Thank you for reading. Thank you for opening your heart and mind. May you have the courage of your conviction to use whatever platform *you* have to do the same. Because at the end of the day, it's usually one person who changes the world. And that's enough for me to continue to fight the good fight. (Albeit, with far fewer futile debates with brainwashed automatons who've lost all ability to think for themselves. Their souls have been swallowed by "The Nothing," and there is no amount of Luck Dragons that can bring them back.)

Unfortunately, one Black man's "good fight" is another white man's burden. Apparently, raising issues of racial injustice is super-inconvenient for some wypipo.

Chapter 19:

Positive Ron

What happens when the nice and "safe" Black man no longer is?

Before writing a deluge of blog and Medium posts about politics, faith, and race relations, my topical expertise and the well from which I most often partook, was the visual arts. The most controversial topics I wrote about were related to editing software and marketing strategies for amateur photographers.

But I also wrote twice as much about topics that inspired photographers and filmmakers to find their inner voice as an artist without letting anyone put it out. I wrote about the importance of positive perspectives in life; that your self-worth as an artist was not based on how many likes your photos or videos got on Instagram or Facebook. I was the funny, articulate, relatively successful, published, and one of the few people of color on the professional videographer circuit.

And I was utterly safe.

What do I mean by that, you ask? Well, you never needed to worry that I would make you feel guilty about your white privilege (assuming you were white). You never needed to be concerned I would challenge you to look in the mirror, question the state of race relations, and see what part you played in it (for better or worse). If you said any colorful jokes around me that were borderline racially insensitive, offensive, or outright racist—there was no cause for alarm that I might challenge you.

So after Trump won the election, and an increasing number of his brainwashed, racially insensitive/racist/tone-deaf followers felt more emboldened to say the stupidest shit, I spoke out. I shared articles and podcasts that broke down what was happening in this country. I contributed to the great conversation that has been going on since Congress signed the 13th, 14th, and 15th amendments into existence. That discussion being: who are Black people in this country, what do and don't they deserve in life, and do we need to keep Affirmative Action around?

Then on June 29, 2018, I shared a video from a 1939 Nazi rally held at Madison Square Garden. You read that right. Twenty-thousand *American* citizens and Nazi sympathizers filled the iconic stadium to spout their vile hatred. It was eerily like a Trump rally. One of the many videographers that follow me on social media responded to that post.

> **Tweedle Dum (not his real name):** Do I only see your division posts? Please tell me you have a positive post that builds people up every once in a while.
>
> **Me:** All you need to do is click my name at the top to see all my posts. If you only see my "division" posts (as you put it), then Facebook's algorithm thinks that's all you want to see from me. :)
>
> **Tweedle Dum:** Nope, want positive from you. From the first day I met you at WEVA 2007 you were a very positive person. I'm guessing Mark Z at facebook likes your posts that have a dividing angle. They get more traction I'm guessing. I would rather see Positive Ron.
>
> **Me:** Oh, you want to see Positive Ron. I get it. Would this help?

At this point, I added that image of Buckwheat in a bellhop uniform with the caption "O-tay!"

> **Me:** I'm sure this makes you much more comfortable. In truth, I don't recall posting anything "negative." Many of the posts I've made ARE uplifting and encouraging, to the right demographic. One man's divisive post is another woman's uplifting encouragement. Or a disillusioned Christian's ray of hope. It's all in your perspective my friend.

> **Tweedle Dum:** Yea, guess you're not the man you once we're. Best of luck sir.
>
> **Me:** Nope. Sorry [Tweedle Dum]. I'm DEFINITELY not the same man I was. Of course, I see that as a POSITIVE thing.

As frustrating as it was to get this response, there was a part of me that felt like little Macaulay Culkin in *Home Alone* yelling, "Yes!" I had risen to a new level of Black power resistance—one in which wypipo, who had once respected and loved me, were falling by the wayside. Is this not the sign of every great resistance leader? You see it in so many stories, since the days of the Bible:

> *Moses gave up his royal life as a Prince of Egypt to lead the Jews.*
>
> *The Pharisee Saul became the Apostle Paul.*
>
> *Malcolm Little became Malcolm X.*
>
> *Jake Sully helped the Na'vi rebel against the human invaders of Pandora.*
>
> *Anakin Skywalker became Darth Vader. (Okay, maybe that's not the best example, but you get the idea.)*

I had entered a new elite club reserved for those warriors of justice willing to sling off their princely robes in favor of donning the people's armor and fight the good fight. Is there any better sign you're on the right path than when the forces of darkness stand up against you?

And just as I'm thinking this, wouldn't you know it, like the cackling echo of the emperor's laugh at the end of *The Rise of Skywalker* trailer, the unmistakable sounds of Sam's laughter can be heard behind me.

> **Sam:** Man! I thought you had lost it when you were telling that breakdance story. But damn! You've taken self-delusion to a whole nutha level of grandeur with this muthafuckin' shit you're spewing.

And with that, it was time for another lesson in Blackness.

Chapter 20:

Waxing Philosophical

Apparently, all these years I've had *Karate Kid* all wrong

Me: I notice you always seem to show up right when I'm feeling good about myself, or when I have a particularly happy or pleasant memory.

Sam: Like when you were reminiscing about all those white bitches you used to like on TV. Oh. I'm sorry. I know that word offends you. Is "hos" better?

Me: Remember when you told me that one man's angel is another man's devil?

Sam: Yeah. Do you realize who I am to you?

Me: Yep. Neither. You're just a pain in the ass.

Sam laughs that wise-crackin' laugh that only Samuel L. Jackson can do. He holds up his hands as if to surrender and says...

Sam: You got me, homie. You figured me out. I'm just one giant, spiritual hemorrhoid!

> **Me:** Well, since you're here, you might as well drop some knowledge. What great words of wisdom does your mighty Blackness want to bestow upon me today?

Sam puts his hands down and into the pockets of his Black suit. He looks me over. It's almost as if he peers right into my soul. It's an uneasy and unsettling feeling. For the briefest moment, he no longer seemed to be Sam Jackson. I can't explain it. It was sorta creepy. It was as if whatever imp (or angel) was behind those eyes, the one wearing this Sam Jackson "costume," for a moment broke character and revealed its true nature.

Then, in a flash, Sam was back.

> **Sam:** Remember the last time I was here, and you so expertly handled me with a barrage of biting repartee?
>
> **Me:** Yes. I recall.
>
> **Sam:** And you said that I "Miyagi'd" you, referring to the 1984 movie *Karate Kid* and how Mr. Miyagi tricked Daniel into learning ka-ra-tay and shit.
>
> **Me:** Well, technically, I was referencing a line from 2011's *Crazy Stupid Love*, which, in turn, was referencing the aforementioned '80s classic. Why?
>
> **Sam:** Nigga. Do you really talk like that?
>
> **Me:** Like what?
>
> **Sam:** Who the fuck says "aforementioned" in a conversation?
>
> **Me:** Well, as you so frequently like to remind me, this isn't a conversation. It's a book.
>
> **Sam:** Touché, Ronald. Touché.
>
> **Me:** Anyway, I assume you were going somewhere with the Miyagi reference?

Sam: Oh. Yes. Right. Thank you. So what was it that made Miyagi's trick so special?

Me: Easy. He got Daniel to learn karate without him knowing he was learning karate.

Sam: Let's see what's on the board. Survey *says*! <EHHHHHH>. Nope. Try again, muthafucka.

Me: There's no trying again. That *is* what makes the trick so special.

Sam: Really? Are you sure about that?

Me: Yes. I'm sure. I think that's obvious.

Sam: Well, what if I told you that the trick wasn't that he got Daniel to learn ka-ra-tay by having him paint his fence and clean all his cars. The trick was getting Daniel to clean all his fucking cars and paint that fucking fence, and then convince him he was learning ka-ra-tay.

Me: Why do you keep saying "karate" like that?

Sam: Isn't that how you're supposed to pronounce it?

Me: If you're speaking Japanese. Anyway, with all due respect to your dumbass theory, let me just say, in your immortal words, "Get the fuck out of here!" That is *not* what was happening.

Sam: Oh really?!

Me: Yes! *Really*!

Sam: You ever heard of Occam's Razor?

Me: I saw *Contact*. Yes, I heard of it.

Sam: And?

Me: And what?

Sam: What does it mean?

Me: Something like, all things being equal, the simplest solution is most likely the right one.

Sam: Correctomundo. So, Einstein. Tell me. What's more likely: that an old Japanese dude who'd seen the horrors of war and got his ass put in a fucking concentration camp by the white racists who ran this muthafuckin' country takes the time to teach some spoiled, *white* ass *I-talian* kid from the valley the secrets of his country's most treasured religion and art form through painting a fence and washing cars? Or, he saw a way to get his fence painted and his cars cleaned, then made up that karate shit? Muthafucka, you actually fucking believe you can earn a fucking Black belt in ka-ra-tay by waxing on and waxing off?

Me: Of course not. It's a movie.

Sam: Yeah, but they had you believing that shit, didn't they?

Sam walks over to me and looks into my eyes.

Sam: You walked out of that fucking theater thinking a limp ass white boy from the valley, with a couple of months at best of "wax on, wax off" and a one-legged jump kick, could advance in a Black belt tournament to the championship match against real ka-ra-tay Black belts who've studied for years?

Sam stands there. Hands in his pockets. Looking me dead in the eye. I swallow hard.

Sam: And then what happens in the fucked-up sequel? He goes to the heart of Japan itself and beats a *young* Japanese dude who probably grew up with that shit. How? With some fuckin' Jack Lalanne hip twist! All the while getting the Japanese people to root for the cute white boy against their own kind. The fuck?!

Me: Well. I, I...guess? It was a movie. You know. Suspension of disbelief and all that.

Sam: They say the greatest trick the devil ever played was getting the world to think he doesn't exist. Well, the greatest trick the Hollywood "devil" ever played was getting a whole world to fucking believe you can become a Black belt with wax on and wax off. You and everyone else were fucking indoctrinated into thinking that shit is so easy that anyone can do it by painting a fence with a limp wrist and shit. In one movie they totally and utterly emasculated one of the most beautiful, meaningful, and difficult-to-master art forms to ever come out of Asia. So in the end, you lost respect for the discipline that goes into it, and you lost respect for the culture behind it.

I must admit. My mind was kinda blown. I had never thought of it like that. I felt the same way I felt after that scene in *Inglourious Basterds* when during the name game with the Germans, we learn about the metaphor of *King Kong* representing the plight of the Negro brought to America in chains. And that's when Sam says...

Sam: You remember that scene in *Inglourious Basterds* when...

Me: Oh yeah. When, during the name game with the German officers, we learn about the metaphor of *King Kong* representing the plight of the Negro brought over to America in chains? I was just thinking about that!

Sam: No nigga. But that *was* a cool scene. No. I'm talking about the end when the Basterds assassinate Hitler and shit.

Me: Oh, that scene. Yes. What about it?

Sam: Remember all the flack Quentin got for writing the end that way. They accused him of revisionist history and shit.

Me: Yeah. I vaguely remember that. So?

Sam: So it's okay to butcher a beautiful art form like ka-ra-tay, but heaven forbid if you portray the assassination of an asshole like Hitler.

Me: I don't know, Sam. I kinda feel like you're all over the place with these analogies. Do you think you can land this plane? Bring it home. Make it plain. What's your point?

Sam: My point is it's going to take more than a metaphorical "waxing on and waxing off" for you to become the Black man we need in this fight. Pissing off a few ignorant-ass white folks on Facebook is hardly a movement on the needle for what needs to get done in this muthafucka, and you basking in the glory of one stupid asshole saying, "I want positive Ron back" is a waste of your fucking time. You need to be Miyagi—but not the Hollywood, sanitized edition that sells out his kind. You need to be the Occam's Razor, muthafuckin' *Black* edition that gets these fascists, racists ass mo-fos to do what *you* want but make them *think* they're getting what *they* want. You, know, like what wives have been doing to husbands ever since some overbearing, patriarchal asshole man invented the concept of marriage in the first place. Second, recognize and wake up to the fact that you've been brainwashed your entire life that the white man can do *anything*. That even a skinny, spoiled white kid can go into the heart of Japan, the birthplace of ka-ra-tay...

Me: I actually think the roots go back to China.

Sam gives me that evil eye.

Me: Sorry. Continue.

Sam: That a white kid can go into Japan, and with a corny-ass Richard Marx soundtrack and a lame-ass Richard Simmons move, kick the ass of a Japanese ka-ra-tay master. Wake up, Mr. Dawson!

Me: I think you meant Peter Cetera.

Sam: What?

Me: You said Richard Marx, but I'm sure you're referencing the song "Glory of Love" by Peter Cetera.

Sam: Who the fuck cares, asshole?! Do you get my muthafuckin' point or what? Jesus. I'm done here!

With that, he turns around, starts to walk out, and vanishes.

Sam says some crazy shit most of the time, but I would be lying if I didn't admit he got the wheels in my head turning. Have I gotten *Karate Kid* wrong all these years?

Shiiiiit! That asshole had me for a minute. Ka-ra-tay, my ass.

Hmmm?

Chapter 21:

There and Black Again

How a Black man lost, then rediscovered, the joy of being Black

Do you remember this exchange between Sam and me back in the chapter about bad words?

> **Sam:** Despite your *Leave it to Beaver* childhood, I understand you actually do have some Black friends?
>
> **Me:** First off, my childhood was actually quite Black, thank you very much. But in answer to your question, yes, I have Black friends.

I realized that at the time, you probably had no idea what the hell I was talking about with respect to my "quite Black" childhood. If my childhood was so "Blackety Black," how did I end up writing this book?

If that question crossed your mind, I don't blame you. So dear reader, let me 'splain.

Omowale Ujamaa

No, that's not the name of some Wakandan Prince. It's the name of an elementary school I attended in the third and fourth grades. In the late '60s and early '70s, there rose out of the Civil Rights movement African-centric elementary schools whose charters were to instill within their populations pride in African heritage. Omowale was one such school near the foothills of Altadena, California, in the mid-to-late '70s. Omowale is Swahili for "the child has returned," and Ujamaa is the fourth principle of Kwanzaa "cooperative economics."

My time at Omowale is some of the most memorable of my childhood. We'd greet the principal every morning with an African dance and ceremony. Then do a similar ceremony at the end of the school day. Instead of traditional numeric grades (e.g., first grade, second grade, third grade, etc.), each grade was named after an African tribe. I was in the Ashanti grade (fourth). My brother, two years younger, was a Zulu. The highest grade in the school was Watusi (seventh). I thought *all* schools did this. It wasn't until I finally left Omowale that I learned that the fifth grade was just boring old grade five and not Yoruba.

I remember learning about Egyptian and Nigerian gods. Since I was raised by Southern Baptist mother, I naturally assumed those gods were sort of "lieutenants" to the "main" god. (It's funny how a fourth-grade, er, I mean, an Ashanti-grade brain thinks.) I remember celebrating Kwanzaa at the school but hiding that we also celebrated Christmas. (Which, as an adult, doesn't make sense to me now because Kwanzaa isn't a religious holiday. The two don't have to be mutually exclusive.)

I remember "corporal" punishment at the school. This was back when parents of all races were still allowed to whoop kids. And you damn well knew Black parents whooped kids. The only thing worse than getting whooped by a Black *parent* was getting whooped by a six-foot, two-inch tall obsidian-skinned math teacher who had a two-foot long, one-and-a-quarter-inch thick paddle and permission by the aforementioned Black parents to take it to yo ass if it got out of line. And in a school like Omowale that was committed to giving their young Black children discipline, "getting out of line" could be anything from talking back to being late for class.

Dear Lord in heaven, you did *not* want to be late for class at Omowale. Because before the pain and humiliation of getting your butt swatted with a thick-ass paddle, you were humiliated by your classmates who would sing the theme song to the '70s cop show *S.W.A.T.* to herald in the certain pain that was coming your way. (At the end of that first melody phrase to the song, we'd add the words "You're gonna get a, get a SWAT!" Kids can be so cruel!)

It should be no surprise that I also remember my crushes at school. (Proof positive that I *did* like Black girls besides Tootie from *Facts of Life*.) Omowale was where I was first introduced to the infamous Black woman head shake. You know the one. You can see it when you piss a sista off and she's about to share some potent words with you.

Apparently, it is either taught at a young age or ingrained in the blood cells of young Black girls. I got it when my "girlfriend" Wendy (we held hands for a few days, I guess that made us married or whatever) got mad when she found out I also like Chini (pronounced CHEE-nee). I must have told Chini I was "broken up" (which I wasn't) because they *both* cornered me to give me pieces of their respective minds (and respective head shakes).

Yeah. Those were the days. Surrounded by Black kids, Black music, Black food, and Black culture, every weekday for two years. My two subsequent years in public schools were pretty racially diverse as well. (As you can see from my fifth-grade class photo.) Then, I went to South Pasadena Jr. High School, and for the next fourteen years, I had little to no interaction with my people.

Then, I made a movie.

Back in Black

It was the spring of 1995. I was a marketing manager at Screenplay Systems, makers of the popular Movie Magic line of film production software and located in beautiful downtown Burbank, California. A year earlier, I had moved down from Cupertino, California (home of Apple), where I had attended De Anza Community College's Film and Television School's Fiction Workshop Program.

Each quarter, the entire class would rally behind one chosen student's film project. Said student would be the writer/director, and everyone else in the class would hold various other roles on a film set. It was an excellent hands-on learning experience. I had been everything from a grip to craft services to production manager. Based on past projects I had submitted, I was confident that I was on track to be a writer/director. But in the spring of '94, I took the new job a Screenplay Systems and never got my shot at the director's chair.

I've always considered myself a go-get-'em kind of person. And if you thought I was going to let a little thing like no longer being enrolled in a film school keep me from making the short film I would've been able to do at De Anza, well, you would be sorely mistaken.

A year into my new gig I was ready to take on the mantle of writer/director and bring my vision to life. I was going to make a film called *Just Friends*, my "Black" homage to *When Harry Met Sally*. It was a short rom-com about what happens when an ex-boyfriend and girlfriend try to be just friends and she learns he slept with a mutual friend shortly after their breakup. (I can't remember whether this was inspired by true events. Let's say, um, it wasn't?)

The problem was, I was no longer in a film school with access to free equipment and free labor. I was in the real world, and that meant using my own money to rent equipment and somehow finding a cast and crew.

Enter Joseph DaShawn Cochran (i.e., JD).

Side note: As of the writing of this book, nearly thirty years into my friendship with JD, I *never* knew what the "D" in JD stood for. I remember hitting him up on group text and asking him when I came to this part of the book. Don't let his biraciality mislead you. This brutha is Black. He's Blacker than Black. He's like from Long Beach (Strong Beach) Black. So I jokingly guessed names like Darnyell, Deyangelo, and Darryl. I was trying to come up with the Blackest sounding "D" names I could think of. I thought his middle name was probably something like David or Daniel, considering his first name was Joseph. Those are all strong biblical names and given his strict Christian upbringing (against which he long ago rebelled), I could see him having such a name. But the fact that it is DaShawn! That was fucking perfect. It's so, so...so *Black*! It's way Blacker than anything I was guessing. This was a perfect example of real life being better than the shit you make up. I could not have asked for a better plot twist. Well, I guess it's not really a plot twist, but more like a literary reveal that perfectly encapsulates the role Mr. DaShawn plays in this story. But I digress.

As I mentioned at the beginning of this book, JD and his wife, Yolanda, are my best friends. The whole reason I'm telling this story of how I made this film (which, when you think about it, isn't really "on brand" for what this book is about) is to set the stage for how these two people came into my life, and the role they play in the Shakespearean melodrama that is my blaxistential crisis.

Obviously, JD and Yolanda are Black. Well, technically, JD is only half-Black (his momma is white). And come to think of it, Yolanda has a bunch of Creole in her, so who knows to what extent her blood is pure, grade A, 100 percent negro (I have no doubt that if they're reading this right now, they are rolling their eyes.) The fact that they are my BFFs is ironically poignant in my story because when I think about it, it's probably all their fault (in a good way) that I'm writing this book and that I'm being "haunted" by the angel/devil Samuel L. Jackson.

Before JD and Yo, the last time I had more than two *close* Black friends (outside of my cousin) was high school and my days hanging with Chris Spencer, and then four years before that when I was in elementary school. Now here was this dude about ten shades lighter than me on the outside and damn near twenty darker on the inside. He was a filmmaker and writer working as an intern at Screenplay Systems.

Black on set

When I was ready to shoot my short-film opus, I hit him up. He was a graduate of USC's film school and theater program and I figured he could hook me up with a cast and crew. He also happened to own a high-end Canon Hi8 video camera and therefore could be my DP (which may sound like an ancient relic by today's standards of 8K RED cameras; but back in the day, it was a pretty sweet setup).

JD did indeed hook me up. He and Yo have this special group of SC friends they call "The Clique." It's about twenty or so African American professionals (and two white people) all in the film and TV business. They're actors in mainstream TV shows, exec producers of HBO, studio execs, editors, and the like. It's an impressive group of friends with a special bond unlike any I've seen. They are tighter than family.

But back in 1995, they were all still film school grads at varying levels of their aspiring careers. And I got a small group of them to crew for my little film. And this is where the introduction of JD and crew represent another key turning point in the story.

For my white readers, I need to explain to you what it's like working on a film set with a group of Black friends from a university located in the middle of da hood (USC is kinda like an oasis of rich white people in the middle of some of the toughest and Blackest parts of LA). Every shoot day was like a nonstop comedy club. Everybody would clown on each other (that is, make fun of, and tease in a harsh, yet loving way). JD and the coproducer Angela would get into it so much I wasn't exactly sure they were friends. But they were tight as two friends can be.

And it was this experience amongst my people that I had long forgotten. I had glimpses of it back in high school hanging out with Chris and *his* friends. I got glimpses of it during large family gatherings with my Jamaican stepdad and his crazy family. I got glimpses of it back at Omowale singing the theme song to "S.W.A.T." as a harbinger of the swats to come to the tardy. It's one of those aspects of the African American experience that makes it special—seemingly nonstop laughter and love expressed in the form of insults, jabs, and barbs.

And it was experiencing this unusual camaraderie that allowed me for the first time in my life to be comfortable in my non-Blackness. Because you know for damn sure I *too* was the butt of many a barb. Whether it was my outdated Cross Colors shorts and Spike Lee jersey, my penchant for crafting sentences in ways that even white people didn't know could be so confusing and overly complicated, or my embarrassing ignorance of the hottest hip-hop stars of the time. But without a doubt, the most targeted aspect of my Ronness was my voice.

I don't sound "Black." Yes, I know even saying that sentence may on the surface feel shallow (see what I did there? Surface? Shallow? No? Okay.

Nevermind). Anyway, but let's be honest, we *all* know what it means to "sound Black." I'm not talking about speaking ebonics or something silly like that. I'm talking about the kind of thing Eddie Murphy's character Axel Foley so classically makes fun of in *Beverly Hills Cop* when he tells the Black cop who's been following him (along with his white partner) how to say, "We're not going to fall for that banana in the tailpipe trick."

So you take a nerdy, aspiring, Spike-Lee-wannabe filmmaker that dresses like the Fresh Prince (in all his '90s glory) but sounds like Carlton, and you can pretty much just put a target on my back for this group of jokesters who pull no punches.

And you know what: I laughed with them. There was a time not too much earlier when being the butt of Black folks' jokes would send me as a still-sensitive college student meandering around the campus of UC Berkeley, feeling sorry for myself and raising fists to God asking why I was such an outcast—not Black enough for the Blacks and too Black for the whites.

By this time, besides just being older and wiser, combined with witnessing how these friends expressed their love for one another in the form of biting repartee, momma jokes, and jabs about jacked-up hair, I felt loved too. (If they *didn't* tease me, I would've been worried.)

I realized what the secret was: *safety*. There was a profound sense that you could be fully and wholly yourself, and still be genuinely loved. You felt safe to just be you.

I wonder what this country would be like if it were like the set of *Just Friends*—a safe place where every man and woman, regardless of race, religion, or political persuasion, could feel safe to say what they think and feel and know that they would still be validated, acknowledged, or loved.

Sam: That is such a beautiful and touching sentiment, Ronald.

I jump back in my seat, startled, as Sam appears out of nowhere. Again.

Chapter 22:

"Mine" Yo Bizness

How wise words from a white wizard help a Black man find a proper perspective

Me: What the *fuck*! Geeze-us! Why the frak do you do that?

Sam: How is it that in one fucking sentence you go from saying "fuck" to "frak"? Goddamn nigga. It's like some kind of emergency profanity alert goes off in your brain or something and prevents you from dropping an f-bomb more than once in a sentence.

Me: I don't know what it is. It just doesn't feel right in my skin, I guess. Anyway, don't change the freaking subject.

Sam laughs at my penchant to iterate the euphemisms I use instead of the "f" word.

Me: What is it you want now?

Sam: I just wanted to drop in and say how touching and beautiful that sentiment was. You know, that thing about people feeling safe and shit.

Me: Oh really. That's what you're doing here?

Sam: Yes.

Me: I don't believe you.

Sam: Why? Can't I come down here and...

Me: You keep saying, "Come down." Are you sure you're not coming up?

Sam: Are you implying I'm some kind of devil or demon or something, coming up from hell?

He makes a classic pose like Nosferatu as he says this.

Me: Well, I don't think you're beaming down from a starship. And I sure as hell don't think you're an angel.

Sam: Oh, yeah, based on what?

Me: Really? I need to explain it?

Sam: Yeah muthafucka. You tell me why the hell you assume you know so much about angels and shit. You ever see one?

Me: Well, of course not.

Sam: Then shut the fuck up about shit you don't know.

Me: You see. I don't think an angel would talk like that.

Sam: Again, upon what theological premise are you basing that hypothesis about the linguistic habits of cherubim and seraphim?

Me: Why in the world would an angel, a servant of the Holy God, use such foul language?

Sam: First, who says the language is foul? Second, even if it is, who says angels can't, don't, or wouldn't use it?

Me: I believe it's Ephesians 4:29 that says, "Do not let any unwholesome talk come out of your mouths, but only what is helpful for building others up according to their needs, that it may benefit those who listen."

Sam: Ain't that what I been doin' with you since I got on the scene? Building you up?

Me: You're joking, right?

Sam: Am I?

Me: Aren't you?

Sam: So you're saying that if you say "frak" instead of "fuck," that absolves you of "unwholesome talk"?

Me: From a certain point of view, yes.

Sam: But if you were on *Battlestar Galactica*, "frak" would sound just as bad as "fuck." Correct?

Me: I guess. Sure. But that's not even a real thing. So using a made-up bad word is different from using a real bad word.

Sam: But the only thing that makes it bad is your perception of it. If the first word a baby hears is "fuck," there is nothing empirically wrong or off to that baby. It's just another sound.

I can't help but think of the first time I ever uttered a bit of profanity. Back at my babysitter's. Remember? The other kids told me to say "shit," I did, not knowing what it meant. Then I was overheard by the babysitter who took me to the bathroom and had my mouth washed out with soap. It left such an indelible effect on me, now over forty years later, I still remember it. Could that be the origin of my issue?

Me: Yes, Sam. I suppose you're right. It's just a word. So please, tell me. Why the fuck are you down here again?

Sam: I told you. I thought that shi—excuse me. That *stuff* you said about feeling safe was moving. And I wanted to compliment you.

I sit and stare at him for a few moments. Trying to figure out if he's telling the truth.

Me: So then, may I go back to telling the story.

Sam: By all means.

Sam sits back and puts his hands behind his head. I stop and try to remember where I was going but can't.

Me: Fuck it. I can't even remember now. See what you did, muthafucka?

Sam applauds.

Sam: Well done, Ronald. Two f-bombs in one muthafuckin' sentence. My nigga.

Me: You are *definitely* no angel.

Sam: Look, I was a tad disingenuous when I said earlier I was just down here to compliment you.

Me: No shit. And?

Sam: Well, you were saying, what would it be like if the world were a safe place for everyone to speak their mind.

Me: Yes?

Sam: Everyone?

Me: That's the idea. Are there some people you would prefer *not* to feel safe speaking their minds?

Sam: Are there *any* people *you* can think of for whom it would probably be best *not* to feel safe to speak their mind?

Me: Obviously not, or else I wouldn't say it.

Sam leans in close to me, looks me in the eye, and says...

Sam: And that is why you fail.

Me: What? Are you the Black Yoda now?

Sam: I can tell you right the fuck now who I don't want feeling safe. Racist muthafuckas who for the past four years have felt "safe" to come out of their racist closets and say and do every fucking racist thing.

Me: I think you're missing my point, Sam.

Sam: No, as usual, you're missing *mine*.

VOMF: I actually think he knows your point very well.

It's been a minute, but out of nowhere comes the voice of Morgan Freeman. Sam wastes no time turning his attention to the sky.

Sam: Man. Not this nigga again. Morgan? Morgan? You barely show up in this nigga's life and right when I'm about to make a very salient point, you gotta intrude and stick your iconic-ass voice where no one asked for it. Can't you mind yo own damn bizness?

Me: Why do you think you're the only one allowed to have an opinion about situations like this?

Sam: It's not that I think I'm the only one allowed to have an opinion. I'm just the only muthafucka up in here making any goddamn sense. We have your confused ass acting like some fuckin' wannabe Huey P. Newton one minute and Mahatma Gandhi the next. Then we have this jive turkey booming down from, what, heaven or some shit, butting in at the least helpful times.

Me: Wait. Did you just say "jive turkey"?

Sam: Excuse me?

Me: You just called the voice of Morgan Freeman "jive turkey."

Sam: So.

Me: So...that seems very, I don't know, outdated of you. I mean, besides that fucked up jheri curl on your head, for the most part you normally seem to have a more contemporary use of urban vernacular. But "jive turkey"? Are you channeling Redd Foxx now? JJ Walker? I think whatever demon, imp, angel, or whatever the hell is under there, that Samuel L. Jackson veneer is crackin'.

The voice of Morgan Freeman starts to chuckle. Sam addresses the sky.

Sam: And what do you think is so funny? Don't you go encouraging this shit!

Sam turns his attention back to me.

Sam: Oh, so you think you're a jokester now? I'm just some clown you can make fun of, huh? I've come all this way because I genuinely care about the cause you're fighting for, man. I see a spark in you, and I want to ignite it. And this is how you treat me? Man, dawg. I had you wrong. I thought there was a decent human being under there. You know, someone with empathy and a sense of honor and integrity. Wow! I can see I was wrong about that shit.

For the first time, I feel guilty. Really, really guilty. Was he right? Had I really given up and sacrificed that part of me that is honorable, just, and forthright? Had I gotten so cold-hearted and callous that I no longer cared about people's feelings? Even Samuel L. Jackson's? I start to drop my head in shame when Sam starts cracking up.

Sam: Ahhhh shit! Man. You should've seen the look on your face. Damn, were you about to cry and shit? *Aaaaaahhhh*. That shit was funny!

Me: Are you fucking kidding me?

Sam: What? Can't take a little joke, Ronald? Is it that easy to get you to feel sorry for someone who, according to you, has been your adversary? A few seemingly heartfelt words and a sullen face, and all is forgiven with you?

> **Me:** You're fucking twisted, you know that? Why are you even here?! *What is your point?!*
>
> **Sam:** Figure it out, muthafucka! *Figure. It. Out!*

And with a puff of smoke, Sam is gone. I stand, reeling with anger and breathing heavily.

> **VOMF:** How are you feeling, son?
>
> **Me:** Oh, hey, Morgan. I forgot you were here. I don't know how I'm feeling, to be honest with you.
>
> **VOMF:** It seems like what Sam said really bothered you.
>
> **Me:** I don't know what it is about him. On the surface he seems like this clichéd narrative device in my life to make me look at issues that are too hard to look at as myself. Like I need him to be some kind of proxy for my conscience.
>
> **VOMF:** That would be a little too "on the nose," don't you think?
>
> **Me:** Exactly! Way too on the nose. So then I think that maybe he's just a way for me to provide some levity in this heavy time of my life. I mean, there is some tough shit going on in my life now. It goes way beyond just that asshole Trump.
>
> **VOMF:** Oh yeah. Like what else?
>
> **Me:** Like, for over twenty years, I've been so assured in my faith. I used to lead those "check out Christianity" dinners like Alpha. I was the guy getting online and defending the faith with all the best apologetic arguments from Augustine to Zacharias.[12] But lately, I've been in a serious season of doubt.
>
> **VOMF:** All because of the evangelical support of Trump?

---

12 This is a reference to the late Ravi Zacharias, an internationally renowned author and Christian apologist. Before his death, he was embroiled in a sex and spiritual abuse scandal. Oh, the irony that I referenced his name in a paragraph of me talking about how the church has failed me.

Me: Well, if I'm being honest, it started before that. But I think it's safe to say his support and damn-near-worshipped status by evangelicals in this country has seriously exacerbated the situation.

VOMF: I can imagine that must be hard for you. In many ways, you're going through a couple of existential crises. One of racial identity and one of faith.

Me: Yeah. I think you're right, Voice of Morgan Freeman. I think you're right.

VOMF: I wonder if I might not be able to offer you a small bit of advice. If you would allow me.

Me: That would be wonderful. I would like that a lot. I could use some from someone other than that Frankenstein-like combination of a Dickens ghost and a poorly written Reginald Hudlin character.

VOMF: Now, if I recall, you're somewhat of a sci-fi/fantasy fan, are you not?

Me: Yes, absolutely.

VOMF: Well, would it be safe to say you've seen *The Fellowship of the Ring*? You know, the first *Lord of the Rings* movie.

I'm a little confused as to where the Voice of Morgan Freeman is going with this. But I play along.

Me: Yes, of course. One of my faves.

VOMF: Good. Good. Now, then I bet you remember the scene when the Fellowship was in the Mines of Moria, and they came to a junction in the path where they weren't sure where to go.

Me: Yes. I remember that scene. But please don't tell me you're going to quote the line where Frodo says he wishes none of these things had happened, and then Gandalf tells him, "So do all who live to see such times, but that is not for them to decide. Yadda, yadda, yadda."

VOMF: Yes! Yes! So you remember that?

Me: Really, Morgan? That's the advice you were going to give me? That's, like, so predictable, man. That's the best advice you got?

VOMF: Tell me, son, what's wrong with that advice?

Me: Nothing. It's great advice. It's a great line. It encapsulates a spiritual message with flavors of many of the world's religions. It's one of my favorite lines from the movie. In fact, whether one claims any kind of spirituality, that line has truth.

VOMF: Well, what's with your negative reaction to my bringing it up then?

Me: I don't know. It's just. I thought you were going to say something I didn't already know. I was hoping you'd give me some insight that I haven't heard before.

VOMF: Well, why would I do that?

Me: Excuse me?

VOMF: Why would I tell you something brand new when the knowledge and wisdom you already have works perfectly fine? I was going to remind you of it. You gotta learn, son, that not every lesson in life that moves you forward is one you haven't heard before. Sometimes the best words of wisdom are the ones you have heard a thousand times, but you must hear it again, and again, and again. The human spirit is stubborn, and we're all too quick to forget the most important things in life. So we must be reminded.

Me: I guess that makes sense. Yeah, I can see that.

The Voice of Morgan Freeman was right. We're all too quick to disregard and shrug off hearing something we've heard before. Sometimes we have to be reminded to be kind to strangers, brush our teeth before going to bed, say "I love you" to our partner, even if we've already said it multiple times that week. Or remember that there's no use worrying about what you can't control. How you handle the things life throws you means everything.

> **Me:** Morgan, could you do me a favor?
>
> **VOMF:** Sure, son. Anything.
>
> **Me:** Would you recite that line? The one you were going to remind me about. Recite it to me in that meaningful, melodic, and memorable way that only you can.
>
> **VOMF:** Give me the cue.

I clear my throat, take a deep breath, then summon my inner Frodo.

> **Me:** "I wish Trump had never been elected. I wish none of this had happened."

And in that slow, deliberate, *Shawshank Redemption*-esque tone that made Zihuantanejo sound as sweet as honey, the Voice of Morgan Freeman replies.

> **VOMF:** So do all who live to see such times, but that is not for them to decide. All we must decide is what to do with the time given to us. There are other forces in the world at work, Ron, besides the will of injustice and racism. Trump was *meant* to become president. In which case, you also were *meant* to have a spiritually challenging self-discovery and racial identity crisis. And that's an encouraging thought.
>
> **Me:** Thank you, Voice of Morgan Freeman.
>
> **VOMF:** My pleasure, son.

I can see now why the Voice of Morgan Freeman is in such high demand. It's always so soothing and calming when I talk with him. Ahhhh...

And I was about to have a revelation that would illustrate just how prescient his advice was.

Chapter 23:

Skool'd, Dazed, and Confused

The third most embarrassing admission in this book

Do you ever have one of those ideas you think is brilliant at the time of its inception? A cool company name or URL? A sweet movie concept? That tattoo of your significant other on your neck? Joining Amway?

Then reality hits and that brilliance quickly fades into a pathetic malaise of self-pity and profound regret.

Well, I had one such idea. Luckily, my dear friends JD and Yolanda talked me down from the ledge.

Don't gimme no Slack

You have to understand that collectively, JD and Yolanda are sort of like the Fresh Prince to my Carlton. If that analogy is lost on you, they are the Fonzie to my Richie Cunningham; the Marty McFly to my George; the Eddie Winslow to my Steve Urkel; the "Dre and Bow" to my Junior. I'm running out of pop-culture comparisons, so hopefully one of those will do it for you.

As I reacquaint myself with my people, in their own loving way, they guide me along when my choices in life are, shall we say, questionable.

The following is a real Slack conversation we had during the writing of this book. (I could write a whole 'nother chapter on why we use Slack

over iMessage, but I'd go over my publisher's page limit, so I'll have to
leave you in the dark on that one. Sorry.)

Me: I have crazy idea. This was something I had wanted to do as
research for my book. I call it...SKOOL'D, DAZED, & CONFLICTED.
Here's the description:

*What happens when a fifty-ish y/o "blerd," who grew up in a white
world, pledges a Black fraternity in order to find his "Blackness." A
funny, poignant, and often cringe-inducing documentary of what the
human spirit can go through when a man facing a possible mid-life
crisis seeks out a connection to his people he never had.*

I would go through all the aches and pains and humiliation the other
pledges go through, so I can have the Black experience I never got in
college. The only knowledge I have is what I remember from Spike's
movie *School Daze*.

Can you imagine me among a group of twenty-year-old Black
bruthas, having to keep up? I'd tune in to watch that. I'm actually
in pretty good shape. I think I could hang. (Would I have to do that
branding thing though? I want it in my rider that I don't have to do
that. Maybe that comes up in the doc. Do they still do that? Seems
like it should be illegal.)

What do you think? Could it be a thing? You wanna direct
it DeShawn?

Yolanda: I have questions. Are you proposing this as a real doc?

Me: Yes. I legitimately wanted to do it at some point as research
before going back to Europe. But as I was watching the Beyoncé
doc, *Homecoming* on Netflix, I was thinking, *This all looks cool
and all. But I know I'm not connecting with it the way I would had I
actually gone to an HBCU, or at least been in a Black frat.* So the
idea expanded.

JD: The frat thing would be ridiculous! I don't think you are aware of
what you are asking, thinking, contemplating. *School Daze* has you

bamboozled! That's the soft, sweet, sugary version of what goes down during the pledging process. The real thing is way worse!!!

Me: Now, by "way worse," are you talking about *12 Years a Slave* beating kinda worse? Getting jumped into a gang kinda worse? What exactly do you mean by "way worse"?

JD: Way worse, cuz! Call me and we'll talk. Much too much to get into, and I'm not tryna write a report or essay here on Slack. I'll say IMHO, there are a lot of folks who have romanticized notions of the pledging process that are way off from reality. I think you trying to enhance your Blackness via a Black frat would be a foolhardy endeavor. It would be funny to experience, but in a bad train wreck type of way.

I was enthralled as to what JD meant. I thought for sure they'd *love* the idea. But he seemed to genuinely think it could even be dangerous. So we set up a conference call on Uberconference[13] to record it, you know, for posterity.

Uber-stupid

At one point during the call, JD says something about the experience of being "online." So I innocently respond, "What do you mean, like online on the computer or something?".

Let me just say, I have never heard these two laugh as hard or as long as they did after that.

JD: Ron. Dude. Are you serious?

Yo: Oh my god! *This* just made the entire conversation worth it.

JD: This shit needs to go in the book. And you need to have Sam Jackson slap you in the face for asking that dumbass question. That is the dumbest shit I've heard all year!

---

13 **Author's note**: Dear marketing teams at Slack and Uberconference—if you're so inclined, feel free to hit a brutha up with some sponsorship cash. Just sayin'.

Yo: It's all love Ron. But...

JD: Dude. I love you, man, but you make it real hard sometimes [laughs some more.] We just gave you another chapter for your book!

As we're on the call, I started Googling, but I don't find anything. So naturally, I say:

Me: I'm not finding anything online about "on line."

More laughter. I can't help but remember my encounter with Viola and her laughter. Except, this time, it's *really* happening.

JD: Wait! Quote this shit dude. Is this recording? Please tell me you're recording this. OH MY GOD! OH MY GOD! I'm about to cry. This shit is hilarious!

Yo: Ron, when you start pledging, that means you're "on line." You're on the line.

JD: Dude. Ron. This is embarrassing. You obviously had NO contact with niggas in college. Didn't you have ANY Black friends in college?

Me: NO. I DIDN'T! That's the whole point of the book!

JD: Dude. This is your strongest chapter right here. It's going to be embarrassin' though. Niggas are gonna be laughin'. But it's golden!

Yo: This is perfect. This is the definition of your book!

I'm not being hyperbolic when I say they laughed for a solid five minutes straight during this conversation.[14] We talked for about another hour, and let's just say, the shit they told me about what a pledge at a Black frat goes through would send shivers down your spine. And with that, I was quickly and most definitely cured of the need to do this little experiment. (No offense to the bruthas out there who crossed

---

14   You can hear a short excerpt from this hilarious conversation in the first episode of the *Dungeons 'n' Durags Podcast*, dungeons-n-durags.com/podcast.

over and joined such a fraternal order. I have no doubt in the end, the brotherhood and experience were worth it.)

After the call, I thought about my exchange with JD and Yolanda. And at one point I got a bit teary-eyed. Not at them laughing. That was cool. I often go back and listen to the recording. (That shit *is* totally hilarious! Even I can see that.)

What hit me and made me profoundly sad was what I had lost. Even as I write this, I can feel tears swell. I missed so much of a connection to my people. I missed out on not just the sheer joy and pleasure that comes out of the unique way Black people relate to one another, but I missed out on being connected to such a rich and vibrant culture all around.

Could this be what the Voice of Morgan Freeman was referring to when he said I was meant to go through this existential crisis? It's only because of that crisis that I was forced to reconnect.

Ode to Odo

At this point, it would be apropos to make a *Star Trek* analogy. It reminds me of the later seasons of *Deep Space Nine*, when the shape-shifting Chief of Security, Odo, finally discovered his long-lost race, known as "The Founders." For years, he thought he was alone in the galaxy— always the only one of his kind among a space station filled to the brim with other races. (Sound like anyone you know?)

In the two-part episode "The Search," he finds his people, and in these and a few subsequent episodes, he ponders all he's lost and what it might mean for him to leave DS9 and permanently rejoin his people. You can tell he's having the equivalent of his own "blaxistential"[15] crisis.

And so, it's only fitting, and not at all surprising, that I find myself on the cusp of yet another confession. And not since my "failure" with Viola did I face someone so challenging!

---

15 It turns out that the Founders were a sadistic race of xenophobic genocidal maniacs, so the "BLAX-istential" analogy breaks down there. That probably makes them more like wypipo. (I'M JUST KIDDING! But it is kinda true, too. Ask Indigenous people.)

Chapter 24:

Spike Jonesing

What do you do when one of your idols shames you?

I was a freshman at UC Berkeley when *She's Gotta Have It* came out. This was Spike Lee's first feature-length film and it immediately put him on the map as a filmmaking force to be reckoned with. However, I didn't see that movie in the theater. At the time I was more interested in being the next "Gordon Gekko" than the next Spike Lee. Six years later, I attended De Anza's film and TV program and I began to start studying his work and style in earnest.

As an aspiring filmmaker—who happened to be Black—Spike's films were practically required viewing and his filmmaking journals (which he published) were mandatory reading. I count *Do the Right Thing* as one of the five films that most influenced my work as a filmmaker.

Now over thirty-five years since Mars Blackmon told Nola Darling, "Please, baby! Please, baby! Please, baby, baby, baby, please!" He's still putting out his "joints" and creating films that have something to say about life, love, and particularly, race relations in America. When Spike speaks, people listen.

He is also known for saying what's on his mind and giving zero f*cks about what anyone thinks, least of all a newly "born" angry Black man who only just recently learned one of the most basic aspects of the Black experience in America. So perhaps it is the universe's sadistic sense of humor that I now find myself on a nondescript corner somewhere in Brooklyn. In front of me is a barbershop. The sign reads, "Joe's Bed-Stuy Barber Shop." That can only mean one thing. I know who I'm going to see next.

No absolution

I walk into the empty barbershop. A basketball game is playing on the TV, and jazz music is playing on a large boombox sitting on one of the chairs. From the back, I hear...

Take a seat. I'll be out in a minute.

I walk up and get into one of the barber chairs and wait. While I wait, I start spinning around in the chair. It's kinda fun.

After about the third revolution, I stop as I see, standing there, looking at me like I'm an idiot, the one, the only, Spike Lee.

> **Spike:** Are you finished? I don't have a lot of time, so let's get this over with.
>
> **Me:** Oh, sorry, Spike. Yeah. Sure. You got it.

I stop spinning, then sit up in my seat, and begin.

> **Me:** Forgive me, Spike, for I have sinned. It's been...
>
> **Spike:** Say no more. I already know why you're here.
>
> **Me:** You do?
>
> **Spike:** Yeah. You're here to confess that you didn't know something as fucking basic as being on line.
>
> **Me:** Yeah. How'd you know?
>
> **Spike:** I know everything.
>
> **Me:** Oh. Okay.

Spike: And you've never been to an HBCU, and you didn't have any Black friends in college.

Me: Um. Yeah. That's basically right.

Spike: And so I take it you're here for some kind of absolution.

Me: I guess. Each one of these confessions has been sorta different.

Spike: Well. I can put you out of your misery early. You're not getting any of that shit from me. No absolution. No lesson. No nothin'.

Me: Wait. What? Are you serious?

The fact that one of my cinematic heroes and earliest inspirations as a filmmaker is refusing to absolve me is not sitting well with my stomach. In my early years as a new filmmaker, I devoured all his behind-the-scenes filmmaking journals and books. From *Spike's Gotta Have It* to *Five for Five*.

Me: May I ask why, Spike? I mean, okay, so I didn't have any Black friends and maybe it's utterly ridiculous and hysterical I didn't know what "on line" meant. But how was I supposed to know if I never pledged? Osmosis? I don't think that...

Spike: That's not why I'm not absolving you. I'm not absolving you because you have no excuses.

Me: No excuses? No excuses for what?

Spike: Staying this ignorant and disconnected this long. I think it's great that orange-skinned muthafucka finally got you off your ass. But man, he wasn't the first. There was Bush 1 and Bush 2. The Clintons weren't innocent either with all that super predator bullshit. And how many deaths of Black men and women by racist cops was it going to take before you felt an urge to speak up and wake up?

Me: Well...

> **Spike:** And haven't you said *Do the Right Thing* is one of the five movies you claim most influenced your work as a filmmaker?

Wow. He really *does* know everything. Enthused that he knows this about me, I get a little bit of excitement in my voice.

> **Me:** Yeah! I thought it was great, Spike! I...

> **Spike:** Yeah, really? I was talking about this kind of shit in that very movie. I fuckin' say "WAKE UP" in the fucking movie! And that was thirty fucking *years ago*!

> **Me:** Yeah, I know, but...

> **Spike:** But what? You been hittin' snooze on that alarm for a long fucking time, my friend.

> **Me:** Okay. But still...

> **Spike:** *Fuck that!* No buts! Enough shit has gone down your adult life that could've woke your ass up. Especially as a filmmaker who wants to tell stories that matter, nothing should have mattered more to you than telling our stories and making a point to right wrongs.

> **Me:** I did want to tell our stories. My first short film was like a Black version of *When Harry Met Sally*.

> **Spike:** Man, I'm not fucking talking about romantic comedies. That's not what we need.

> **Me:** So what? I had to make movies about growing up in the hood? Why? That wasn't my experience.

> **Spike:** And growing up in the South as a bisexual Black woman beaten and tortured by an abusive husband wasn't Spielberg's experience, but that didn't fucking stop *him* from making *The Color Purple*. The fucking Farrelly brothers didn't grow up Black in the Jim Crow South. That didn't stop them from making *Green Book*. I don't want to hear that shit about it "not being your experience." That's a bullshit excuse, my brother. White people have been making shit

that wasn't their experience for years. You have eyes and ears and a degree from fucking UC Berkeley. You can read and do research. So sorry, I'm not buying it.

I'm starting to get really uncomfortable now.

Me: C'mon, Spike. Can't you go easy on a brutha? That's the whole reason I'm writing this book. You know. I mean. Fuck. Geeze. Don't I get credit for at least *finally* comin' 'round?

Spike: No. Not in my book. For years upon years, you sat and listened to some of your ignorant friends say some of the stupidest shit, and you sat there and did and said nothing. Now, twenty and thirty years later, you want me to absolve you of all that just because you wrote one fucking book? As the aforementioned Bush used to say, "Not gonna do it. Wouldn't be prudent at this junc-ture."

Me: Wow. That's kinda cold, Spike.

Spike: Yeah, well. You made that bed, so sleep in that shit.

Me: Okay then. I guess that's it.

Spike: No. Not yet. I said I wouldn't absolve you of your past sins, but that doesn't mean you can't make a difference going forward, which at some point may earn you my absolution.

At this point, I'm a little defensive.

Me: Man. Fuck this. I don't need your absolution.

Spike: Okay. Fine. Suit yourself. See ya.

Spike gets up and starts to walk away.

Me: Wait. Hold up. What were you gonna say? Just out of curiosity.

He turns back around and points at me.

Spike: Speak out.

Me: Speak out?

Spike: Yeah. That's it.

Me: Um. Isn't that what I'm doing?

Spike: I'm not just talkin' about this book. I'm talking about after the book comes out. And you get any amount of notoriety. Use it to speak out. Don't make excuses not to say what has to be said. And I don't mean fighting with assholes on Facebook or Twitter either. If you end up on *Good Morning America*, *The View*, *The Breakfast Club*, or fucking *Fox and Friends*, you need to channel me and say what shit's got to be said. Without worrying about what people are gonna think.

Me: I think it's pretty safe to assume that will be the case, don't you think? I mean, if you knew some of the stuff I'm writing in this book.

Spike: Man, I know the deal. It's one thing to say whatever you want when you're nice and safe behind a computer like some fucking anonymous coward on Reddit. It's another thing when you're sitting across from Whoopie or Gayle King or some shit.

Me: Wow. You think that could happen? That would be cool.

Spike: Motherfucker! Are you listening to yourself? This isn't about it being cool for you to get your fifteen minutes of fame. It's about having the balls to say what needs to be said when twenty million people are watching you. It won't be so easy then to be as free and flowing as it is now typing away on a MacBook Air at two in the morning. You wanna show me you've really changed? Come back at me when you've had a chance to speak your mind on that platform. If you squander it, don't even bother looking me up again. But if you use it to actually do some good to open people's eyes in this country, we'll see. As of now, I got a Knicks game to attend.

Spike gets up and starts to walk out. Just before he heads out the door, he turns around and says...

Spike: Ronald.

Me: What?

Spike: Stay Black!

He then laughs and walks out the door.

I turn and look into the mirror. After a moment of reflection (no pun intended), I take a deep breath and in my best Captain Picard voice, say...

Me: Ensign Crusher. Engage!

I then start spinning around in my seat and yell...

Me: *Cry havoc and let slip the dogs of war!*

I promise to make you proud, Spike.

But before I get too cocky and confident in my abilities to garner Spike's affections, I need to address something we touched on earlier. An aspect of African American culture that is undeniably perhaps the most influential in America—music—and my relative knowledge (or lack thereof) as it relates to Black folk.

Chapter 25:

Hit 'em Up—Politics and Evangelical Edition

What happens when a newly "born" angry Black man channels his inner Tupac

As friends often do, JD, Yolanda, and I kept in touch via text messages. We'd frequently have these epic-long iMessages back and forth over all sorts of topics (usually filmmaking, the movie business, or politics). They became so long and unwieldy that we started using Slack (did I already mention that sponsorship by Slack is open for consideration?) We've had countless debates and discussions via Skype (and eventually Zoom), which I would conveniently record for use in podcasts.

As I said, we've had conversations about all sorts of topics. And in one such conversation, the topic was Tupac.

> **Me**: So I, um, just heard "Hit 'em Up" for the first time. (Somehow, I missed this hit.) He really don't seem too fond of Biggie. I mean, I know they had bad blood, but d-yam, he REALLY, REALLY didn't have very nice things to say 😂
>
> **JD**: No worries. You're just 22 years late. 😜😂

Me: For the record, I KNEW of the Pac and Biggie feud. But when I heard the end of that song, he's like f- ANYBODY that likes east coast. Like that is some serious anger issues.

JD: Errbody knew about the Pac & Biggie beef. My granny, God rest her soul, knew about the Pac & Biggie beef. So that earns you no street cred points.

Yo: Ron. I'm a dork who doesn't listen much to the radio, doesn't know lyrics, song names and artists. And I know these things. You, my friend, are off the chart.

JD: But we still love you, bro.

Me: Ha! Much love to you two also. You're probably the only two Black people I could admit this to (not including, perhaps, the world when I share my story). But again, let me repeat. I *knew* these things. It was just the degree of his anger I didn't know. I thought it was more like a publicity stunt kinda thing. Or maybe something like Cal vs Stanford or 'SC vs UCLA kinda thing. But have you HEARD the end of that song? That is one brutha in serious need of a Talkspace subscription. Perhaps two of our greatest artists would be alive today if they spent some of those Benjamins on, like you know, a counselor's couch.

My 'Pac epiphany

I started listening to Tupac and Biggie again in early 2019. Partly to get into the headspace to write this, but largely to relieve the stress and anger I was dealing with at the time. (Fodder for a different book.) And as I'm sure white people do when they listen to Metallica and play air guitar secretly in their bedrooms, when I listened to Tupac spit those mad lyrics, I *became* him. My walk and talk transformed me into the hard, don't-give-a-shit, best-not-mess-with-me, gangsta type that would go off on any muthafucka that even looked at me sideways. (Which, I must admit, aside from the fact I have more melanin in my skin, me doing "air gangsta rap" is akin to the Michael Bolton character in *Office Space* rapping to 'Pac during the opening credits.)

What was I doing in those moments? Just dancing and beboppin' my head to some dope tracks? Or was I trying to be something I never was but wished I could be? Something in between? What was it about this song that connected with me so much? Deep inside, I knew it was more than just living a fantasy in my head of being a truly hard "nigga."

So I put the song on again, donned my earphones, and listened to 'Pac verbally annihilate his foes.

Then I heard a line in that song that hit me like a bolt of lightning. A line that, in some strange way, could explain the impetus for this book (or at least the version of this book you're reading).

In between lyrics, 'Pac addresses the audience, and at one point near the end, he says…

> "Now, when I came out, I told you it was just about Biggie, then everybody had to open their mouth with a muthafuckin' opinion!"

Eureka! That was it! That is exactly how I was feeling! When I came out online, specifically my altercation with Mr. Dufus Asshole, it was just about the House Negro Daneen Borelli; but then he had to come out with a muthafuckin' opinion.

And you could take that analogy one step further. Overall, when I came out with my anger about what was happening in this country, it was just about Trump. But then his supporters (and even a few who weren't necessarily supporters but white men longing for a return of "Positive Ron") came out with *their* muthafuckin' opinions.

As I had this revelation, I channeled the spirit of 'Pac:

> *When I came out, I told you it was just about Trump, but then everyone had to open their mouth with a muthafuckin' opinion. Well, this is how we gonna do this!*

> *Fuck Dufus Asshole!*

> *Fuck Mr. Positive Ron!*

> *Fuck right-wing evangelicals as a group, a political movement, and as a muthafuckin' crew!*

And if you wanna be down with Trump...

Then fuck you too!

As cathartic as that all feels, I know that's not me. I'm mad as hell, but I'm about as "gangsta" as Justin Timberlake (actually, JT is way more "gangsta" than me even).

And a sentiment like that is probably why I find myself facing yet another confessional. (Didn't I just have one of these?)

Chapter 26:

In the Dogg House

Never underestimate the wisdom of a dog. Or a lion?

"This is the song that is going to play in my documentary when I shoot the establishing shot of gentrified Oakland."

—YouTube User Aklikyano in the comments of the
Dan Heely version of "I Got Five On It"

I find myself on a deserted street on a sweltering hot day. Tumbleweeds bounce by as a warm, salty breeze fills the air. The fact that there's no one on the streets and dried vegetation from the desert is bouncing past me must mean one of two things. Either a) I somehow got sucked into a cliché dream sequence from a psychological thriller, or b) I'm about to face yet another "confession."

There, in front of me, on top of a corner store with a bright yellow top, is the sign, "V.I.P. World Famous..." I am standing in front of the legendary record store in Long Beach, California, made famous by Snoop Dogg's "Who Am I? (What's My Name?)" music video.

I walk into the store and make my way down a row of records, tapes, and CDs. And then, like magic, I hear "Lodi Dodi" play over the speakers. Not the original Slick Rick and Doug E. Fresh version, but Snoop Dogg's version. And as soon as I recognize it, I see standing there behind the counter is Mr. Doggy-style himself.

Me: What the hell! You're Snoop.

Snoop: In the flesh.

Me: This is crazy. I can't believe you're the next person I need to confess to. Ain't that some shit.

Snoop: Come into my office and let's get this over with.

Me: Yessir, Mr. Dogg.

Snoop: Mr. Dogg?

Me: Oh. Sorry. I mean, Mr. Lion? Mr. Broadus. I gotta be honest, I really can't keep up with all the different names you rap personalities take.

Snoop: Nigga, just get in here.

Me: Got it.

I follow Snoop into the back office. He takes a seat behind a desk, and I sit in a short chair in front of it.

Snoop: All right. I'm ready. Let's get this shit on.

Me: Got it. Um. Forgive me, Snoop Dogg, for I have sinned.

Snoop: When was your last confession?

Me: I don't really recall. A couple of chapters, at least.

Snoop: And what do you have to confess?

Me: I actually have three confessions, but they're all kinda related.

Snoop: Okay. Shoot.

Me: Okay. First, um, I was reading *The Root* the other day, and Michael Harriot wrote a post about one of the whitest things he's ever seen, and number four was an acoustic rendition of "I Got Five on It" by Dan Heely.

Snoop: Dan who?

Me: Heely.

Snoop: And?

Me: And, I kinda liked it.

Snoop: *That's* your confession? What was wrong with it?

Me: Oh. I don't know. I guess because, you know, it was like this acoustic guitar, sort of bluegrass version of "I Got Five on It" sung by a white guy.

Snoop seems unmoved.

Snoop: What else you got?

Me: Oh. Okay. Number two is…I also kinda like Justin Timberlake.

Snoop: JT's my boy. What's so sinful about that?

Me: Aren't like a lot of our people pissed off at his appropriation of our culture?

Snoop takes a puff of his blunt I hadn't even noticed he was smoking before. I guess it kinda explains the mellow nature.

Snoop: What makes you say that?

Me: Well, I often hear Kid Fury and Crissle rip into him.

Snoop: Kid who and Chris what?

Me: Kid Fury and Crissle? You know. From *The Read*.

Snoop looks confused.

Me: *The Read*. It's like one of the most popular podcasts on Apple Podcasts.

> **Snoop:** Podcast? Man, I ain't got time to listen to that shit. Do they speak for all Black people or something?

> **Me:** Well, no. Of course not. But they seem to have the pulse of what's going down in the Black community. I definitely feel, like, you know, closer to my people when I listen to them. And their listener letters and reads are often hilarious. Admittedly, I don't know half the people they be talkin' 'bout during the pop culture part of the show. Makes me feel kinda old.

Snoop looks totally and utterly uninterested in anything I'm saying. He takes another drag off his joint.

> **Snoop:** I wouldn't know about nothin' like that. Is that it?

> **Me:** Well, the last one is...well, you see, I didn't totally hate Taylor Swift's version of "September."

And with that, Snoop's eyes squint, and in an outrage, he jumps up from the chair, over the desk, pulls out a Glock, and points it at me.

> **Snoop:** *What the hell did you just say, muthafucka! Take that shit back right now nigga, or I swear to God, I will bust a cap in your muthafuckin' bitch ass!*

I drop to the floor and duck for my life under the small chair. Screaming for my life.

> **Me:** *Whoa! Whoa! Whoa!* Chill out! Chill out! *Jesus!* What the hell is going on?!

Snoop starts laughing his ass off.

> **Snoop:** Nigga. Git the fuck up. You *really* thought I would shoot your ass over some shit as stupid as that?

> **Me:** Niggas get killed over shoes and colors, so yeah! I fuckin' thought you'd shoot me over some stupid shit like that.

> **Snoop:** Nigga, pleeze. You watch too many goddamn movies. Who do you think I am? I'm past all that shit. This ain't even a real gun.

With that, he holds the gun up to his joint, pulls the trigger, and a small flame comes out of the barrel. After relighting his blunt, he whacks me across the head with his hand. The big-ass ring on his finger stings like hell.

> **Me:** Hey! What the fuck was that for?

> **Snoop:** That's your penance, muthafucka. How dare you come into this holy hall talkin' some shit like "You like that fuckin' abomination." Taylor Swift? "September"? Shiiiiit. Those two words shouldn't even be in the muthafuckin' same sentence. If her birthday is in September, she better move it to October and become a Libra or some shit. *You feel me?*

> **Me:** Well, technically, you could *still* be a Libra if your birthday is in, like the last days of Sept—

Snoop cocks his head. Annoyed.

> **Me:** Sorry. Anyway, I didn't say I *liked* it. I just said I didn't *hate* it.

> **Snoop:** What's the fuckin' difference?

> **Me:** I thought the version was stupid and, like, you know, totally weak…and shit.

Snoop looks at me side-eyed.

> **Snoop:** Uh huh?

> **Me:** I just wasn't as up in arms about it as some others, present company included.

Snoop leans against the desk across from me and offers me a hit from his blunt.

Me: No thanks. I, uh, am cutting back. Thanks though. I hear the medicinal properties are—

Snoop: Muthafucka, you talk too much.

Me: I've been told that. Once or twice. Maybe thrice.

Snoop: Looky here. I understand that the appropriation of our culture is a big deal and one that needs to be addressed, know what I'm sayin'?

Me: Yeah. Sure. That's kinda why I brought it up.

Snoop: Are you being smart?

Me: No! I'm serious. That is literally the reason I'm here. I thought that was obvious. My quote, unquote "sin," is liking (or not disliking enough) Black culture appropriators.

Snoop: Anyway, there's a balance that's got to be met when people who don't know us don't care about us and don't look like us wanna *be* us.

Me: Yeah. Yeah. It's like the movie *Get Out*.

Snoop: Man, don't be talkin' about that now!

Me: Why? This is a good point.

Snoop: Because muthafucka, if we start goin' down the path I *think* you're going, you're gonna spoil that shit for a bunch of readers.

Me: Oh. Snap. I didn't think about that.

Snoop: Yeah, not thinkin' gets you in trouble a lot, don't it?

Me: I'll plead the fifth on that one. But don't you think that by the time anyone reads this, if they haven't seen the movie yet, it's like kinda on them?

Snoop: Let me ask you this. You're a big movie fan, right?

Me: Oh, yeah. The biggest. I mean, I don't have the kind of Library of Congress mental vault of cinema knowledge like Scorsese or Tarantino or anything, but I think when you consider all the little nuances and subtle nods to cinema I like to make, you can make a fair assessment that I reach a certain caliber of cinephile that—

Snoop: Goddamn, muthafucka! Shut the fuck up! Do you just like hearing yourself talk all the time?! Shit!

Me: Oh. Sorry. I just, I don't know. I like movies. That's all.

Snoop: Yeah man. But damn. Learn to just be quiet. Shit. I ain't never met a brutha in more need of indo than yo monkey ass. Shit. I don't even remember what the fuck we were talking about now.

Me: The appropriation of Black culture and how the brain transplant procedure in *Get Out* represents a satirical metaphor of that culture among white liberal elites.

Snoop takes another hit.

Snoop: No. That wasn't it. We were talking spoilers.

Me: Oh right. Spoilers. You didn't want me to spoil *Get Out*.

Snoop: Right. Now, as I was saying, you're a cinema-phile, right?

It takes all the strength and willpower in me not to correct him.

Me: Yes, that is correct. I am a *cine*-phile.

Snoop: Now, as a cinema-phile...

I squirm...

Snoop: Would you tell someone who's never seen *Citizen Kane* what the meaning of "Rosebud" is?

Me: I see where you're going with this. No, as a *cine*-phile, I would want to preserve that amazing revelation for anyone seeing it for the first time.

Snoop: Exactamundo. And as a cinema-phile who appreciates film, why wouldn't you want to preserve that revelation about *Get Out*.

Me: Because, as a *cine*-phile, I believe certain films earned that right to never be spoiled. I just don't think *Get Out* is one of them.

Snoop: Why? Who determines what cinema-philes can or can't spoil?

I just can't take it anymore and I snap.

Me: *It's cinephile! Ci-ne-phile!* Not fucking cinema-phile!

With that, he smacks me across the head with that thick-ass ring again.

Me: FRAK! What did you do that for?

Snoop: Because you *just* couldn't let it go, could you? I knew I'd get you to crack.

Me: What? You mean you were mispronouncing it on purpose just to test me? That's fucked up, Snoop.

Snoop: Let me ask you somethin'. Why the fuck couldn't you just let it go?

Me: What? Why do you ask?

Snoop: Because there is something behind that shit. I could see it making you squirm every time I said "cinema phile." It was like eating you up inside. Right?

Me: Well, I think that's a tad hyperbolic.

Snoop: First, I don't know what the fuck "hyperbolic" means. But I'm sure what I said is not it. And I know it's not because we were having

> an engaging conversation about the philosophical merits of when it's okay or not okay to spoil a movie, and instead of just letting yourself get drawn into a deep and emotionally connecting conversation with the person across from you, you just *had* to correct that person. *Correcting* me became more important than *connecting with me.*

What the fuck is going on that I'm getting this kind of deep introspection from fucking Snoop Doggy Dogg?

> **Snoop:** I think you need to do some deep introspection into yo'self, homie, and find out what drives you to do that. I hazard to guess it's what's caused more than your fair share of unneeded conflict on Facebook. And if I may be so bold, I would guess that topic has reared its ugly head with your wife once or twice. Maybe even *thrice,* as you like to say.

Okay. Now he's hitting below the belt. But I can't argue.

> **Me:** I can see your point, Snoop. Yeah. I think I could think about that.
>
> **Snoop:** So for now, let's just agree not to spoil *Get Out.* You feel me?
>
> **Me:** Um...suuurrrrre. You got it.

He takes another hit, and I am secretly thankful for the mind-numbing powers of cannabis.

> **Me:** So let me ask you one last question, in the spirit of connecting and all. Why is someone like JT or Eminem okay, but Taylor Swift or Dan Heely aren't? I mean, what's the difference?
>
> **Snoop:** Man, you're asking the wrong question.
>
> **Me:** Well then. What's the right question?
>
> **Snoop:** I have no fucking idea. What I *do* know is that you still have a lot of growing to do. And when you *do* find the right question, it won't make you happy. Or sad. And it won't necessarily have an answer. In situations like this, the best questions just lead to more questions,

and so on. And each question can have a "multitude and plethora" of answers.

Me: Wow. A multitude *and* a plethora?

Snoop: Fo' shizzle!

I'm not quite sure what he's saying, but I'm pretty sure he agrees with me. So I respond in kind.

Me: For, um, shizzle.

With that, he gets up and starts to head toward the door.

Me: Hey, before you go, does that mean I'm absolved? After my last confession, I feel like I'm behind the eight ball, which is ironic, considering the whole theme of this book and all.

Snoop: You one dense muthafucka. I just dropped a whole lot of philosophical knowledge about questions and answers and shit, and you ask me that? Damn! Give some bruthas a forty and they still can't get a buzz.

Hmmm? I'm not quite sure what that means either. I sit in disappointed awe as Snoop turns around and heads out the front door, leaving me with a headache. But not necessarily from his thick-ass ring.

Chapter 27:

He Was a Fifth-Grade and Grown-up, Nerdy Negro People Pleaser

A romp through the past brings up issues in my present

I've come to learn an invaluable lesson on my path to "negro spiritual salvation." *I like to please people.* There's something inside of me that can't stand if I find out someone doesn't like me. (Except for Trump supporters. I couldn't give fewer f*cks if one of them doesn't like me.) This need to please has undoubtedly played a role in my reticence in telling white and Asian friends over the years when they've said something culturally insensitive. (Asking me to get the dancing started, fascination with the palms of my hands, commenting on how eloquent I am, etc. You know. Your run-of-the-mill, everyday micro-aggressions.)

I've also learned through years of personal coaching, therapy, and marriage counseling, that we can learn a lot about who we are today, by looking at our childhood. I can go back over forty years to find what may be the earliest clue of this need to please.

Mellow drama

Consider the following story "inspired by true events." It was a long frakking time ago (over forty years) and I cannot attest to the 100 percent accuracy of every minute detail. But the point is that it expresses the theme I want to convey, which plays a key role in my overall story. (More about that at the end of the chapter.)

My best friend in the fifth grade was Johnny. He was a skinny little Armenian kid with a John Travolta-style hairdo who spoke seven languages. I don't quite remember how we became best buds, but all I remember is that my friendship with him was deep. We were Ronny and Johnny. Two peas in a pod. Inseparable friends.

That is until, you know, girls.

It just so happens we both had a crush on the same girl (as Sam would say, "Ain't that a bitch!"). Her name was Caitlin, and she was the quintessential girl next door. Shoulder-length, sandy-brown hair in barrettes, knee-high socks and sandals, pink girly dress, and blue eyes. (Or were they brown? I forget.) It was the meeting of our eyes that made my little fifth-grade heart go pitter-patter. We were both looking down at something, looked up at each other, and that was it. I was gone. She looked just like the young Jan Brady I used to fawn over. That was right before Christmas vacation. Never in my young life did I ever wish so hard for a Christmas break to end.

Caitlin must have cast quite the spell because, in addition to Johnny and me, Greg liked her too (not his real name, I don't think).

I remember the day that this "crush quadrilateral" soap opera came to a head. It was raining, and while waiting for the bus, one of the girls asked Caitlin who she would like more between Greg and me. Apparently, her answer was me. My heart was elated. I remember Greg coming up to me, putting his hand on my shoulder, looking at me in the eye, ten-year-old to ten-year-old, and saying, "The best man won. Take good care of her." I replied, "Um. Okay. I will." I didn't even know we were in a contest. But sure. (To this day, I'm fascinated by what memories stick with us through the years.)

As Greg walked off into the distance, I was ready to do my finest impression of Gene Kelly and go sing in that rain. But my elation was short-lived.

Later that day, when talking to Johnny on the phone, he told *me* that someone told *him* Caitlin liked *him*. (*Da fuq*?!) He was so excited and couldn't wait to share the news with his best friend. (Apparently, I hadn't expressed to him my feelings for Caitlin or else I don't think he would have been so excited about delivering this information.)

In an instant, I went from a Gene Kelly singin' in the rain to Rutger Hauer as Batty in *Blade Runner*, ready to give a transcendental death soliloquy on behalf of my dead heart.

Well, such is fifth-grade romance and drama. But things only got worse from there.

Johnny and I would later have a rift in our friendship because one day I forgot to wait for him when I went out to play for recess (that's all I remember as to the origin of our disagreement). That rift ended with him becoming new BFFs with my then-rival Fred (again, not his real name). That resulted in Johnny taking my place to dance with, you guessed it, Caitlin in the talent show that year. She, Johnny, Jennifer, and I were all going to do a Bee Gees dance routine for the school musical revue. (Or was it from *Grease*? I think it was *Grease*. Again, my memory is a tad foggy on all the details.) Anyway, I was supposed to be in it. But given the state of our friendship, I bowed out.

I'm not sure how I did it or what I said, but I went to Johnny, apologized, and probably begged to be his friend again. I should never have left him alone when I went to play, and I desperately wanted him to be friends with me again. I'm sure now, with 20/20 hindsight and four decades to the day—give or take a few months—this was some form of early codependency. (If my therapist is reading this book, this may be something worth discussing in a later session.)

Whatever you want to call it, Johnny and I made up, and on the day of the musical revue, as I sat in the audience instead of being on stage, I cheered Johnny, Caitlin, Fred, and Jennifer on. I'm just that kind of a guy.

One of the last performances of the show was a boy and girl singing the Peaches & Herb classic "Reunited" (it was at the top of the charts that year). The significance of these two singing it was that rumor had it they had broken up, then got back together. (Although, I must say, fifth and sixth grades seem kinda young for two kids to be singing that song. But, you know, it was the '70s.)

As I listened to that song, I realized that Johnny and I were kind of reunited too—and my pathetic reconciliation was apparent to some of the other kids. I remember one of them teasing me for "sucking up" to Johnny to be his friend again.

And the moral of the story...

As I mentioned at the top of the chapter, this desire to so easily forgive and want to be friends is something that would follow me well into adulthood. (Remember my encounter with Sam back in the "Mine Yo' Bizness" chapter, when Sam made me feel bad that I insulted him, only to discover that he was teasing me...again?) This is perhaps why for so many years, I could not (or would not) challenge idiotic or borderline racist comments. "Why rock the boat? I know they don't *really* mean it. I don't want to lose their friendship."

There's nothing like a racist, egotistical, lying, hypocritical bigot to weed that right out of a person. After four years of debating assholes and idiots online, I had officially reached the "zero f*cks to give" level on the "White-Safe Ron Tachometer."

Or rather, I *thought* I had...

Chapter 28:

When Pigs Sigh

Breaking the proverbial back of the proverbial camel with the proverbial straw

I wasn't always this angry. As I wrote earlier, it took the gradual and consistent vitriol of Trump supporters to be the "gamma radiation" that transformed me into an SJW "Hulk." It got to the point where I no longer desired to civilly dialogue with anyone who supported that vile human being, especially if they were Christians.

But if I'm honest, I couldn't help but admit to myself that my judgment of these TSCs (Trump-Supporting Christians) for lauding and following someone so antithetical to the Christian doctrine they proclaimed was in many ways almost as bad as their support of him. Did not my faith say I was to love my enemy? To speak with love and peace? To be the bigger person?

So in one thread, when my every action to a TSC was combative debate and attack, I did something I never expected.

Olive branch

You remember that Trump-supporting woman I mentioned at the beginning of the book? The one who claimed she didn't give Trump a pass on his treatment of women, but then went on to do exactly that as she gave an excuse for men in power who harass women? It was one of *her* posts where I made a pivot.

It was right after Brett Kavanaugh was confirmed to the Supreme court in 2018 (every time I type that, I have to fight back the anger), and she posted this:

"Winning!"

I then commented:

"Spoken like a real recipient of white privilege."

As expected, her fellow TSCs came out and attacked. But I expected it. And, frankly, I deserved it. I had no intention of having civil discourse. I was pissed and wanted to vomit *my* vitriol on her thread.

I later had a moment of clarity. Particularly after a conversation/ discussion/minor argument where my wife said something to me that kinda upset me but had a ring of truth. I honestly don't remember what it was. I'm sure it was a comment that convicted me and threw me into deep introspection. So much so that it prompted me to write this post on that woman's thread:

APOLOGY AND OLIVE BRANCH

Last night my wife said something to and about me that upset me, but had an air of truth to it. But I was too caught up in my emotions of HOW she said it to see the message she was trying to convey.

I realized that is what I did to you all on this thread. And I sincerely apologize.

I would like to try something. I want to extend an olive branch. I believe that beyond the partisanship and politics, we all might actually be people who would genuinely like one another in real life, if we just knew each other. We all speak past one another without really listening.

So if you're game, I'll start.

I was born in Philly, PA. Son of a mother from Winston-Salem, NC. She separated from my dad when I was about 4 and...

Sam: What in God's name are you doing?

Sam was back. And he did not sound happy. Which doesn't necessarily say a lot because he seldom sounds "happy." But today, his exasperation seemed to be at an eleven.

Me: Sam? Um. What. Why. How did you get here? I haven't seen you in a while. What brings you 'round here?

Sam: Muthafucker, I show up whenever I goddamn please. Now tell me. What the fuck are you doing?

Me: What do you mean?

Sam: Don't play stupid with me. This blog post. What's this shit about?

Me: It's Facebook.

Sam looks annoyed.

Sam: What?!

Me: You said blog post, but it wasn't a blog post. It was a Facebook post. Actually, it wasn't even a post. Technically it was a comment on...

Sam: Shut up, asshole! You say potato; I say po-*tot*-to. Who gives a shit?! You see, it's stupid replies like that that piss your wife off. Do you think it matters, Ronald?

I remember my confessional with Snoop and cringe on the inside.

Me: I guess not. But anyway. Why does it matter?

Sam: It matters because I've spent a great deal of time mentoring your ass, and I don't like the fuck where this post is going. Are you actually trying to make amends with this bitch?

Me: I'm trying to be a bigger person. I'm trying to be a role model for the kind of American...

Sam: Nigga. *Shut the fuck up!* Man, you've said and done some dumb shit during the course of this book, but damn, if this don't take the cake.

Me: What is your problem? What the hell is wrong with this?

Sam: And did I see you write another post where you actually praised one of these muthafuckers for treating you with decency?

He's referring to another post where I praised one of the Trump supporters I often debate. I gave him props for being a civil person when debating me.

Me: Um. Oh. That. Well. I wanted to give credit where credit was due. He was literally the first Trump supporter in two years on Facebook who said he welcomed hearing my ideas and that we all may have differing opinions, but it's worth having civil dialogue. I wanted to just show that I honored that mindset.

Sam: So let me get this straight. Some dude actually treats you like a human being, is polite, and not rude, something which we teach our kids when they're fuckin' four! And you wanna give him a Nobel fucking Peace Prize?! Really? Do you also praise adults who wipe their asses with toilet paper?

Me: No. Of course not. But...

Sam: Isn't this the same dude who posted a meme that Florida would become a socialist state if Andrew Gillum became governor?

Me: Yeah, but...

Sam: The same dude who posted a meme saying that Caitlyn Jenner claims Bruce fondled her for fifty years. Same dude who reposts all the dog whistle memes about illegal aliens committing violent crimes? Same dude who reposted a meme saying, "Instead of taking

down every statue in America, how about teaching history again?"
Same dude you even referred to earlier who said that if he were a
negro in this country, he would be so thankful for the sacrifices of
his forebears to have suffered the horrors and indignities of slavery
to carry his DNA and RNA to the land of opportunity and hope." And
this is the same asshole you want to be your new BFF?

Me: No. Of course not. You see, though, what I was thinking was...

Sam: No, Ronald. You weren't thinking. You were feeling! And that's
the fucking problem! This is more of that shit about being liked, isn't it?

Me: Now. Just wait a minute. I...

Sam: Where is your super suit?

Me: What?

Sam: Where. Is. Your. Super. Suit? You know, the one you
referenced back in Chapter 2. Your "super suit of Blackness."

Me: Oh. Yeah. That. What do you mean? Why do you want to know?

Sam: Because Ronald, I'm beginning to think you don't have the balls
to really use it. I'm beginning to think you're acting like a little bitch.

Me: Why? Just because I think there can be a better way? Just
because I feel deep inside that the tenets of my faith have some
merit? That what Dr. King wrote about the power of love is
something that rings true?

Sam: Aren't you the one who wrote on Medium, and I quote: "After
nearly two years of trying to have cogent, coherent, and reason-
based discussions with them, I've come to the conclusion that
debating a Trump supporter is literally like debating with a flat-
earther. You can't use reason and logic. You can't use recorded
video and audio that demonstrably show how horrible an American,
leader, or even a human being he is. It doesn't even matter if you
traditionally vote Republican and uphold what some would consider

true conservative values. If you speak out against Trump in any way, to them, you are an infidel"? Unquote.

Me: Wow. You remembered all that? Anyway, yes. I wrote that but—

Sam: And did you not also write, "At this point in the game, anyone who still vehemently supports Donald Trump lacks either the intellectual capacity, morality, and/or grip of reality to waste your time. So why bother"?

Me: Yes. I wrote that too. And I meant it. But I'm not—

Sam: Isn't this woman on whose *Facebook* post you're now commenting, the same woman who constantly posts headlines from Fox News and Breitbart?

Me: Yes.

Sam: And despite all of that, you're attempting to make amends with her, tell her your life story, and expect her and her Trump-loving friends to suddenly look at you like you're their best friend?!

Me: Well not exactly...

Sam: You read the Bible, Ron?

Me: What?

Sam: Do you read the Bible?

Me: Is that supposed to be a rhetorical question? You know I do. You're not going to give me your Ezekiel 25:17 monologue from *Pulp Fiction*, are you? That line you quoted in that movie wasn't even what the verse really says.

Sam: First off, I didn't write that shit. Second, the verse I'm referencing this time is very *much* real. It's Matthew 7:6: "Don't give that which is holy to the dogs, neither throw your pearls before the pigs, lest perhaps they trample them under their feet, and turn and tear you to pieces." I've been thinking about that verse a lot, Ronald, during this literary adventure of ours.

Me: Oh. This is *our* adventure now?

Sam: Nigga. Shut the fuck up and listen. For the longest time, I thought the "pearls" were the words and lamentations *you* offered to these dumb ass muthafuckers who don't have the sense that God gave them if they think that muthafucker in the White House is really some vessel of the Almighty who cares about them. *They* were, therefore, the swine. But I've come to realize, Ronald, that *I* am the pearls, and *you* are the swine.

Me: Oh, really? *I* am the swine?

Sam: You damn skippy! And with this post, you have torn me asunder. I've overlooked a lot of the dumb shit you've done in your life. A lot of the stupid, idiotic platitudes you've expressed. I even looked past the fact that there wasn't *one* fuckin' sista on TV other than a preteen on skates that you ever had the hots for as a kid. But I can see now, my wisdom and work are utterly lost on you. From here on out, you're on your own man. I'm done with you.

And with that, Sam turned around, strolled away, and vanished. Never to be seen again.

I take a seat, look out my window, lean back, and sigh. As I do, I fall into a daydream of all my encounters with Sam. The good times and the bad. It's like one of those slow-motion montages. There were times when he really pissed me off. But I must admit, there were times when he really made me think. If I'm being honest, there were more times I appreciated his presence than I didn't. He made me laugh more times than I care to admit. And he emboldened me to be the kind of person I've wanted to be for a long time.

As I drift deeper into this stroll down memory lane, I could swear I hear Barbra Streisand's "The Way We Were" playing in the background.

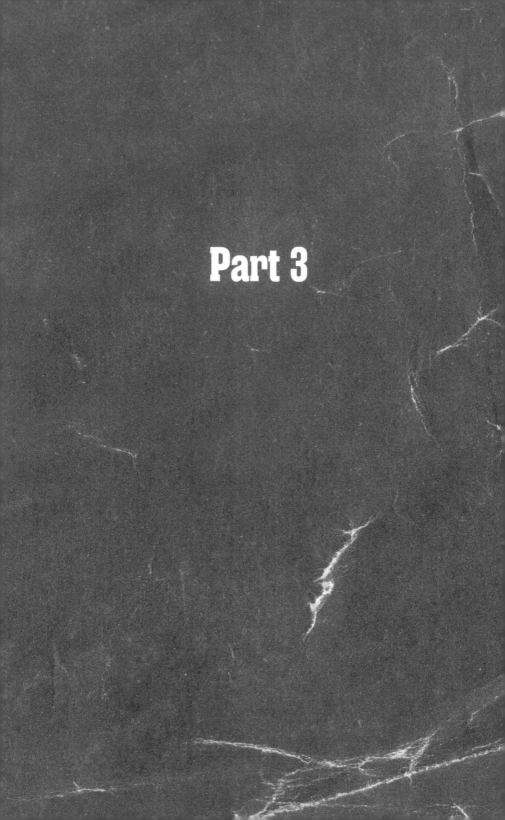

Part 3

Chapter 29:

"Dude, where's my church?" —Jesus

Those frakking white evangelicals

One of my favorite movies is 1986's *Aliens* by James Cameron. At the beginning of the film, Ripley—played masterfully by Sigourney Weaver in what I believe was an Oscar-worthy performance—is addressing a room full of executives about the destruction of the ship *Nostromo*, from the movie's predecessor, *Alien*. (Trust me. I *am* going somewhere with all of this.)

These business types are pissed that Ripley destroyed one of their most expensive ships and an extremely expensive payload. They're not buying her story about this alien that gestates in a human host and has concentrated acid for blood.

Then one ignorant junior exec asks, "Are there species like this hostile organism on LV426?" (The planet where Ripley and the crew from *Alien* picked up their "friend.") Then another vacuous exec (a woman with an Edna Mode haircut and a cheap suit) says after exhaling smoke from her cig, "No. It's a rock. No indigenous life."

Then, in one of the most quotable lines from the movie, Ripley turns from the wall where photos of her deceased crew members are being projected and says, "Did IQs just drop sharply while I was away?"

I fully believe this will be the first thing Jesus Christ will say when, and if, he ever comes back to this god-forsaken planet.

"What the hell have you done with my church?" is what I think he'll say next.

Now, it's not lost on me that I have no idea what Jesus will say when he comes back. My even suggesting I do, or suggesting I know how he'll respond, is in a way as theologically problematic as the millions of Trump-supporting evangelicals who somehow have found a way to deify, worship, and laud one of the most empirically anti-Christian men to ever hold the office of POTUS.

Notice I said *anti-Christian*. As in, "opposite of what Christ stands for." I in no way think he's the Antichrist. Quite frankly, he's far too overtly "evil" and ignorant to be the Antichrist. The AC will supposedly charm the entire world before he twists his proverbial mustache and rains down havoc.[16]

Except for the thirty-five million or so brainwashed, brain-dead, and/or morally bereft followers who love this man, the entire world thinks he's a fucking moron and hates his ass. You had the British government get their knickers all up in a bunch arguing to keep him from setting foot on their island. So no, he ain't the Antichrist.

And I have to say, he may be ignorant (of history, politics, economics, geography, the Bible, or basically any other characteristic or experience needed for a true leader), but I won't say he's stupid. The muthafucker knows exactly what he is saying.

What I fail to understand, and what has got me in one of the greatest spiritual existential crises of my life, is how my so-called fellow brothers and sisters in Christ can so thoroughly love and praise a man who quite literally represents the exact opposite of every one of the fruits of the spirit and wholly embodies every one of the seven deadly sins.

---

16 I would be remiss not to mention a blog post by progressive Christian, theologian, blogger, and fellow "heretic" in the vein of Rob Bell, Benjamin L. Corey. In Corey's blog post "Could American Evangelicals Spot the Antichrist?" he makes a legitimately freaky and believable case for Trump to be *the* AC himself based on eerily coincidental biblical predictions with Trump's life (his insinuation that MAGA hats could be the "mark of the beast" is fucking brilliant!).

Oh, sorry, if my Christian-speak is leaving you perplexed. The apostle Paul (you know, one of the greatest heroes in the New Testament. The man who single-handedly wrote about two-thirds of it), in his letter to the churches in Galatia (what is now Chapter 5 of the book Galatians), lists nine attributes every follower of Christ should theoretically display.

> "But the fruit of the Spirit is love, joy, peace, patience, kindness, goodness, faithfulness, gentleness, and self-control."
>
> (Gal. 5:22–23)

Now you tell me. Which one of those attributes does Trump possess? I'll wait.

I've already raised the issue of white evangelicals in general supporting the former Cheeto in Chief. And I knew there were pastors in the world who did. But I hadn't actually come across one on Facebook. That is, until shortly after the midterm elections of 2018.

As you might expect, Facebook algorithms were all ablaze, dumping frustratingly dense political memes and posts right into my feed. (I honestly think Mark Zuckerberg is sitting up in his office, looking at my feed, and cracking up as he pulls the trigger to dump the most mind-numbing Trump-supporting and right-wing conservative drivel into my feed. Why don't I ever get all the cute videos of kittens playing tag with bulldogs?)

Anyway, while wading through the toxic sludge that was my Facebook feed, I came across this post by Mr. Clueless Christian (not his real name, but I can't necessarily deny the initials may or may not be similar):

> Pray for our elected leaders! And if you haven't had time to do your legwork - vote "No" on all the amendments. 1 Timothy 2 says, "I exhort therefore, that, first of all, supplications, prayers, intercessions, and giving of thanks, be made for all men; For kings, and for all that are in authority; that we may lead a quiet and peaceable life in all godliness and honesty. For this is good and acceptable in the sight of God our Savior."

This is one of the ways Trump-Supporting Christians justify their support of this sexist, egotistical, lying, hypocritical bigot. They are just praying for their president. Once again, the Bible is being used to support morally reprehensible actions.

So then, this pastor chimes in. Let's call him Pastor Tom.

> *I preached on this passage to my congregation yesterday. Prayers are more powerful than protests.*

Whenever anyone in this country says, "prayers are more powerful than protests," you can bet your house it's a white evangelical. I feel confident that *Pastor* Dr. Martin Luther King Jr. would not have been as effective if *all* he did was pray. Just sayin'.

I sat there at my computer debating: "Do I, or don't I?" I waffled back and forth on whether to dive into this thread, knowing it would be a total shit show. And I can't help but now hear Sam's words echoing in my ears.

Against my better judgment, I jump right in. And you won't believe what transpired.

Chapter 30:

Letters to a Trump-Supporting Christian

A social media beatdown fit for the history books!

One of the leading resources Christians love to share when attempting to convert someone to the faith is Greg Boyd's *Letters to a Skeptic*. It's a compilation of real-life letters Christian author and teacher Boyd shared with his agnostic father, Ed. Greg invited his father to ask any tough questions about Christianity, and Greg would answer as honestly and thoroughly as possible. The exchange of letters ultimately led to Ed becoming a Christian.

It would appear I had a similar situation brewing with the Pastor "Tom." But instead of questions about God, faith, and the empirical contradictions in the Bible, this would be a "dialogue" about Trump, politics, and the role of a pastor with respect to letting the world know his political leanings.

So I dive right into the deep end of this cesspool of mutual admiration between Pastor Tom and Mr. Clueless Christian.

> **Me:** I'm curious, "Pastor Tom." What are your thoughts on the rest of 1 Timothy 2 that states: "women should adorn themselves in respectable apparel, with modesty and self-control, not with braided hair and gold or pearls or costly attire, but with what is

proper for women who profess godliness—with good works. Let
a woman learn quietly with all submissiveness. I do not permit a
woman to teach or to exercise authority over a man; rather, she is to
remain quiet"?

I was eager to see what he would say about this controversial verse.
Did he agree with it, which expressing publicly would reveal his
fundamentalist complementarian mindset and set the stage for the
kind of Christian he was? Or would he attempt to twist his way out of
answering it, or worse, say he didn't believe in that part of the verse, in
which case, his preaching on the first part comes into question.

My trap was set. But his response was unexpected.

Pastor Tom: That's a great question! Don't know why you are asking
so can you give me a little heads up? What is your particular interest
in this passage? And on the Bible in general? Are you writing as a
fellow Christian, or a non-Christian seeking dialogue? Thanks!

Oh. I see what you're doing here. You're hoping I'm some inquisitive
atheist or agnostic and perhaps this is an opportunity to save another
soul. Sorry, Mr. White Evangelical Trump Supporter, this brutha has
come packing Proverbs and some badass exegesis. Bring it!

I reply:

Me: Thanks for the inquiry, Pastor Tom. I AM a fellow believer. I've
taught, read, and studied apologetics for years. I'm no theologian,
but I've been around the biblical block a few times. I, like many other
followers of Christ, am utterly dumbfounded at the full-sail praise,
and dare I say, worship other believers put in a president who quite
literally represents the opposite of every one of the fruits of the
spirit, and is a walking manifestation of every one of the seven
deadly sins. Every time I see a believer use some verse of the Bible
to support their complicity in this administration, and particularly
this president's actions, I want to vomit. So when I see "Clueless
Christian" here use this verse in particular, I want to know if they
(and you since you mentioned you preached on it) are prepared to

address the very provocative additional verses in this chapter. I can see from your Facebook wall that you are yet another such Trump Supporting Christian. It would appear that you, like Clueless, are fond of conflating Republican ideology with Christian virtue. To be honest, I find many of the posts on your Facebook thread rather sad and disappointing coming from a "man of the cloth." But given what I've seen from the overwhelming number of white evangelicals that support this modern-day Ahaz, I'm not at all surprised. So yes, I more than ever now would like to know your take on the rest of 1 Timothy 2, and I would particularly like to know YOUR excuse for the support and praise for a man like Trump.

Where's Sam? He'd be so proud of me! Pastor Tom's response was interesting:

Pastor Tom: Dear Ron, Thanks for your email. I'm glad to know you are a brother in Christ.

It's actually not an email; it's a Facebook reply. But, you know, whatever.

Pastor Tom: That is by far the most important thing to know about anyone.

Really? That is the most important thing to know about anyone?

Pastor Tom: But as I read your message, I don't sense that there is peace in your heart by the way in which you address me.

You don't sense a peace in my heart? Really?! No shit mutha...okay. Calm down, Ron. This is a pastor. So far, he's been cool. Don't go Sam Jackson on him. Yet.

Pastor Tom: Christ promises us a peace that passes understanding. This thought gives me great comfort as I walk through this life, to know that I am in Christ and Christ is in me.

*Ahhh. To be an old, white, conservative, male evangelical Christian
in Trump's America. It's like they walk around in orgasmic states of
existential bliss fueled by privilege and denial.*

> **Pastor Tom:** Whether I agree or disagree with someone's politics, I
> still can respect and love them as a person.

*Lie. As you'll soon learn, he may love them, but he definitely doesn't
respect them.*

> **Pastor Tom:** With regard to politics, here is a suggestion. Since
> you find my support of President Trump so upsetting in many ways,
> would it be okay if you would help me get a handle on this discussion
> by choosing one area of concern you have about Mr. Trump or
> his policies?

Only one? How about racism. How about that one? FFS.

> **Pastor Tom:** I seriously want a dialogue but addressing one area at
> a time would be helpful. Please tell me why you object to one area of
> concern, and why you think it is wrong biblically. In this way it is my
> desire to keep the conversation respectful and policy-based, not
> personality-based.

*In other words, "Let's forget the fact that Trump is a petulant man-child,
bereft of any moral character, and even though you are a negro, let's
also forget all the racist and dog-whistle language Trump has made.
Even though I'm a pastor and those kinds of things should matter to me
if I'm going to put my faith in a leader who has his finger on the proverbial
button and who should ideally be some sort of moral role model for
the country."*

> **Pastor Tom:** I like to think that my opinions or preferences are well
> reasoned and not the result of bias...

*Sam talked about my reality distortion field? The Borg shields ain't got
nothin' on this dude's reality distortion. Again, as you'll soon learn, for him
to think his opinions are not based on bias is utterly laughable.*

> **Pastor Tom:** But feel free to challenge them in any way you like. If I can be shown that I am wrong, I want to be a big enough person to admit it and ask God to change my heart. Respectfully Yours, Pastor Tom

He then added his phone number and address and the name of his ministry. I just realized he must be emailing these replies (Facebook allows you to do that). So I don't know whether he thinks I'm emailing him directly or he realizes these are Facebook replies coming into his email.

I am not quite sure how I want to respond to this dude. This feels like some kind of Jedi-Mind-Trick-level shit. Is he trying to use kindness and decency to win me over and have me listen to his Trump-supporting poison?

With Sam Jackson's voice firmly ringing in my ears, I think back to all the posts I've seen this "pastor" put on his wall. Think of every frustrating, Fox-News-supporting, ignorant meme you've ever seen a Trump supporter post. This dude had them all and then some:

- Links to articles criticizing Christians who criticize Trump and praising Trump's negotiating process.

- A meme that said, *"Democrats riot in the streets and violently destroy the country they hate. Republicans work hard, pay their taxes, and pray for the country they love."*

- Memes supporting Brett Kavanaugh in conjunction with a link to the article "10 Red Flags About Sexual Assault" meant to discredit people like Dr. Christine Blasey-Ford.

This is the same dude who said we should "pray for our president" because it's the "Christian" thing to do. Hmmm? Do you think he was praying for Obama during his presidency or posting memes like these? If you think the former, I have a failed Trump casino in Atlantic City I'd like to sell to you.

I read through about eight weeks' worth of posts. It was too emotionally draining to read any more. I am sure as hell not gonna look at this guy as the kindly, reasonable, respectable, friendly neighborhood pastor who wants to have a conversation that he's making himself out to be.

Channeling Sam

So with all that crap firmly imprinted in my brain, and Sam's voice
rooting me on, I offer my response:

> **Me:** Dear Pastor Tom, I find it interesting you started your reply,
> "Dear Ron." Perhaps you see this as a sort of "letters to a skeptic"
> kind of scenario? Hmmm? The question is: which one of us is Greg
> Boyd and which is Ed?

*That's right, my nigga. Ease into it. Put the muthafucka in a state of false
security. All Sun Tzu and shit.*

> **Me:** I appreciate that you are willing to have a civil conversation
> about politics, and that you are open to having your "mind changed"
> if you are proven wrong. But with all due respect, I no longer have
> debates with Trump supporters about their support of him.

Hello! It's about to get real up in here!

> **Me:** There is nothing really to discuss. I assume you are as privy to
> news on the internet as I am. If after everything you've seen and
> heard from him, you still support him, I don't know what I could say
> that would sway you. I doubt I will tell you anything you have not
> already heard many times.

Many, many times!

> **Me:** Besides, I've read a number of the colorful articles you've posted
> on your wall that praise Trump's intellect and international political
> prowess, or how we Christians that oppose him are hypocrites and
> should be thanking God for Trump (do blog posts like that come with
> barf bags, or do you have to purchase them separately?).

*That's right, Ron. You tell him, dawg. You got this, bruh? Set this white
boy straight.*

> **Me:** At the end of the day, I think any person (let alone a "man of the cloth") who praises and supports *any* man the way Trump supporters support Trump is antithetical to what Jesus teaches.

Ahhh yeah. You droppin' the big words, "antithetical" and shit. Yeah, yeah. Keep goin'!

> **Me:** Add to that the empirical evidence that Trump is by all accounts the equivalent of a modern-day evil King of Israel (e.g., constantly sows divineness, lies on a level never before seen, sexual sin in the form of adultery, assault, and lascivious behavior that he brags about, conspiring with other evil "kingdoms," etc.)—it is even that more tragic when a pastor so fully supports him.

Trump is a straight-up Ahab, my nigga.

> **Me:** Contrary to what American white evangelicals seem to believe, the president is not appointed or anointed by God the way Kings of Israel were.

Truth!

> **Me:** And he has not earned a lick of it, definitely not from me anyway (and it would appear that a majority of the world feels the same).

Can I get an amen! Who's the preacher up in here? Continue.

> **Me:** This man swore to uphold the Constitution, yet when a group of football players decided to *peacefully* protest racial injustice by kneeling during the anthem, he attacked them and began this pathetic, embarrassing battle. Their protest is something fully supported by the first amendment of the Constitution, and something that most would say is at the heart of what *actually* makes America great—the ability to speak out against the country or the President without fear of reprisal from the government.

School House Rock this fool! "Conjunction Junction" and "I'm Just a Bill" ain't got nothin' on you, nigga!

Me: In order to cater to his base, he not only spoke out against these men, he used the power of his office to force the NFL to punish those who continue to protest like that. If that doesn't scare you to your core, you're either blind, deaf, dumb, or so numbed by your white privilege you fail to see it.

Yeah! Yeah! Yeah! That's what I'm talkin' about. Bring it home, dawg! Put this false prophet in his place, homey!

Me: I bet you a million dollars that if Tom Brady or Tim Tebow kneeled during the anthem in protest against abortion legalization, you would be giving them a standing ovation.

You know that shit is right!

Me: A real presidential response, one that doesn't break the POTUS oath to uphold the Constitution, would be to express your personal feelings about the flag and why you support it and may disagree with these men, and at the same time vociferously support their right to do it and show how this is what makes America the special place it is.

This is some real Zig Ziglar-leadership-seminar-level shit! You need to get an infomercial.

Me: You say you are a pastor and therefore lead a flock. That flock will turn to you for leadership and guidance. How would I trust you to lead me when *you* put so much trust (or *any* trust, for that matter) in such an empirically vile man (I think it's apropos that vile is an anagram for evil, by the way)? And if you can't see that about him, then our debate/discussion will be DOA.

Dead as a motherfucker!

Me: But I can't say that I'm surprised. From 2011 to 2016, the percentage of white evangelicals who believe a president can still perform his duties ethically, even if they commit immoral acts in their personal life, jumped from 30 percent to 72 percent! More than twice as many evangelicals now believe there is no correlation between a president's personal morality and his ability to ethically lead. Hmmm? Why is that?

Oh, snap! This is like some Gallup-poll-level shit! Is this your book or a scene from The Great Debaters?

Me: The only answer I can see for the reason white evangelicals so enthusiastically support Trump is what I mentioned earlier, that they have conflated conservative, right-wing Republican ideology with Christian virtue. And you are just another clear indication of that. I saw the meme you shared on your wall that demonizes all democrats as violent USA haters and praises Republicans as hardworking, praying lovers of their country. That is so reductive and childish, it's pathetic. I don't know what kind of a church you pastor, but I wouldn't go near it with a ten-cubit pole.

Leopard-ass muthafucka is showing his spots. Rip that sheep costume right off the pale, pimply back of that wolf. (And I love that little cubit and pole joke. Very biblical of you.)

Me: You're all for being "pro-life" and getting Roe v. Wade overturned, but you're hell-bent on protecting people's rights to build up a stockpile of AR-15s.

Is this asshole's picture next to the word "hypocrisy" in the dictionary? Oh shit. It is! Continue!

Me: Trump can get you the judges you need to overturn Roe v. Wade and attain the "holy grail" that right-wing conservatives have sought since the mid-70s. That is a primary reason the Federalist Society was created in the first place. No, Pastor Tom, I appreciate the invite to discuss politics, but I'll pass on that futile endeavor. I would still very much like to know your answer to my *first* question—about your thoughts on the rest of 1 Timothy 2. Is that how you believe women should be treated? What is your stance on women being pastors or church leaders? Are you for or against?

All right, my nigga, let's land this jet. Bring it home.

> **Me:** I would much rather have a theological discussion than a
> political one. If you're not interested in that, I will respect that and
> move on. But I do not want to waste either of our time discussing
> Trump and your political belief system. The day is just too beautiful
> and time is too precious.

And with all of that, I link him to my now infamous "Flat Earther" Medium
essay where I argue that debating Trump supporters is like debating
flat-earthers (the one Sam referenced when he abandoned me).

> **Me:** "Yippe ki-yay, motherfucker!"
>
> **VOMF:** Now, if I recall, wasn't it a white action hero that said that?

The unmistakable echo of Morgan's resonant voice can be heard
beaming down. Gosh darn it! Not now, Voice of Morgan Freeman!

Chapter 31:

Wonder and...Awww!

Sometimes you cling to anger and hate to keep you warm

Me: Morgan. Is it you?

VOMF: Hi, son. How you doin'?

Me: I'm doing just fine, actually. Feeling very refreshed and energized.

VOMF: That's quite the exchange with that pastor you had there.

Me: Yeah, well, I'm not exactly sure what kind of "pastor" he is. I pray to God he's not like one who leads a whole church.

VOMF: Just curious. I noticed he said he was open to being convinced he was wrong.

At this point, I'm not liking where the Voice of Morgan Freeman is taking this conversation.

Me: Yeeaaah. Aaaaand. Your point?

VOMF: Oh. I don't have a point. Just an observation, that's all.

Me: You don't just make observations. Is there something you want to say? Just say it.

VOMF: Well, and again, this is just an exercise in curiosity.

Me: Uh-huh.

VOMF: But what if he was serious? What if he was truly open to having his mind changed?

Me: You can't *possibly* be serious, can you? First of all, the dude is a Trump supporter. Have you not been paying attention? Dyed in the wool Trump supporters don't change their minds. Secondly, did you not read the crap he had on his Facebook feed? You really think a social media political debate with that guy would have changed him? People like that cannot—

VOMF: I know, I know. They can't be reasoned with. But just humor me. What if he was?

Me: No. I don't want to humor you. There's nothing humorous about any of this.

VOMF: True or false. Instead of insulting you and calling you names, he complimented you on being a fellow Christian and was more than just civil; you could say he was polite.

Begrudgingly, I answer.

Me: True.

VOMF: True or false: out of all the Trump supporters you encountered, he was the first one to say he would be willing to change his mind.

Gritting my teeth.

Me: True.

VOMF: And true or false, like you are fond of doing, he was willing to avoid ad hominem attacks and just look at the facts and figures of Trump's presidency.

Me: Where the frak are you going with this, Morgan? Are you saying I should be the Charlie Brown to yet another Trump supporter's Lucy and try to kick that ball, only to have her pull it away again? Is that what you're suggesting? Because, if that's what you are, then you might as well save your iconic breath. I'm not trying to kick that ball any longer.

VOMF: Yeah. I can understand your feelings, son. And believe me, I am the last one who can truly understand what you've been through. I can only imagine.

The fatherly, soothing, reassuring tone of Morgan Freeman's voice makes my soul and spirit squirm with doubt and ambivalence. I don't like it.

Me: He's a Trump supporter, Morgan. There's nothing to like. They are all fucking alike.

VOMF: Didn't you say this guy replied to you as if he were emailing you, as opposed to posting directly on a wall?

Me: Yeah. So. He's old. He's probably as internet inept as all those old white dudes questioning Mark Zuckerberg a coupla years ago.

VOMF: Perhaps. But what if, for whatever reason, he really *did* think it was an email sent directly to him from you.

Me: I wouldn't be surprised. The kind of shi—er, stuff he put on his wall suggests he's not the sharpest tool in the shed.

VOMF: But don't you see? If he really thought it was some private email exchange, then we know he wasn't trying to put on a public show for his followers. As far as he was concerned, this was a private, one-on-one conversation between you and him.

Okay. Morgan's reason and logic are starting to piss me off.

Me: And?

> **VOMF:** And so, it's safe to assume he was sincere. He may have been really willing to have his mind changed.

At this point, my foot is incessantly tapping, my arms are folded, and I'm getting a headache from all the teeth grinding.

> **VOMF:** Do you remember *Wonder*?
>
> **Me:** What?
>
> **VOMF:** *Wonder*. The movie starring Julia Roberts, Owen Wilson, and Daveed Diggs.
>
> **Me:** Oh. Yes. That movie. What about it?
>
> **VOMF:** What did you think of it? Not when you saw it, but when you first saw the trailer.
>
> **Me:** I thought it looked like a crappy ABC after-school special and I was shocked a star as big as Julia Roberts would make something that looked like a reject from Hallmark.
>
> **VOMF:** Yeah, you did. But then you watched it on a long flight home, right?
>
> **Me:** Only because my wife made me.
>
> **VOMF:** Regardless. You watched it on your way home, and what happened?

You know that feeling you get when every core of your body wants to stay mad, but then some wise, benevolent, deity-like voice (whether from a real pastor, a teacher, a mentor, a parent, or the voice of some old, warm Black man) starts opening your eyes and heart to something else? Something that would require you to, you know, let go of that anger and hate. But you don't want to let go of that anger and hate because you've held onto it for so long that it's comforting. It's warm. It even gives you meaning and fulfillment.

So your mind goes back to all the things that made you hate in the first place. Like Jack Dawson on that tiny floating door in the icy Atlantic, you're grasping onto that hate, hoping it can keep you afloat. Or like Robert in the original (i.e., good) *Red Dawn*, who's carving notches of all his kills on the butt of his rifle, and Powers Boothe's character, the colonel, says to him: "All that hate's gonna burn you up, kid." And Robert responds: "It keeps me warm."

Part of me wants to stay warm.

But maybe, in reality, love and understanding represent the door, and hate and unforgiveness are the icy deep. And a better part of you is trying to keep you from sinking.

> **VOMF:** Son, what happened when you watched it?

My eyes start to well up as I hear Morgan's soothing, fatherly voice. I take a deep breath. And answer.

> **Me:** I loved it.
>
> **VOMF:** And what did you love most about it?

Sighing that begrudging sigh one does when one doesn't want to admit he's wrong, I answer. (As a film lover, I would be remiss not to tell you that there is somewhat of a spoiler in my answer. Nothing major. But if you haven't seen *Wonder*, I encourage you to do so.)

> **Me:** I loved that every person in the story, no matter how horrible they seemed at first, had a back story that explained why they were the way they were. It gave you a whole new perspective on them, even allowing you to empathize with them.
>
> **VOMF:** Son. Isn't it possible this Pastor Tom guy has a backstory that would give you a different perspective? And by engaging him, maybe, just maybe, you might see him different? And maybe, he'll see a perspective in you he didn't expect, and he'd see you different. And maybe, perhaps, you *just might* change his mind? And if he

is the pastor of a church, maybe his conversation with you might reverberate throughout a whole community.

I have to say I feel rocked to my core. The guilt and shame started welling up inside. Never in a million years after reading Pastor Tom's puke-inducing Facebook wall would I ever imagine having the slightest bit of interest in engaging him in any meaningful way. But I cannot ignore what the Voice of Morgan Freeman is saying.

He then tops it off with one more point I find frustratingly logical and poignant.

> **VOMF:** You saw him one way based on what little you saw on his Facebook feed. But that was like a trailer, son. It's not the real movie. Once you get to know him, you may be surprised like you were about the movie *Wonder*. But you'll never know if you don't try. For all you know, this man could be your "Boo Radley."

Damn you, Voice of Morgan Freeman!

Chapter 32:

My Last Confession

Black Panther, personal demons, and lessons learned

I'm a Black man caught between two worlds. On one hand (or "shoulder"), I have my proverbial "devil" in Sam Jackson, encouraging me to drop f-bombs left and right and go marching through the streets with my fist permanently raised in defiance to the white man.

On the other shoulder, I have Morgan Freeman (or rather, his voice) encouraging me to "go high," rise above rote stereotypes of angry Black men and even make me feel guilty about hating Trump supporters. What the frak! (I mean, er, fuck! Whatever!)

If nothing else, the push and pull between these two aspects of being a Black man in America speak to our rich diversity. And there is perhaps no better microcosm of this than a good ol' healthy debate about Marvel's *Black Panther* (the movie, not the comic).

Wakanda forever

I'm a huge fan of the Marvel Cinematic Universe. Out of ten years of MCU movies, there are only two or three I wasn't too crazy about. I yelled and nearly leaped out of my seat with a kid-like joy in that one movie where that one guy wields that one thing and uses it during you-know-what against you-know-who. (I'm trying not to spoil it. If you've seen them all, and particularly if you're a comic geek, you know exactly what I'm talking about!)

As a Black man who's recently come into his Blackness, I was also a huge fan of *Black Panther*. Everything from the Afro-futuristic design of Wakanda to the storyline of Killmonger (easily one of the most complex villains in the MCU, right up there with Loki IMHO). As big as a fan as I was, though, I didn't think it was a perfect movie. And I fell into the camp that questioned its worthiness for Best Picture. Which probably explains why I had this exchange with JD and Yolanda on Slack.

I shared an article from a white film reviewer who wrote this in response to *Black Panther*'s nomination for Best Picture:

Now, call me old-fashioned, but I believe that any Best Picture trophy should go to, you know, the best movie of the year. And this year has seen some great films. Bradley Cooper's A Star is Born *seems to be the favorite for Best Picture, Alfanso Cuaron's* Roma *has received stellar reviews and buzz so far, and those are just the obvious ones. If Beale Street Could Talk, BlacKkKlansman, Sorry to Bother You, The Favourite, Crazy Rich Asians, and Green Book have all earned grand praise and been the talk of the town at the Golden Globes. Black Panther has the same kinds of high ratings, and blew the box office to pieces before* Infinity War *came along and snapped out the pieces. Black Panther is good, but it's not the best movie of the year, for one reason. The last forty-five minutes of the film are lousy.*

This is an excerpt from our convo on Slack.

Me: If I'm being honest, I can't disagree with anything this guy is saying.

JD: And this is where your Sam Jackson character materializes, slaps you in the face, and grabs you by the shoulders and says, "Snap the fuck out of it!!!"

Yo: I DAMN SURE don't have time for this discussion. But I'll say this. MOST of the writer's silly rhetoric actually argues IN FAVOR of getting the award. Since when the fuck does CULTURAL RELEVANCE DISQUALIFY you for best pic????

JD: Imma start calling Ron, bamboozled!

Me: Ok, I'm gonna say it... Black Panther is the "Black" LaLaLand of Oscar noms!

Yo: Ron, I'm going to slap you for that La La Land comment.

Yolanda has some real issues with *La La Land*. She pretty much hated it. Something about the movie's call back to an old Hollywood era during the same year Trump was running and spreading his Make America Great Again rhetoric. In essence, the movie harkens back to an era that Trump and his Magats were calling for. Oh, and the fact that the greatest champion of jazz music in the film was a white dude. But that's a topic for another book.

Now, back to our Slack convo.

JD: I'm not saying BP is perfect or the best film I've ever seen, but it sure as hell holds up to the others Homie mentioned. He was acting like it was a cut below them.

Me: all the reasons you're saying BP should win best picture are all the reasons ppl gave for LLL being nominated. Come on you two. I expect more and higher standards.

Yo: *La La Land* did NOT have cultural relevance. Ima give you a list about what goes into a movie: Writing, Direction, Casting/ Performance, Production Design, Cinematography, Costume Design, Editing, VFX, Sound Design, Music, Production Execution. PLEASE! PLEASE! PLEASE! PLEASE! SOMEBODY!

It's worth noting Yolanda is a studio executive, producer, PGA, and Academy member, so she *does* have a deeper insight into the machinations of the Hollywood machine.

Me: Is cultural relevance a key factor in best pic? Also, I can give you a list of issues with BP that detracts from it being "best pic" worthy. LLL had all those things (except for maybe VFX).

Yo: Tell me WHICH of the movies were hitting the HEIGHTS in EACH of those categories as HIGH as BP this year? WHICH?

JD: Bamboozled!!!

Yo: NONE. That's which.

JD: Where's Sam Jackson when we need him?

Yo: LLL is NOT nominated this year. GTFOOH

JD: Nigga, let's talk this weekend! Ain't got time for this Slacking bs.

Me: We're debating two different points. 1) does BP as a piece of cinema on its own stand out as a "best pic," and 2) Based on what else is nominated, WILL it win (or should it win). I'm debating point #1. Y'all are debating #2. Listen to the *Low Key* podcast I told you about. Then I'm going to find a time for us to hash this out. Ya dig. Sho nuff!

JD: This weekend! And stop using tired '90s catchphrases!!!

So there you have it. Another glimpse into the world that is my complex yet deeply loving friendship with these two. This Slack thread was followed by a heated ninety-minute debate over Skype. It genuinely was one of the most heated convos we've had as friends in our twenty-five-year history. That's what happens when you get passionate filmmakers debating. Especially passionate *Black* filmmakers debating such a "Black" film.

I have no doubt that that discussion was the impetus for my next and final confession.

All hail the queen

I step into a large square room, approximately twenty feet long by twenty feet wide. The room is completely white. On the other side of the room is an African American woman, with long, dark braids, writing on a chalkboard. Her back is to me. Behind her (and therefore in front of me) is a teacher's desk. It too is white.

I step in, close the door behind me, and walk into the room and toward the desk. In front of the desk is one of those old-fashioned student's desk and chair.

I continue to look at the woman who probably hasn't noticed I walked in. So she keeps writing.

Woman: I'll be with you in one moment.

Oh. Apparently, I was wrong. She does know I'm here.

She sighs, drops her shoulders, and puts the chalk down. I would swear her timing and reaction seemed a little too coincidental. Like, as soon as I wrote, "Apparently, I was wrong..."

Woman: Just have a seat already.

She turns around and there in front of me is none other than Miss Angela Bassett. A little awestruck, I don't sit down.

Angela: Did you not hear me?

Me: Oh. Yes. Sorry.

I sit down. But I can't take my eyes off her. I know this is my imagination and all, but damn, she looks amazing for her age. Does she even age?

She sits down at the desk and proceeds to take papers out of the drawers and put them on the table.

Angela: Do you normally stare uncomfortably like this with everyone you meet?

Me: Sorry.

She takes out a Mont Blanc pen and starts writing on the papers.
Without looking up from her work, she asks me...

Angela: I assume you're here for a confession?

Me: Yes.

Angela: What was your last confession?

Me: Oh. Did you say "what" was my last confession?

She continues to write calmly as she responds.

Angela: Yes, I did.

Me: Oh. That's weird. Usually, people ask, "*When* was your
last confession?" No one has ever asked, "*What* was your
last confession?"

Angela: You'll find I'm full of surprises.

Me: I bet. Can I ask you something?

Angela: No, you may not.

Me: I can't ask you one question?

With that, she puts down her pen, sighs again, and looks up at me.

Angela: I just told you that you could not ask me a question, yet you
did so anyway.

Me: No, I didn't.

Angela: Yes, you did.

Me: With all due respect, I did not ask you a question. That was my
point. I *wanted* to ask you one.

Angela: You asked me if you could ask a question, correct?

Me: Yes.

Angela: I told you no, correct?

Me: Yes.

Angela: The next sentence out of your mouth was, "I can't ask you a question?" *That*, sir, is a question.

I roll my eyes.

Me: Come on, really?

Angela: Excuse me! Who do you think you're talking to? Did you just roll your eyes at me?

Me: Sorry.

Angela: I bet you have to say that word a lot.

Why do people keep telling me that? Anyway, I gulp and sink into my seat. Ms. Bassett looks back down at her papers and begins to write.

And write.

And write.

I fidget, tap my feet, and play the drums section from "Shout" by Tears for Fears.

Ms. Bassett raises her head then shoots me a glare. It takes a few moments for me to notice that she's looking at me. Once I do, I stop.

Me: Oh. Sor—I mean. I'll stop.

She opens another drawer, takes out a small pharmacy bottle, and places it on the front of her desk.

Angela: Here.

Me: Oh. What's that?

Angela: Your meds. It's obvious you haven't taken them.

Ouch. That hurts, Angela.

Me: No, thank you. I'm fine.

Angela: Okay. Suit yourself.

She then places the bottle back into her drawer and returns to writing.

And writing.

And. Writing.

An ungodly amount of time seems to go by. It feels like an eternity. So I break the silence.

Me: Should I come back?

Angela: You've been here a whole five minutes and you're already ready to walk out the door?

Me: Five minutes? I beg to differ. Maybe you've lost track of time, but it's been much longer than that.

Angela: When you walked through that door, it was exactly 12:06.

She looks at her watch, which I must say is very bling, bling.

Angela: It is now 12:11.

She looks back down and begins writing again.

Me: Actually, I think I *will* take those meds.

Without taking her eyes off her writing, she reaches into the drawer, takes out the bottle, and places it back on the edge of the desk.

After taking the pill, I sit quietly, clasp my fingers, close my eyes, take a deep breath, then meditate. I meditate and wait.

After another "eternity," Ms. Bassett *finally* stops writing, puts her pen down, and then looks up at me.

> **Angela:** Okay. Let's try this again. When was your last confession?
>
> **Me:** I thought you asked "what" was my last confession?
>
> **Angela:** Well, I'm changing the question. Like I said. Surprises.
>
> **Me:** I don't know. I kinda liked that last question.
>
> **Angela:** Then why didn't you answer it when I asked it?
>
> **Me:** It just threw me for a loop, that's all. I wasn't expecting it. But I'm ready to answer it now.
>
> **Angela:** That's wonderful. But that ship has sailed. So let me repeat myself, which, let me warn you, is not something I like doing, so I strongly suggest you don't make this a habit during our brief encounter here. Are we clear?

I gulp.

> **Me:** Yes, ma'am.

I fight the urge to say "Sorry" and continue.

> **Me:** My last confession was a few chapters ago.
>
> **Angela:** With whom?
>
> **Me:** Snoop Doggy Dog.
>
> **Angela:** And what did you learn?
>
> **Me:** Oh. Um. Wow. What did I learn? Let me think about it.
>
> **Angela:** Take your time.

I sit up and try to remember my interaction with Snoop. I remember I brought up a white version of "Five on It," then we were talking about the appropriation of Black culture, which led to a discussion of *Get Out*, which led to a discussion about spoilers, which led to him annoyingly saying, "cinema-phile" instead of "cinephile," which led me to correct him, and then...

> **Me:** Oh! I remember! I learned that I have a penchant for correcting people in inappropriate situations instead of just letting them talk.
>
> **Angela:** I would say that was more like a revelation. Not a lesson. What did you actually *learn*?

I pause to think for a second. Or two.

> **Me:** I guess, maybe, I learned that I shouldn't do that?
>
> **Angela:** Really? So you learned that you shouldn't correct people?
>
> **Me:** Well, not in inappropriate situations.
>
> **Angela:** Who determines when a situation is appropriate or not?
>
> **Me:** I don't know. Etiquette?
>
> **Angela:** I would say the lesson you learned is the importance of being present in the moment, connecting with the person you're communicating with, and basing everything you say and do in the presence of that person based on empathy and the connection you're having. That may, or may not, require correcting them.
>
> **Me:** Huh? Yeah. I can see that.
>
> **Angela:** Although, I would strongly advise that for you, just lean toward *not* correcting. It'll be safer that way.
>
> **Me:** You're probably right.

I laugh as I say this. Ms. Bassett doesn't.

> **Angela:** So what are you here to confess now?

I had totally forgotten this was supposed to be a confession.

> **Me:** Yes. Right. Let me see. Oh yeah. I didn't necessarily feel like *Black Panther* was a "Best Picture" worthy movie.

I cringe a bit as I say this, knowing that I'm sitting in front of Queen Ramonda herself. She raises her left eyebrow and tilts her head as she responds.

> **Angela:** Oh, is that right?

Tentatively I respond.

> **Me:** Don't get me wrong. I *loved* the movie and the message it had for Black and brown people as a whole, the milestone it was for African American cinema, having a Black director direct the highest-grossing movie of the year, that Black cast, the first win for a Black set designer, the feeling of pride and power it instills in Black youth, the sheer spectacle of it all, the complexities of Killmonger as a villain, all the effects and music, and the powerhouse acting, it was all great.

She leans back in her seat, crosses her legs, places her elbow on the arm of her chair, and leans her head against her forefinger and thumb.

> **Angela:** And yet?
>
> **Me:** I don't know. I mean. I gave it a solid 8.5, maybe even 8.8 or even 8.9.
>
> **Angela:** Okay?
>
> **Me:** That's out of ten.
>
> **Angela:** Yes. I gathered that.
>
> **Me:** I guess I should rephrase. I mean, when you list all those qualities, it does sound like it's worthy of Best Picture. I guess what

I really mean is that when I saw it, I wasn't thinking, *Oh, this should be Best Picture.*

She continues to stare at me.

Me: And I'm not the only Black person who has thought that. I remember listening to the bruthas on the *Low Key* podcast, and I have to say, they had some of the same issues I had. Particularly in how some of the third act progresses. Although, on subsequent viewings, I will admit some of the issues I had in act three weren't as bad as I originally thought. So it's just that first viewing I think that affected me. Maybe the second and third viewing.

Angela: How many times have you seen it?

Me: Oh, I don't know, maybe three or four. Four and a half.

Angela: In what period of time?

Me: A year. We originally saw it in Amsterdam while traveling, then got the VOD version and watched it again because, you know, even though we saw a version in English, the subtitles for all the Wakanda and Korean language was in Danish.

Angela: Okay.

Me: And I don't speak Danish. Or Wakandan. Or Korean, for that matter. So, you know, I saw it again. Then maybe a couple of times later that year and into the next. So yeah, within a year.

Angela: For a movie you don't think was worthy of being Best Picture, you sure did watch it a lot.

Me: Well, there are lots of movies I frequently watch that I wouldn't necessarily think Best Picture. I mean, I could watch *A Christmas Story* every one of the twelve days of Christmas and never get tired of it. But I wouldn't say it's Best Picture worthy.

Angela: Are you comparing *Black Panther* to *A Christmas Story*?

> **Me:** Oh no! Not at all Queen Ramonda—um, I mean, Miss Bassett. *Ms.* Bassett.

Angela leans forward onto the desk then begins writing again.

> **Angela:** Okay. That's all. You're dismissed.
>
> **Me:** Oh. I'm sorry. Did I offend you? Like I said. I really liked it.
>
> **Angela:** Yes. I know. I heard you.
>
> **Me:** So what? That's it?
>
> **Angela:** Yep. That's it.
>
> **Me:** You have nothing else to say?

Ms. Bassett puts her pen back down and turns her gaze back to me.

> **Angela:** What exactly do you think these confessions have been about?
>
> **Me:** Confessing my Black sins?
>
> **Angela:** Nigga, please!

I must admit, I am taken aback at her dropping the N-word.

> **Angela:** You are smarter than that, Mr. Dawson. Black "sins"? Really? That's what you've been doing all your life? Committing sins against the Black community? And even if that *were* the case, what the hell makes you think confessing them to African American icons in your life is going to absolve you of them?
>
> **Me:** Hey, it wasn't my idea to go through this often embarrassing, albeit sometimes enlightening, metaphorical journey. This is Samuel L. Jackson's doing?
>
> **Angela:** You mean allegorical journey, don't you?
>
> **Me:** Yes, right. Allegorical. Thank you.

Ms. Bassett laughs, stops writing, gets up, and walks around the desk and sits on the edge of it, folds her arms, then addresses me.

Angela: I was joking, Ron. My bigger point is this: you absolutely have demons in your life that you're struggling with regarding how much you have or have not connected to your Black brothers and sisters. I can tell it's been hard on you.

Me: Yeah. I guess it has.

Angela: And the act of talking to people like me, or Snoop or whomever else you've encountered on this fantastical campaign, I'm sure has been a very comfortable way for you to ask tough questions and engage in challenging discussions in a sort of dissociative way. And I commend you for your bravery to be so vulnerable. But the truth of the matter is that the only "sins" you've committed have been against *yourself*. And only when you really grab ahold of what *that* means will you be able to truly reconnect or connect with *any* race or people or *person*, for that matter, in a way that is authentic and filled with integrity. If you can't be authentically yourself, in the way that God made and formed you, no matter what that looks like, no amount of f-bomb dropping, African American history reading, or Facebook fighting is going to bring you peace. Especially if you're engaging and debating with a bunch of idiots on social media. Do you honestly think that will move the needle or make a difference?

Me: Well, I just thought...

Angela: It's a rhetorical question, Ron.

Me: Oh. Yeah. Of course.

Angela: Look. You're not going to find true peace this way. True peace comes at being comfortable in who you are, embracing it, loving it, forgiving yourself for the *real* hurt you might have done to people in your life, seeking absolution from *them*, and then moving forward in your *truth*. And that truth may indeed be this evolution you've seemed to have undergone these past few years to be the "angry Black man" that you've never been, cussin' out racist-ass white folks and duped evangelicals. And that's okay.

But it's also okay if the real you wants to forgive a Trump-supporting asshole. It's also okay if the real you wants to engage in conversations with whom you vehemently disagree. It's also okay if you don't like chicken and waffles. And it is for damn sure also okay if your immediate reaction to *Black Panther* was that you didn't think "Best Picture," despite the litany of excellence you rattled off to me a few minutes ago. I mean, damn, nigga, if *that* don't qualify a film for Best Picture, what does?

And with that, she got up from the table, walked back around to her seat, sat down, and continued to write.

I take a big sigh, still trying to process all that she just said. I then get out of my chair, turn to the door, and walk toward it. But before I leave, I turn to her and...

Angela: No. You may not ask me another question. That is all I'm going to say. Good day, Mr. Dawson.

Me: Good day, Ms. Bassett.

Angela: Angela.

Me: Excuse me?

She looks up from her writing, smiles, and says...

Angela: You can call me Angela.

I smile and respond.

Me: Thanks, Angela. Bye.

Angela: Good day. Please make sure the door is closed all the way on your way out.

Me: Yes, of course. Bye.

And with that, I leave the white room and conclude my final confession.

As I walk outside and head back home, Keegan-Michael Key, dressed in a dapper 1940s double-breasted suit, comes up to me.

> **Keegan:** Excuse me, sir. Are you Ron Dawson?
>
> **Me:** Hey. Wow. This is so cool. You're Keegan-Michael Key. Yes. Yes. I'm Ron Dawson.
>
> **Keegan:** I have this for you.

He hands me a letter.

> **Keegan:** See ya.

Keegan-Michael Key then runs off like he just robbed a bank or something.

I open the envelope and read it.

> **Me:** *What*!? I've just been served papers by Keegan-Michael Key. Ain't that a bitch!

It's a fucking summons! And you'll never believe what I'm being summoned to court for!

> **Me**: *Get the frak out of here!*

Chapter 33:

Reunited (and It Don't Feel Too Good)

Ronald Dawson v. The People of African America

"And they say it's the white man I should fear
But, it's my own kind doin' all the killin' here..."

—Tupac Shakur, "Only God Can Judge Me"

It's a hot summer day. The town courthouse is all abuzz. A hush comes over the courtroom as the defendant and his attorney enter the room. The defendant looks nervous as he surveys the room and sees an ocean of Black faces. Dark ones. Light ones. Round ones. Thin ones. Some shake their heads in disgust. Others seem to be encouraging him. Alfonso Ribeiro, dressed in a red sequined jacket, and wearing shades, pumps his one white-gloved fist at the defendant and yells "Woot! Woot! Woot!"

Seated in the balcony are the surviving cast members from *The Brady Bunch*, *The Sound of Music*, *The Partridge Family*, *Lost in Space*, and an assortment of other random white people. Eve Plumb and Angela Cartwright sit next to each other. They hold hands, comforting each other as they look down on the crowd.

The attorney and the defendant take their seats. Name placards on the tables tell them where to sit.

Defense Attorney: Don Cheadle

Defendant: Cleve Ronaldo Dawson Jr.

Opposing counsel enters the courtroom and the room erupts into cheers and applause. A smooth, dashing, dark-skinned brutha who looks like he just stepped off a cover of *Gentleman's Quarterly* saunters down the aisle to his desk. He places his Louis Vuitton leather attaché case next to his name placard.

Prosecuting Attorney: Blair Underwood

The bailiff enters the room, and it's none other than Reginald VelJohnson. He finishes his chocolate-covered donut, gulps down the rest of his lukewarm coffee, and calls the courthouse to order.

RVJ: "Settle down, everyone!"

He clears his throat. And begins.

RVJ: Aw yeah! Aw yeah! Aw yeah! All rise for the Honorable, the Chief Justice, and HNIC of this court of law. Aw yeah! Aw yeah! Aw yeah! All bruthas and sistas having business before the Honorable, the Chief Justice, and HNIC are admonished to draw near and give their attention, for this court is now sitting. God save the Black men and women of these fucked-up United States. Aw yeah! Aw yeah! Aw yeah!

The crowd stands to their feet as Reginald opens the court. Once he finishes, a squeaky whine erupts from the speakers in the ceiling. Everyone covers their ears. The annoying sound stops.

A bell from an alarm clock rings over the speakers. And we hear a DJ.

DJ Voice: Waaaake up! Wake up! Wake up! Up ya wake, up ya wake, up ya waaaake! This is Mr. Señor Love Daddy, your voice of choice.

Ize only plays the plattas that matta. And that's the truth, Ruth. Let him who has an ear hear. Y'all ready?

The sound of a needle dropping on a turntable is heard. The familiar sounds of a scratchy record now ooze from the speakers.

And then... they hear it. The smooth, soulful sounds of Al Green's "Let's Stay Together" start to play.

The crowd reacts with a jubilant celebration. The sistas swoon. The bruthas bounce. It's like the spirit of God coming down on Pentecost.

"*Aaaahhh*, shit! Yeah! Now that's what ahm talkin' about!" someone says from the crowd.

I look around and adjust my collar. Don attempts to calm me down.

Don: Don't worry. Just keep lookin' straight.

The door to the judge's chamber opens from behind the large, looming bench. As the judge climbs the bench and takes his seat, my heartbeat jacks up and I practically turn white (no pun intended).

The judge takes his seat. His name placard is a small blinking neon sign that reads:

HNIC: Samuel L. Jackson

I can't help but exclaim loudly.

Me: *What the hell! You've got to be fucking kidding me!*

Judge Jackson takes his golden mallet and pounds.

Sam: *Shut the hell up mutha...*

He clears his throat.

Sam: I mean. Order in the court, young man. We'll have none of these shenanigans in my courthouse.

Don Cheadle turns to me.

> **Don:** Man. Are you trying to lose this case before it starts? What the
> hell was that all about?!
>
> **Me:** Don. He *can't* be the judge. This ain't right. This ain't right. Oh
> man, oh man, oh man, oh man!

Don looks around and tries to calm him down.

> **Don:** What? What *is* it?

I lean over and whisper into his ear. From his bench, Judge Jackson
sips on a long straw from his soda, then gives me a mischievous wink
and a nod.

I finish whispering to Don. Don does not look happy.

> **Don:** Dude. Why are you just now telling me this?! Are you
> shittin' me?
>
> **Me:** How the fuck would I know he'd be the judge?
>
> **Don:** Cuz it's *your book*, muthafucka! That's how.
>
> **Me:** I know. But the "me" in here is not the same me writing. I don't
> know. This whole meta thing is weird and hurting my head. Anyway.
> Doesn't he have to recuse himself or something?
>
> **Don:** Hold on. Let me see what I can do.

Don Cheadle gets up and addresses the judge.

> **Don:** Permission to approach the bench, Your Honor.

Judge Jackson gives a coy smile.

> **Sam:** Be my guest.

He kicks his legs up on the table as Don and Blair approach. Don leans in and whispers.

> **Don:** Your Honor, it seems my client feels that you may have a biased opinion of him based on a rather contentious past relationship, and I must therefore ask that you recuse yourself from this case expeditiously.

Judge Jackson chuckles.

> **Sam:** Ooooh. Those are some mighty big words there, counselor. You want me to recuuuuse myself. Well. Allow me to retort. I don't give a fuck what you think. I'm the muthafucka assigned to this case. The world is filled with judges who shouldn't be fuckin' wearing a robe. This is the real world. I'm running this muthafucka like a graduate from Georgetown Prep. I'm your Brett "Muthafuckin'" Kavanaugh, baby, and if you don't like it, you can take yo Black ass home and I'll get Harry Hamlin in this muthafucka to take your place. Ya dig?

Don gives him a side-eye.

> **Don:** Yeah. I dig.
>
> **Sam:** Now get the hell up out my face, muthafucka, and do your job. And don't worry 'bout me, 'cuz I *will* do mine.

Don gives him a stern look.

> **Don:** You like to say muthafucka a lot, don't you?

Judge Jackson takes his feet off the table, puts down his soda, and leans in close to Don. Don can feel the judge's breath and smell the unmistakable scent of THC.

> **Sam:** Yeah, muthafucka. I do! Now take your Black ass back to your seat and let's get this shit started. I have a violin concerto to attend tonight, and I don't want to be late.

Don grits his teeth, turns away, and heads back to his seat. Blair smiles at the judge and gives him a pound.

Don returns to his seat next to me.

Me: So what did he say?

Don adjusts his collar.

Don: It's cool. It's cool. I worked it out. It'll be okay.

I lean back and look up at Judge Jackson as he bangs his gavel. Reginald calls for me to stand.

RVJ: Will the defendant please stand?

Don and I stand.

RVJ: On the charges of not being Black enough and tryna perpetrate a fraud up in here by appropriating the Black culture you for so long have ignored, how do you respond?

Me: Um. Not guilty?

Judge Jackson and the rest of the crowd start cracking up.

Sam: Awww, shit. This is gonna be good.

Don: Your Honor. Please!

Sam: Okay, okay. Settle down. Whatever, counselor. Calm yo ass down. It just struck me as funny, is all. Sit down and let's get started.

Don and I take our seats. Blair Underwood smiles.

Sam: Mr. Underwood.

BU: Yes, Your Honor.

Sam: Call your first witness.

BU: Thank you. I would like to call to the stand Derrick Howard.

I shake my head.

Me: Oh man. This is going to be a long day.

Derrick, my old housemate from the UC Berkeley African American house back in the summer of '87, takes the stand.

Reginald holds up *The Autobiography of Malcolm X* for him to swear on.

RVJ: Raise your right hand and place your other hand on this book. Do you promise to tell the truth, the whole truth, and nothin' but the double-truth, Ruth?

DH: Sho nuff.

Reginald nods to Blair.

RVJ: He's all yours.

Blair Underwood approaches the stand.

BU: Hello. Would you please state your name for the court?

Derrick: My name is Derrick Howard.

BU: And can you please tell the court how you happened to come into the acquaintance of the defendant?

Derrick: Sure. He was one of my housemates in the African American house at UC Berkeley during the summer of '87. We were both working during the summer at the Unit 2 residence halls.

BU: And what were your jobs there?

Derrick: Cleaning up after privileged rich kids attending school during the summer.

BU: And how would you describe Mr. Dawson during his time there?

Derrick: Well, he was a rather odd bird.

BU: What do you mean by that?

Derrick: Well, we were staying at the house right at the beginning of the NBA basketball championships that year. The other bruthas in the house and I would always go down and watch the games. But not Ron. He stayed up in his room. I mean, it was like he didn't care about basketball.

The crowd gasps in shock and surprise. Judge Jackson bangs his gavel.

Sam: Order.

Don Cheadle stands up.

Don: Objection, Your Honor. Relevance? What in the world does liking or not liking basketball have anything to do with being Black?

Blair responds.

BU: Your Honor, back in 1987, over 80 percent of the players in the NBA were Black. That '86–'87 season was one of the most iconic in basketball history. The golden era. Michael Jordan became the second player in history to score three thousand points in a season. Given the state of basketball that year and its influence on the Black community, it stands to reason that a *real* Black man would be into it.

Judge Jackson takes a bite out of a cheeseburger and responds.

Sam: I'll allow it. Proceed.

Don shakes his head and sits down.

Blair continues.

BU: Thank you, Your Honor. Now, Mr. Howard. Were there any other aspects of Mr. Dawson's character that seemed, how shall we say, white?

Derrick: Well, yeah. He talked white.

Don: Objection.

Sam: Overruled.

BU: Continue, Mr. Howard. What do you mean he talked "white"?

Derrick: You know. Like, he didn't sound like a brutha. I get it that just because a Black man speaks proper English don't mean he talks white. But come on. We all know the deal. When you're hangin' out with your boys, you talk one way, and when you're at the office with the wypipo, you talk a different way. Ron wasn't like that. He sounded and talked the same, regardless.

BU: Thank you, Mr. Howard. I have no further questions, Your Honor.

Sam: Okay. Well. There you go. Closing arguments, gentlemen.

I freak out and exclaim...

Me: What?!

Don stands up.

Don: Your Honor! I get to cross-examine the witness!

Judge Jackson starts cracking up.

Sam: Man. I'm just shittin' ya. You shoulda seen the look on your face. Go ahead and ask your little questions.

Don approaches the stand.

Don: Mr. Howard. Are you familiar with W.E.B. DuBois?

Derrick: Of course.

Don: James Baldwin?

Derrick: Yes.

Don: Oscar Micheaux?

Derrick: Oscar who?

Don: Micheaux. He's widely regarded as the first prominent African American feature filmmaker.

Derrick looks confused.

Derrick: Okay. Not too familiar with him.

Don smiles.

Don: That's okay. How about Frederick Douglass? I'm sure you know him.

Blair stands up.

BU: Objection, Your Honor. Where is this all going?

Sam: Sustained. Get on with it, Mr. Cheadle.

Don: Sure. Sorry, Your Honor. Mr. Howard, would you not say that all these men represent paragons of what it means to be Black in America?

Derrick: Sure. I guess so.

Don: Did any of them watch basketball or NBA championships?

The audience laughs. Derrick responds.

Derrick: Of course not.

Don: So you *can* be considered a "real" Black man, despite having no interest in or even seeing one basketball game.

Derrick: Well, I guess, if you put it that way. Yes. But...

Don: Thank you. I have nothing further, Your Honor.

Blair stands up.

> **BU:** Permission to redirect, Your Honor.
>
> **Sam:** Permission granted.

Blair stands up, buttons his top suit button, then asks one
final question.

> **BU:** Mr. Howard. On June 3, 1987, you cleaned out one of the empty
> dorm rooms at the Unit 2 residence Davidson Hall, correct?
>
> **Derrick:** Yes, sir.
>
> **BU:** Whose room was that?
>
> **Derrick:** Well, as it turns out, it was Ron's very room that past
> school year.
>
> **BU:** And as you cleaned out the room, what did you find?
>
> **Derrick:** A photo of him. He must have dropped it while packing up at
> the end of the semester.
>
> **BU:** And was there anything unusual about that photo?
>
> **Derrick:** Yeah. A white girl had her legs wrapped around him and was
> licking his face.
>
> **BU:** And what was his expression in the photo?
>
> **Derrick:** He was smiling ear to ear.
>
> **BU:** What did you do then?
>
> **Derrick:** I handed the photo back to him and just kinda looked at him.
> I then teased him a bit and pulled the photo away. Then started to
> hand it to him, then pulled it away. Then handed it back. Then pulled
> it away. That shit was funny. I was just givin' him a hard time, seeing
> as I kinda figured he looked like the kinda dude that would stash

away a photo of a white girl wrapping her legs around him. But shit. That was a fucking strange experience.

BU: I'm sure it was. Thank you, Mr. Howard. No further questions, Your Honor.

I drop my head into my hands. Don addresses me.

Don: Do you have any more surprise photos you need to tell me about? Any photos of you at a Young Republican convention or something? Please let me know now.

Me: No. What?! I'm supposed to remember every frakkin' photo I've ever taken with a girl? It was a high school graduation trip, for crying out loud. We were flirty friends. Geesh! That was, like, over thirty years ago.

Don throws his pen on the table and puts his head in his hands. Then he sits up and looks me in the eye.

Don: And one more thing. For the rest of this trial, there's a moratorium on the word "frak." You got that? You're fucking fifty years old, man.

Me: Geeze. Fine.

Don sighs.

Don: This is gonna be a long day.

Judge Jackson addresses Blair.

Sam: Call your next witness.

Blair Underwood proceeds to call witness after witness, making his case for my being a disgrace to the Black race and the last person on earth to be mounting any kind of woke protest against the establishment.

But Don responded masterfully. In each cross-examination, he was able to show that the definition of "Blackness" is not tied to any of those things. He brought up example after example to counter Blair's witnesses—from Roscoe Lee Browne and his inestimable acting and directing career as a counter to the "voice" arguments, to former National Republican Committee Chairman Michael Steele as an example of a conservative brutha who's still "down."

But then, it happened. The eventuality that Don and I knew was inevitable.

Blair addressed the bench.

BU: Your Honor, for my last witness, I call to the stand the defendant, Cleve Ronaldo Dawson Jr.

Awwww shit!

Chapter 34:

Faith, Evolution, and the Unforgivable Sin

There are some things you need to know about me

I was probably about seven or eight when, one Wednesday evening, my little brother and I came home from some kind of church event being held in the Cross Creek Village community room of Playa del Rey, California. When we got back to our apartment, we enthusiastically shared with our mother all we learned and told her we were ready to say "it." The prayer of all prayers. The holy grail of prayers. The prayer to "rule them all." *The Sinner's Prayer.*

Da-da-da-dummmmm! (Cue "Hallelujah Chorus"!)

On the night we said that prayer, according to the Bible, a whole host of angels had an old-fashioned, down-home house party! Two more souls were saved and washed clean by the blood of the Lamb. Before this night, apparently, my brother and I, despite barely being old enough to understand why gravity works, and who still believed a bearded, jolly, red-suited, overweight white man came down the chimney every Christmas (ignoring the fact that as apartment dwellers, we didn't even have chimneys), had we died, these two ign'ant Black boys would have spent an eternity screaming and hollerin' and gnashing our teeth in hell. (To this day, I still don't know what it means to "gnash your teeth.")

As the sons of a Black woman raised in the South by strict Southern Baptist parents, it was only a matter of time before we would have said "the prayer." But there was something special about that night. There must have been because over forty years later, I remember it. Anything someone remembers so vividly so many years ago must be something that has meaning.

And for many years, my faith had lots of meaning. It evolved and grew to define me as a man.

As is the case with anyone on a path of truth-seeking or enlightenment, the strength of my faith ebbed and flowed. Sometimes it was white-hot (no pun intended) and I was "on fire for Jesus," as they would say.

And other times it was more lukewarm-ish (which, if you are a die-hard Bible reader, you know is even worse for a believer than not believing at all).

As I grew into adulthood, my faith has had five significant evolutionary jumps.

#1. Personal ownership

The first major evolutionary jump was in high school, running for Chaplain of the Senate in Youth & Government, the YMCA's state-wide model legislature and court program. Up until that point, the extent of my faith was being "forced" to go to church every Sunday—and let me tell you, sitting in a Baptist church from 10:00 a.m. to 2:00 p.m. was, in some cases, worse than going to school. First you got the Sunday school, then you have singing, then the announcements, then more singing, then more announcements (why didn't they just make these announcements with the first announcements?), more singing, then the sermon, then the altar call, then having all the altar call people introduce themselves, then closing announcements (again, with the announcements).

When you're a fourteen-year-old kid going to a church like that, every week, when the pastor *finally* excuses the congregation, you feel like the dude that just got his parole papers and is walking out of the state penitentiary after serving ten years of an eleven-year sentence.

But when I ran for chaplain, I was doing so because I had a sincere love for Jesus and wanted to spread that love. For the first time, I owned my faith on my terms.

#2. Freaky Friday

The second evolutionary shift in my faith was in college when I had what I'll just call a "freaky" experience with a church, which shall remain nameless, but let's just say, it was "of Christ." This experience was so bad that it pushed me *away* from going to church. They would have these sessions with you where they'd try to get you to admit all the sins you've committed in your life.

During one of my "confessional" sessions, knowing how much I liked dancing and how dancing can lead to sexual lusts, they tried to get me to admit which sexual sins I might have committed. Yeah. True story. (Ironically, as of that time in my life, I didn't have any sexual sins to speak of. But if I had, I tell you, it would have been none of their damn business!)

The final straw with them came one Friday morning when I woke up from a nightmare where I felt like an evil spirit was tormenting me. Minutes after I awoke, members from that church were knocking on my door, checking up on me because I hadn't been around for a while. *Freaky!*

After this experience, I stopped going and entered my twenties "church-free" (and pretty much lived life like a "church-free" bachelor). However, I never stopped believing in God.

#3. Back to church and back on track

The third and one of the most profound evolutionary jumps in faith was in my late twenties when I started attending a church in Eagle Rock, California, called Christian Assembly (CA). I went the first time because I was invited by a girl I kinda had a thing for (I know, it's a terrible reason to go to church. But God can work in any number of ways to get his children back in church. And if it takes a girl, so be it). But attending CA was such a big deal for me because I went *back* to that church—*sans* girl—and I genuinely loved it.

It was unlike any church I'd ever attended. For one, the pastor, Mark Pickerill, wore Hawaiian shirts and shorts. After years of either Episcopal or Baptist church attendance, this was the first pastor I ever saw that didn't wear a suit. In fact, this was the first church I attended where you didn't have to wear your "Sunday best." You could wear just regular ol' clothes. And Mark was self-effacing and a brilliant and funny orator.

From its pastor to the racial diversity to the amazing worship music lead by internationally renowned worship leader Tommy Walker, CA felt like "heaven on earth."

I first went to CA because of a girl. I stayed because of God. For the first time in my adult life, I had joined a church and truly made my faith my own again. After ten long years, I was back on track.

#4. Defender of the faith

Evolutionary jump #4 was a few years later when I moved to Silicon Valley and joined another church, similar in style and feel to CA. It was called The River, and while there, I joined a seeker's ministry geared to reach people who have questions about the Christian faith.

I first joined as a member, then eventually became a group co-leader. I had a passion for apologetics (the practice of defending and/or explaining the faith). You've heard that saying that if you want to become good at something, then teach it? That's what I did at The River. For pretty much the rest of my adult life (up until 2016), apologetics were my passion as a follower of Christ.

#5. "My Dark Period"

But then came evolutionary jump #5, which represented one of the legitimately scariest moments in my life.

It was about a week or two after 9/11, and I was sitting at my desk at work, typing away on some business report, when I swear I heard the audible sound, "F*** Jesus." (And no, it was not "Frak Jesus." It was the *real* f-word.)

What the hell?!

I had no idea where it came from. It seemed like a whisper. As I tried to figure out how that phrase could possibly enter my mind, I thought it again. The first time seemed undeniably audible. The second time was just me thinking it.

The more I tried *not* to think it, the more it happened. And happened. And happened.

Every day during my waking hours, every few minutes the phrase "F*** Jesus" or "F*** God" would pop into my brain. And every time it did, I fought against it. And the more I tried to stop it, the more it kept coming.

There are no words to describe how emotionally and spiritually debilitating this was. I would stay up all night, playing my favorite albums from Chris Tomlin, Tommy Walker, and other popular Christian worship leaders and rock stars, trying like the dickens to drown out my "blasphemous" thoughts.

Why was this happening to me?!

I scoured through the Bible, looking for answers. (It's hard and guilt-inducing to read the "good book" when every other sentence you're thinking, *F*** God, F*** Jesus*. It was like a little Tourette's demon was sitting on my shoulder or something.) But then matters got a whole lot worse.

In my Bible reading, I came across Mark 3:28–29: "Verily I say unto you, 'All sins shall be forgiven unto the sons of men, and blasphemies wherewith soever they shall blaspheme: But he that shall blaspheme against the Holy Ghost hath never forgiveness, but is in danger of eternal damnation.'"

No sooner did I read this passage did the next thought enter my mind. You guessed it: *F*** the Holy Spirit.*

That was it. I was done for. The little boy who took to his knees all those years ago and said "the prayer" had thrown it all away. I was headed for H.E. double hockey sticks.

I immediately emailed my pastor at The River and set up a time to meet with him about what I had done.

I was a total mess when I met with him. "Am I possessed or something?"

"No, Ron. As a Christian who has accepted Christ into his heart, it is impossible for you to be possessed."

As we talked, I teared up and said, "I'm going to work as hard as I can to win as many people for God as possible. If I'm going down, I'm going to save as many people as I can along the way!" We then sat and prayed together that these thoughts and hounding from spiritual forces would leave me. All the while, I was thinking... well, you know.

As the days went by, it just got worse. I spent my birthday, October 2, trying to enjoy the special time spent with my good friends, putting on a good face and smile, but underneath, a chaotic storm was raging. By this time, the thoughts were nonstop. *F*** Jesus, F*** God, F*** Jesus, F*** God, F*** Jesus, F*** God, F*** Jesus, F*** God, F*** Jesus, F*** God, F*** Jesus, F*** God, F*** Jesus, F*** God, F*** Jesus, F*** God, F*** Jesus, F*** God, F*** Jesus, F*** God.*

All. Day. Long.

I finally decided to go to a Christian psychiatrist.

It was Thursday, October 25, 2001. As I sat in his office and explained my story, he could clearly see the stress and strain I was under. He spoke in a calm and encouraging voice.

"So Ron, tell me. What do you think it means to 'blaspheme the Holy Spirit'?"

"I'm not quite sure, actually. I thought that's what I had done."

"I would suspect the fact that you feel so bad about it suggests you really didn't do that. Blaspheming the Holy Spirit in that context isn't about profanity."

"Well, what about these thoughts? I mean, this can't be a good thing in the eyes of God."

"I suspect that God understands what you're going through. He, more than anyone, knows about how the brain he created works."

"What do you mean by that?"

"Tell me. If I tell you not to think of a pink elephant, what's the first thing that comes to mind?"

"A pink elephant."

"And the more you try to *stop* thinking about a pink elephant, the more you *will* think of one. That's how the brain works."

"So how do I stop it?"

"By not trying. The next time one of those thoughts enters your mind, just let it hang out. Don't fight it. Just let it be."

"Huh. Really? Just let it be."

"Yep. Try it. How often do they come?"

"I'm thinking it now."

"Okay. Just let it be."

I left the doctor's office thinking, *Could it really be that easy?* I must admit, it seemed like a hokey way to exorcise these "evil" thoughts. But what did I have to lose?

So over the next day or so, whenever one of those dreadful thoughts entered my mind, I ignored it. I didn't fight it. I was like, "Hey there, Mr. F*** Jesus. How are you today?"

And guess what? In a few days, they had all subsided. What hours upon hours of nonstop worship music throughout the night, laying on hands, and incessant prayer couldn't do, good ol' fashioned neuroscience cured in a few days. After about a month of debilitating and demoralizing "spiritual" warfare, I was finally "healed."

I refer to this time as my "Dark Period," and it taught me a valuable lesson about learning how to balance faith and science. It taught me that while we *may* fight against powers, principalities, and spiritual forces of evil, sometimes we are indeed fighting against flesh and blood, and simple science and medicine will do just fine.

Ironically, I've used the story of my "Dark Period" as a personal testimony to other Christians, or those considering the faith, that there's nothing too terrible from which they can't find the grace of God and Jesus Christ.

The real question is: will my people, the Blacks, be as forgiving when they find out about my other "dark sin"? Perhaps the worst sin a Black man could commit against his people. Because when I mentioned "faith, evolution, and the unforgivable sin," I wasn't talking about dropping an f-bomb on the Holy Spirit. I meant that *other* unforgivable sin.

Chapter 35:

The Other Unforgivable Sin

The #1 most embarrassing admission in this book

This entire tome is about self-reflection and facing personal demons. Along the way, I've made several confessions related to my life as a Black man in America that are empirically embarrassing. Luckily, I'm self-aware and self-effacing enough to deal with it and laugh at myself. I've even alluded to a couple as my second most embarrassing confession (never having dated or been with a Black woman) and my third most embarrassing confession (not knowing the meaning of the fraternity term "on line").

I'm sure one question has been eating you up this whole time: "What on earth is the most embarrassing admission?" Against my better judgment, and for fear of losing any modicum of credibility I *might* have garnered during the time you've been reading, today I will share with you the answer to that question. And it isn't particularly funny.

Lord Jesus, have mercy.

The story I can no longer avoid telling <gulp>

The 2008 US presidential election cycle was an exciting time in United States politics. And at the center of all that excitement was America's first African American candidate by a major party for the president of the United States: Barack Hussein Obama.

I didn't know this at the time, but Barack was a man devoted to serving the public and making a real difference in the community. I would learn more about his career ten years later during the *Becoming Obama* podcast series. His was an impeccable pedigree: At twenty-eight, he was elected the first Black president of the *Harvard Law Review*; he had passed up a prestigious offer with a definite partner track to be able to lead community development programs in some of the poorest communities of Chicago.

His famous speech opening the 2004 Democratic National Convention proved that he was not only a powerful and eloquent speaker but a savvy political strategist.

His commitment to serving his community proved his leadership and desire to use his abilities and prestige to better the lives of African Americans. And as a magna cum laude graduate of Harvard Law, we know he was one smart brutha as well.

After eight years of George Dub-ya, Obama would be a refreshing leader in the Oval Office. Politics had never been my thing. But this was one presidential election I was eager to participate in—the voting of the first African American president.

But then, a funny thing happened on the way to the voting booth.

A few months before that history-making November, I was hanging out with some friends who were, you know, Christians. And, um, Caucasian.

Me: My wife and I are excited about voting for Barack Obama. It'll be cool to have our first Black president.

White Christian Friend: Oh no, Ron. You don't want to vote for him. Have you read his policies?

Me: No. Why?

WCF: If he's elected president, he'll unleash an army of evil and satanism, the likes of which this world has never known! All of us good Christians need to not vote for him.

> **Me:** Oh. Wow. I didn't know that. Evil *and* satanism?
>
> **WCF:** Yeah, it's true. Now you know.
>
> **Me:** Thanks?
>
> **WCF:** Sure thing. Vote Republican!

Now, I must be honest; she didn't say anything about evil and satanism. (At least I don't think she did.) My guess is, whatever issue she brought up, it was probably related to abortion and/or homosexuality and how liberal Democrats just love them some baby-killing gay lovers.

All I know is I was now deeply conflicted. On one hand, I wanted to vote for the first African American president of the United States. I wanted to partake in that historic event.

But what about Jesus? What about God? What about the vow I made during my "Dark Period" when I thought I was hell-bound? How could I vote for someone who would advocate for things I was supposed to be against?

And so, I eventually did *not* vote for Barack Obama in 2008. And for some reason—I honestly cannot tell you why—I'm pretty sure I didn't vote for him in 2012 either. My guess is for similar reasons. Because of... Jesus.

Cue my walk of shame down a cobblestone street of Black folk throwing all manner of nastiness at me.

Am I a tad melodramatic about my voting record? Maybe. I'm sure there are plenty of reasonable, defensible, and perfectly logical reasons why a Black person wouldn't vote for Obama in either election.

But I don't have any such reasons. I wasn't into politics. I didn't do research. I wasn't listening to the popular political podcasts or radio shows of the day.

If I had a firm grasp of all the issues at the time. If I knew *any* of the candidates' stances in-depth; if I had my finger on the pulse of the goings-on of world politics that I have now; and then with all that information, decided not to vote for Obama, I may still be slightly embarrassed about not voting for him, but I wouldn't feel shame about it.

But I didn't do any of those things. My only "excuse" is that I was just a conflicted Christian man, torn by a promise I made years earlier to God and thinking that somehow, voting Democrat would break that promise.

Most of this book was written before the Democratic primaries for the 2020 presidential election. JD and Yolanda had both read the manuscript, but due to her busy schedule, it took Yolanda longer to get to the end. So it was early spring of 2020 by the time she got to the chapter you're reading now. They knew of my "shameful" voting record, but apparently, she didn't know why. She had assumed that I was just another conservative Republican brutha who had lost his way and come back. She assumed I *was* versed on the issues and had a healthy voting record. When she read that was not the case and that my reasons for not voting for Obama were due to some stupid-ass Christian wypipo, she was livid! (Rightfully so, I might add.) In one of her comments on this part of the book, she wrote:

> "Do you KNOW the BLOOD and TREASURE that our forefathers and our ancestors gave for you to have the rights and privileges that you so cavalierly were waltzing through life with??? You took it for fucking granted? Our parents went to fucking segregated schools, dude!!!
>
> "I'm sorry. I don't accept this bullshit toss off. The more I think about this, I think i'm just going to have to make a definitive CHOICE to put this book aside for now (I was going to say forgive you, but then found it patronizing). And it's SOLEY...SOLELY on the basis that I love you. And nothing more."

Later, we even got into a heated debate over a comment I made after watching Bill Maher. He commented that Democrats need to stop pussyfooting around and play hardball like the Republicans. And I agreed with him. So did Yo. But she got irate that I would dare comment on the situation given my apolitical stance in life.

In the twenty-five years I've known them, that was the angriest I've seen her get at me. (Not that she gets angry at me that often anyway. I am still a nice guy.) But she, like the rest of the country during that time, was distressed at the state of the nation. Elizabeth Warren had just bowed out, which was already shortly after Kamala Harris. And Trump was still up to his foolishness. The idea that a Black man in this country would ever squander his vote was so foreign to her. Especially someone she knew so well.

It's hard to fully encapsulate the indoctrination of a religious faith. It's no secret the disdain I have for Trump and his supporters—especially his evangelical ones. But if I'm being honest, a part of me understands. While I don't think *not* voting for Obama is anywhere near as bad as voting *for* Trump (let alone continuing to support him), I have the proverbial log in my eye when it comes to making political decisions based on religious conviction. I may be able to justify that my decisions are not as egregious, but that's all it would be—a justification.

At the end of the day, I felt as bad as a Trump supporter.

Never again would I vote like that. But is it too late for Black redemption?

Chapter 36:

Can I Get a Witness?

Time to take my medicine

Blair Underwood, looking as fly and suave as ever, stands and addresses the judge.

> **BU:** Your Honor, for my last witness, I call to the stand the defendant.

Blair Underwood makes his request of the judge with confidence and vigor. Those in the audience start to throw out their commentary on the situation.

> **Audience:** Awww, shit. It's about to get real up in here! Time to go back to Whiteyville, Ronald, and your tofu burgers on gluten-free cwah-sawnts.

The fellas in the audience start laughing and high-fiving each other as I make my way up to the stand. But there were some people on my side. Alfonso Ribeiro yelled...

> **Alfonso:** Keep a stiff upper lip there, Ron. You can do this.

Angela Cartwright and Eve Plumb yell down their support in sync, smiling and waving.

"We believe in you, Ron!"

A hush comes over the whole audience as everyone looks up. Angela and Eve slowly sit back down.

The crowd erupts in laughter again.

Don starts to bang his head on the desk. And Blair and Sam both smile at each other.

As I walk onto the stand, Judge Jackson makes a gun symbol with his hand, points it to me, then bends his thumb to represent shooting me. He winks and smiles that coy, mischievous smile that only Sam Jackson can smile.

Reginald VelJohnson comes up to me, and he holds up the copy of *The Autobiography of Malcolm X*.

> **RVJ:** Do you promise to tell the truth, the whole truth, and nothing but the double-truth, Ruth?
>
> **Me:** Yes. I mean. I do. I mean...

At this point, I break into my best hard-ass Black man impression.

> **Me:** Straight up, my nigga! Yeah boy!

Reginald looks at me like he just saw a hairless Siamese cat riding on a skateboard down Rodeo Drive.

> **Me:** I didn't really sell that, did I?

He leans in, puts his hand on my shoulder, and says...

> **RVJ:** Just be yourself, son. Just be you. No matter what happens, they can't take that from you.
>
> **Me:** Thank Reggie. I will.

I take a seat and Blair Underwood approaches the bench.

> **BU:** Please state your name for the court.

Me: Ron Dawson.

BU: And in what year were you born?

Me: 1968.

BU: That was quite a year in the history of Black people, wasn't it?

I nervously lean into the mic.

Me: Yes. Yes, it was. On April 4 of that year, Dr. Martin Luther King Jr. was assassinated. It was also during the Olympics that year when Tommie Smith and John Carlos raised their fists in protest and solidarity for the plight of all disenfranchised people.

BU: My, my. Impressive. One could also say another Black milestone that year was, it was the year *you* were born?

Blair gives me a wink and a smile. The sarcasm is thinly veiled.

BU: We've had an opportunity to hear a lot about your life. You are indeed a man caught between two worlds it would seem.

Me: I guess you could say that.

BU: I guess the thing I'm trying to determine is... which world do you want to be a part of?

Don Cheadle stands and exclaims...

Don: Objection. Badgering the witness.

BU: Sorry, Your Honor. I'll rescind. Mr. Dawson, in the summer of 1991, you began work as a real estate appraiser, am I correct?

Me: That's correct.

BU: And when you were in the office, was the radio ever played?

Me: Sure. Of course.

BU: What did you all listen to?

Me: Excuse me?

Don stands up again.

Don: Objection! Relevance?

Sam: Overruled.

BU: The question is pretty simple. What would you all listen to?

Me: Well. We listened to all kinds of things, I'm sure. It was a long time ago.

BU: Is it not true that you played Rush Limbaugh's show in your office?

Don: Objection! Relevance? Since when does listening to a conservative talk show host make one less Black?

BU: Your Honor, no one denies the legitimacy and even the values for a Black man in the country to uphold and adhere to ideals, which some may say are conservative. Conservative stances on family, faith, and even economics are ones that can be fairly argued are beneficial to the African American culture and advancement. But there is no denying a certain bent of the postmodern conservative movement that is intrinsically steeped in a historical connection to systemic and institutionalized racism and furtherance of belief, values, and philosophies, which have heretofore, forthwith, and beyond been a pain in the proverbial ass for the Black man. Rush Limbaugh and shows like his have contributed to the aforementioned said racial bereavement and ergo and et cetera represent a most untrustworthy and even incontrovertible impediment to our desired advancement as a people.

The crowd cheers, woots, and hollas in approval.

"Preach, preacha!"

"Amen!"

"Come on now!"

Don is not impressed.

> **Don:** What the fuck does that even mean?
>
> **Sam:** I'll allow it.
>
> **Don:** You've *got* to be kidding me!
>
> **Sam:** One more outburst like that, counselor, and I'll hold you in contempt and throw your Black ass in jail faster than a Black man jaywalking in Mississippi.

Don sits back down, visibly pissed.

> **BU:** Thank you, Your Honor.

Judge Jackson addresses me.

> **Sam:** Answer the damn question.
>
> **Me:** Well. Um. Yes, we did listen to Rush. But it was really my workmate Chris that played it.
>
> **BU:** And it never occurred to you to ask Chris to turn it off?
>
> **Me:** Well...I...actually no. Karen would, though. I think she would get annoyed.
>
> **BU:** Any reasonable person would. Was she a sista?
>
> **Me:** No. She was white. Is white. She is white, cuz, you know, she's still alive.
>
> **BU:** So let me get this straight. A WHITE woman named KAREN of all things was the one who asked for this Chris fellow to turn off Rush?
>
> **Me:** Um. Yes.

BU: How is it that in this entire office, it took a "Karen" to request this. There weren't any other Black people in this office?

Me: No, actually. I was the only Black person.

BU: That seemed to be a common theme with you.

Me: I guess.

BU: So as the only person of color in this office, it took a white girl, named Karen no less, to ask this Chris fellow to turn off *The Rush Limbaugh Show*?

The crowd mumbles and grumbles and shakes their heads.

Me: I guess.

BU: So are you telling this court that you never listened to Rush Limbaugh in your car?

Me: It's possible there were some occasions. But I don't think he was as bad back—

BU: And did you not also listen to the Dennis Prager and Larry Elder shows?

Me: Those sound vaguely familiar. But I listened to a lot of different shows. Howard Stern. Dr. Laura.

BU: Howard Stern *and* Dr. Laura. Yes. Yes. Very Black of you, indeed.

The audience laughs.

Me: I just meant, I listened to a lot of different shows.

BU: Did you listen to any predominantly Black shows, Mr. Dawson? I mean, besides the House Negro Comedy Hour with Mr. Elder?

Cue Don.

Don: Objection!

BU: No need. Withdrawn. So, Mr. Dawson, besides Mr. Elder's excellent political analyses, which other predominantly Black shows did you listen to?

Me: I can't say I recall.

BU: That's okay. I'll move on. Mr. Dawson. For the past thirty-two years, you've been of voting age, is that not right?

Me: Yes. I guess that would be right.

BU: And in all that time, there have been eight presidential elections, correct?

Me: Yes. I believe that is also correct.

BU: In how many of those elections did you vote?

Me: I don't think I can be expected to remember all those elections.

BU: Go ahead. Try. We have time.

I think back to all the times I recall voting in a presidential election.

Me: Well, I definitely remember voting for Ross Perot, I believe, in '96. But to be honest, I never was really big on politics. To be frank, I didn't ever really like or trust any politician. I was sort of apolitical.

BU: So essentially, you squandered the very rights so many of our people bled and died for?

Me: No. No. I just had a profound sense that politicians were inherently dishonest and corrupt, so I didn't vote. It's why I *did* vote for Perot.

BU: Well, I'm sure Sojourner Truth and Frederick Douglass will be very moved by your reasons once you meet them on the other side.

The crowd laughs. Blair unbuttons his expensive Italian double-breasted jacket, walks over to his table, then opens a folder. He then asks the question I dreaded yet knew he was leading up to.

BU: Mr. Dawson, for whom did you vote in the 2008 presidential election?

My heart races. I look around at all the faces looking at me. Waiting for my answer. My palms get sweaty, and I wipe them on my pants.

BU: Did you not hear my question?

Me: Oh. Sorry. Could you please repeat it?

Blair Underwood smiles, buttons his double-breasted coat again then walks over to the stand. He stands directly in front of me, looking me straight in the eyes.

BU: Who. Did. You. Vote. For. In. The. 2008. Presidential. Election?

I clear my throat and adjust my collar. I then mumble something unintelligible into the microphone.

BU: I'm sorry. Could you please repeat that?

Me: McCain.

The audience gets unsettled and starts yelling from their seats.

"Guilty!"

"Case closed, judge!"

Right then, Tag-Team's "Whoomp! (There It Is)" starts playing over the loudspeakers. But the people in the audience are cheering...

"Whoop dat ass! Whoop dat ass!"

Don is looking around, shaking his head. Blair Underwood walks back to his table, and the judge is out of his seat doing a jig too!

Don: Your Honor. Objection! Objection!

Judge Jackson stops dancing.

Sam: Oh. Sorry. Order in the court, everyone. Y'all settle down.

The crowd settles down.

Me: Can I please explain myself. It's not really that...

BU: So, Mr. Dawson. Let me see if this is right. You had an opportunity to vote for the very first African American to ever become President of these United States of America in its two-hundred-year history, and instead you voted for John McCain?

Me: It's not that simple.

BU: Actually, it is. You had a choice to join with your fellow bruthas and sistas in the most historic political achievement in our history as a people in this country and *you* chose not to participate. Actually, *worse*. You *did* choose to participate but *against* our first Black president.

Me: I wanted to vote for him! I really did! In fact, I was going to.

BU: And you didn't because?

Me: Well...I...some friends of mine said that he would not be good for the country.

BU: Oh really? And why was that?

Me: Well, because... you see, as a liberal Democrat, he would enact laws that could lead to things that, you know, weren't good for Christianity. Or something. I don't really recall the exact things they told me. I just—

BU: Were these friends of your white?

Me: What?

The judge intervenes.

Sam: Nigga, are you hard of hearing? You say "what" and "excuse me" a lot. You heard that shit. Answer the muthafuckin' question!

Me: Yes. Yes, they were white. But deep inside, I wanted to vote for Obama. I was conflicted. I just wasn't that educated on the issues. In fact, I remember being thrilled that he won. I bought like four or five newspapers as souvenirs to commemorate the occasion.

BU: Well, there's nothing like buying multiple copies of a white-owned newspaper to absolve you of your guilt for not voting for the first Black president.

The crowd laughs.

Me: No. That wasn't why. I was genuinely excited and secretly glad he won.

BU: Oh. You were *secretly* glad, huh? Couldn't let your white evangelical buddies know you were a closet Obama fan?

Me: I wouldn't put it like that.

BU: Mr. Dawson, who did you vote for in the 2012 election?

Me: What?

Judge Jackson springs out of his seat, raises his gavel, and points it at me.

Sam: Say "what" again! I dare you! I double dare you, muthafucka! Say wha—

Judge Jackson pauses mid-sentence and looks up at the audience. Their energy is palpable as they lean forward, waiting for the ubiquitous and egregiously over-used phrase that has become so intricately and iconically connected to Mr. Jackson.

He sits down then sternly addresses the audience.

Sam: Nuh-uh. Y'all can get off your fuckin' pins and needles. I ain't no muthafuckin' cliché vending machine. I ain't saying that shit again.

The audience in the courtroom sinks back into their seats. Deflated.

Sam: Answer the question, Mr. Dawson.

Me: Wh...what was it again?

Judge: Goddammit. That's it!

Judge Jackson springs up again and points the gavel at me.

Sam: Say "what" again! I dare you! I double dare you, muthafucker! Say what one more goddamn time and I'm going to hold you in contempt!

The audience jumps back up and begins cheering and woot-wooting, pumping their fists. Judge Jackson raises his arms toward the audience.

Sam: *Are you not entertained*?

More woot-wooting and cheering from the crowd. Judge Jackson sits back down, chuckles, and says under his breath...

Sam: Niggas.

He kicks his feet up onto the desk and tosses some popcorn into his mouth.

Sam: Repeat the question for this asshole, Mr. Underwood, and let's get on with this shit. And Mr. Dawson, I strongly advise avoiding the "W" word henceforth.

BU: Yessir, Your Honor.

Blair Underwood turns back to me.

BU: So. Mr. Dawson, again. For whom did you vote in the 2012 election?

I give a deep sigh.

Me: I didn't. I abstained.

The crowd really goes crazy.

BU: So instead of voting for Barack Obama this time, possibly making up for that first lame-ass decision, which you claim you regretted, you chose to not vote at all?

Me: I voted for the other stuff on the ballot that year. Just not, er, um, president. I knew in my heart I couldn't vote Republican again. But I was still conflicted about voting for a Democrat.

BU: And was this also due to the same "Christian" guilt at the thought of voting for a liberal Democrat.

Me: As crazy as it sounds, yes.

BU: Mr. Dawson, do you know that when asked about his Christian faith, in 2010, President Obama answered: "I came to my Christian faith later in life, and it was because the precepts of Jesus Christ spoke to me in terms of the kind of life that I would want to lead—being my brothers' and sisters' keeper, treating others as they would treat me. And I think also understanding that Jesus Christ dying for my sins spoke to the humility we all have to have as human beings, that we're sinful and we're flawed and we make mistakes, and that we achieve salvation through the grace of God. But what we can do, as flawed as we are, is still see God in other people and do our best to help them find their own grace. That's what I strive to do. That's what I pray to do every day. I think my public service is part of that effort to express my Christian faith."

Me: No. I didn't know that about him at the time.

BU: Apparently there were a lot of things you didn't know. Is ignorance an excuse you've used for all your shortcomings in life, Mr. Dawson?

Don: Objection!

BU: Withdrawn. I have nothing further.

Don sits back down. Blair Underwood walks confidently back to his seat. Judge Jackson addresses Don Cheadle.

Sam: Cross-examination, counselor?

Don: No questions, Your Honor.

I respond, shocked.

Me: Are you sure? I'm ready to answer anything you have. Ask me something.

Sam: That will be all, Mr. Dawson. You heard the man. No more questions. Go back to your seat.

I slowly get up and walk back to my seat. It feels like the longest walk in my life. For the first time in two decades, I feel like that young, conflicted, sad, scared, and depressed college kid stuck between two worlds.

My feeling of depression and despair is made worse as I go take my seat, and Don Cheadle just sits there, staring ahead. He won't look at me. Won't acknowledge me. He won't say it, but I know what he's thinking. He too is shocked, dismayed, and disappointed. He too is conflicted. That he must defend someone like me.

I sit and stare straight ahead also. The laughing and jeering fade into the distance as my life flashes before my eyes. Eyes that are now watering. As a single tear drops, I wipe it and look up at Sam. He looks me in the eye, his smile fades and he bangs his gavel.

Sam: We'll dismiss and reconvene tomorrow for closing arguments.

BU: I'm ready to go now, Your Honor. We can get this done lickety-split.

Blair smiles and winks at Judge Jackson. The judge gives him a stern glare.

Sam: I said, we'll reconvene tomorrow. You have a problem with that?

BU: Oh. No. Sorry, Your Honor. It's cool. Tomorrow is fine by me.

With that, Judge Jackson gets up and quickly walks out. In fact, the whole courtroom empties, leaving just me and Don Cheadle. Not looking at each other. Not saying a word. Then...

Don: Well, I gotta go prepare my closing arguments. See you tomorrow, man.

Without looking at me, Don gets up, closes his briefcase, and walks out of the room. He turns out the light, and I'm left alone. In the dark.

Chapter 37:

A Surprise Confession

Of all the imaginary, old-fashioned court houses in the world, I'm glad he walked into mine

I've seen some pretty crazy shit during this D&D campaign. And I'm sure it all sounds pretty unbelievable to you. Trust me. If you think it seems unbelievable to *you*, imagine what it's like for me. Samuel L. Jackson. Viola Davis. Snoop Dogg. Angela Bassett. The Voice of Morgan Freeman. All these encounters are ones I'd never expect to happen to me in a million years.

But none of it would compare to what happened next.

As I sat there in the dark, reminiscing about my life and the choices I made to get me to where I am today, I heard over my shoulder...

"Bravo Othello is on the move. Notify all stations that target is here, just where we were told. Area has been swept. Coast is clear."

I look over my shoulder, and there in the doorway to the courthouse is what looks like a Secret Service agent. If I didn't know any better (and if I wasn't told by my grandmomma over thirty years ago that it was a sin to do this), I'd swear to God it was Agent Coulson—you know, of Avengers fame. Of course, it's probably just any regular ol' white man in shades, a Black suit, and an earpiece. From this distance, who else would he look like?

The lights come on, and three more agents enter the courthouse, walking with a determined walk, right toward me. And within seconds, I see what the hullabaloo is about.

Not five feet behind them, dressed in the flyest, coolest, taupe suit you ever saw, was the one, the only, Barack Hussein Obama—the last "real" president of the United States of America (as of this writing).

You know when you watch a sitcom with a television audience, then a really big movie star walks into the scene as a guest star; then when he or she does, you get like twenty to thirty seconds of the audience cheering and applauding? (Think Brad Pitt guest-starring on *Friends*.) Well, that's kind of what this moment felt like. Except, there was no audience.

Once the president reaches my seat, he whispers to the other agents and motions them to leave. The head agent gestures to the other men, and they exit the building.

> **Obama:** Mind if I have a seat?
>
> **Me:** No. Of course not. Please. Sit down, Mr. President.

Of all the encounters I've had, this one by far is the most surprising (which is doubly weird since I'm the one writing this book).

> **Obama:** So I hear you had kind of a challenging day.
>
> **Me:** You heard I had a challenging day? Who told you that?
>
> **Obama:** I have friends in high places, one of whom paged me and let me know what was going on.
>
> **Me:** Wow. Really? I'm at a loss. I'm flattered. I think. But honestly, I'm not quite sure why you're here. Why would you care?
>
> **Obama:** Because I believe you represent a group of people who need to hear from me. I believe you are the solution to that one thing that is perhaps the most detrimental blow to the American people.

I look around the room to make sure he's talking to the right person.

> **Me:** Are you sure you're talking to the right brutha? I don't see how that's possible.

President Obama laughs that charming laugh. You know the one. The one we were so used to seeing during all those press correspondent dinners.

> **Obama:** Yes. I'm sure I have the right brutha.
>
> **Me:** And what is it exactly I represent?
>
> **Obama:** You, my friend, represent the abolition of apathy. You represent those men and women who have come to a grand inflection point in their lives and determined that no longer can they stand by the wayside and let the status quo go unchecked. And you're doing it at the possible cost of friendships, followers, and being laughed at.
>
> **Me:** You think I'm being laughed at?

The president sees the look of concern on my face, then tries to play it down.

> **Obama:** Well, you might not get full-blown guffaws, but there might be a few chuckles thrown your way. I wouldn't worry about it.
>
> **Me:** I don't know. You seem to be kind of playing it down. Should I be worried and put the kibosh on this whole book?
>
> **Obama:** Look, when you grow up with a name like mine and ears like these, man, whatever *you're* going through will pale in comparison to what I had to endure—and I became president. I would've never made it if I worried about what people thought about me.
>
> **Me:** I guess that makes sense.

Obama: But my point was, you're doing all of this even though it's hard. To put yourself out like this, in front of the world to see, warts and all, to share and fight for a cause you believe in. That represents the best in all of us.

Me: I'm assuming you're familiar with my voting record?

Obama: Oh yeah. I had a peek at it. It's admittedly not my favorite part of your story.

He laughs again as he says this.

Me: And you still want to talk to me?

Obama: Look. What is it I always tell the audiences that come to my campaign speeches? Don't get angry...

Me: Vote.

Obama: And that's what you did. And you did it in a way that was true to your heart at the time. I believe that is one of the greatest duties any American can have. Do you think I would really want you voting for me if the only reason you did it was because of my skin color? That would be no better than those who *didn't* vote for me just because of my skin color.

Me: But I think it's safe to assume there were a lot of bruthas and sistas who voted for you for no other reason than the color of your skin.

Obama: Is that so? And you know this how?

Me: I don't know. Seems natural, I guess. Who wouldn't think that?

Obama: Anyone with an ounce of sense wouldn't, that's who. Black folk aren't that dumb or gullible. You really think if Ben Carson ran against, oh, any halfway-decent white Democrat, that the majority of Black folk would vote for him?

He sits up then leans in the chair toward me.

Obama: Don't you see what you just did there? You made a gross generalization about Black people that you've been accusing conservatives and Trump supporters of doing throughout this entire book.

He has a point.

Obama: But regardless, I'll tell you another reason why I *do* think many of them voted for me. Because I represented hope. And change. And a profound movement in American politics that would forever change the course of their futures. Now, for whatever reason, that wasn't *your* story or your need at the time. I wouldn't expect you or anyone else to vote against their conscience. Nor would I want you to.

Me: I appreciate you telling me all that, Mr. President. But you don't have to say all of that just to make me feel better.

Obama: Man, do you think I came out all this way, giving up precious time on the golf links, just to make you feel better?

Another excellent point. And since I don't know how soon again, if ever, I'll get a chance to ask President Obama a personal question, I take advantage of the situation.

Me: Have you ever felt caught between two worlds? Ironically belonging to both, but not really fitting in any?

Obama: My name is Barack *Hussein* Obama, son of a Nigerian father and a white mother who grew up and went to high school on a Polynesian island. I was also a centrist Democrat who was too liberal for conservatives and often not liberal enough for my constituency. What do *you* think?

Me: Yeah. I guess by definition, you had to be.

Obama: You damn skippy.

I sometimes forget how cool and funny President Obama could be.

At that moment, "Agent Coulson" comes back in and whispers in his ear. (And for the record, it wasn't Agent Coulson. Just looked like him from afar. As I suspected. He was just another random white guy with chiseled facial features.)

> **Obama:** Well, Ronald. I must go. I'm glad we had this little chat.

I stand up as he does. He then reaches out to shake my hand.

> **Me:** Thank you, Mr. President. It's been a real honor.
>
> **Obama:** You're welcome, Ron. Just remember: In everything you do, be yourself. It's the one thing no one in this world can take from you.

I smile as he tells me this.

> **Me:** I will, Mr. President. I will.

And with that, he gives me a quick nod, then heads toward the door, Secret Service close behind. And right before he leaves, he stops, turns back to me, and says...

> **Obama:** One last thing. The next time you *do* vote your conscience, just make sure it is *your* conscience, not someone else's.

He then walks out the door and is gone.

Having President Obama visit me like that gave me renewed hope. He tends to have that effect on people. Even people who didn't vote for him when they had the chance. Whatever happens to me tomorrow, I'm now ready to face the music.

Chapter 38:

Closing Arguments

Can a Black man earn redemption from his people?

A hush comes over the courtroom when the judge asks Blair Underwood to make his closing argument. Blair stands up from behind his desk, buttons his Armani suit, then approaches the jury.

> **BU:** I want to first thank all of you fine people for taking time out of your very busy schedules to show up and represent. And let me start by saying that I understand and empathize that the decision you have before you today is a hard one. How can we as a people move forward and move on if in addition to fighting the institutionalized racism in our courts, businesses, and politics, we also continue to be forced to fight amongst ourselves? Black-on-Black crime feels like it's on the rise. A Black man is eight times more likely than a white man to die via homicide and more likely from another Black man. And despite the fact we had a Black president for eight years, given the events since 2016, we have seen that hate crimes based on race have also been on the rise.
>
> Bottom line: we need strong, intelligent, powerful bruthas to make a difference and bring about change. So the last thing we need to be doing is attacking or disparaging our fellow bruthas on the front lines.

> Nothing that happens here will prevent the defendant from going about his merry way and continuing to do his part in making that difference. In fact, it is my sincere desire that despite what happens here today, he will continue to do what he has been doing. In some cases, he seems halfway decent at it.

Blair turns in my direction and smiles at me. I'm a little confused about where he's going with this. I soon find out. He turns back toward the jury.

> **BU:** I would be remiss if I didn't point out that in every war, you have your generals, your captains, your sergeants, your corporals, and your Gomer Pyle privates. Each must play their role in the grand scheme of things. So you must ask yourself, who do you want to see as your captains and generals? Who deserves to hold the mantle and continue the legacy of the Martin Luther Kings and the Malcolm Xs? The James Baldwins and Langston Hugheses and Alex Haleys? Who will your little Black boys turn to and say, "That's who I want to be when I grow up!" and take up arms to fight the racist power structures that keep this nation going? Who can stand alongside the Colin Kaepernicks and the LeBron Jameses of today? Who do you want to put on that highest of pedestals, the top of the Google results page gallery of images when you search for "modern-day African American voices of civil rights and justice"?

Don rolls his eyes and puts his head in his hands. Blair unbuttons his Armani suit, then leans on the banister of the jury box.

> **BU:** I submit to you fine people of the jury that only the finest and strongest paragons of the African American experience should be at the top of those search results. Proud Black men and women who are fully, wholly, and unequivocally steeped in the culture and experiences that make our people as special as they are. Only men and women like this can truly connect with and make the strongest cases for our advancement. Warriors who have a greater sense of loyalty to the Black *people* rather than a blonde *Jesus*.

There is a lot of head-nodding going on in the jury.

BU: Speaking of Jesus, Mr. Dawson has spoken of his faith. And it is a commendable quality. We all know that for years the church has been a foundation and backbone of the African American community. Our greatest singers have come out of church choirs, and some of our greatest leaders have come out from behind church pulpits.

There's a term in the evangelical community known as the "baby Christian." It's a sort of an affectionate term used to describe someone newly indoctrinated—er, I mean, who has recently accepted Jesus as their savior. They profess to follow the faith, but they still kinda act like heathens, if you catch what I'm sayin'.

The jury laughs. Apparently, they are catching what he's saying.

BU: In many ways, Mr. Dawson is to Black folk what a baby Christian is to the church. You wouldn't have a baby Christian pastor a church, lead a mission, or write for a major Christian magazine. But you might have them usher. You know, pass the plate down the aisle and greet folks at the door. Yeah. Yeah. That's a perfect analogy. Door-greeter. At this stage of Mr. Dawson's coming of age into his "Blackness," he should be a "door-greeter." Or the deacon at the front of the sanctuary with the white glove who holds his hands up to welcome people to the pulpit during the altar call.

With time and a few seasons of *Atlanta* or *Queen Sugar* under his belt, I could see a fine young, or rather, older, brutha like him advancing up to the equivalent of a small group leader. But for now, make no mistake: this ex-Rush-Limbaugh-listening, only recently converted Democrat who's never played bones, never had chicken and waffles, and probably couldn't even tell you what team LeBron James plays for right now.

I immediately jump out of my seat and yell...

> **Me:** Not true! He plays for the Lakers! The Lakers! He plays for
> the Lakers![17]

The judge bangs his gavel.

> **Sam:** Order in the court! Nigga, are you outta your goddamn mind?!
> You best keep your client in check, counselor!
>
> **Don:** Yes, Your Honor. Sorry.

Don turns to me, annoyed, and yanks me back down to my seat.

> **Don:** Man. Sit down!
>
> **Me:** But that's not true. I know who he plays for.
>
> **Don:** That's wonderful. I'm proud of you. Now shut the fuck up!

Blair smiles and continues.

> **BU:** As I was saying—and I hate to put it this way—but sometimes you
> just have to call a spade a spade: he is just not "Black" enough right
> now to be the person he's trying to be. As they used to say back in
> the day, "this brutha is straight-up perpetratin' a fraud." Don't be the
> sucka that gets duped.

And with that, Blair Underwood re-buttons his Armani suit, turns
around, and walks back to his seat. On the way back, he and Judge
Jackson give each other an air fist bump.

Up next is Don Cheadle. I hope he can pull a rabbit out of his ass because
I gotta say, Blair Underwood's closing argument was killer.

Don gets up, opens his briefcase, and takes out a copy of the Bible. He
then opens it, finds a verse, and walks over to the jury.

---

17 As of this writing, LeBron *does* play for the Lakers. Just, you know, making sure *you* know that *I* really do
know. Okay. That is all.

> **Don:** Matthew, chapter 18, verse 3: "And truly I say unto you, unless you change and become like little children, you will never enter the kingdom of heaven."

Don closes the Bible and looks up and down the jury box. Then he repeats the verse. Slowly.

> **Don:** Unless you change and become like little children, you will never enter the kingdom of heaven.
>
> "It is easier to build strong children, than to prepare broken men," Frederick Douglass. "There can be no keener revelation of a society's soul than the way it treats its children," Nelson Mandela. "Children are a wonderful gift. They have an extraordinary capacity to see into the heart of things and to expose sham and humbug for what they are," Bishop Desmond Tutu. "If we are to teach real peace in this world, and if we are to carry on a real war against war, we shall have to begin with the children," Mahatma Gandhi.

Don turns and points to Blair.

> **Don:** My esteemed colleague compared my client to a child. A young sapling of a Black man, only now beginning to learn how to walk and talk. Well, I say he is right on the money. All throughout history, from the time Jesus Christ walked this earth and trained his disciples, the philosophers, storytellers, and leaders of all kinds have seen and understood the extreme value and worth of children and seeing the world through a child's eyes.
>
> A study commissioned by NASA in 1968 showed that 98 percent of five-year-olds were creative geniuses.[18] They followed those kids and checked up on them every five years. Five years later, among that same group of kids, that number dropped to 30 percent. At age fifteen, only 12 percent were creative geniuses. By the time

---

18 *Think Like a 5-Year-Old: Reclaim Your Wonder and Create Great Things*, Len Wilson, United Methodist Publishing House.

they were adults, only 2 percent were creative geniuses. Children have a gift.

My client has been compared to a child. A man who is just a "baby" in his Blackness. Now, if you set aside the absolute ridiculousness of that statement, even if it were true, it's actually a *good* thing.

We are seeing political movements and shifts in the socioeconomic landscape the likes of which we never have before. Perhaps we need allies who can look at and approach our challenges through the eyes of a child. With a freshness, a sense of creativity, and hope we've never had before. Someone who has been on both sides of the proverbial aisle. Someone who understands how the other side thinks and feels. Looking at these issues facing Black America through the eyes of a "child" may be just what we need in this country.

Lastly, I would like to quote Al Green himself. From the very song that played when Your Honor graced us in this court.

> *Oh, baby*
> *Let's stay together*
> *Lovin' you whether times are good or bad, happy, or sad*
> *Oh, oh, oh, oh, yeah*
> *Whether times are good or bad, happy or sad*

Now. Just replace the word "baby" with "Black folk." We need to stay together. We need to support one another, accept our differences, and relish in the truth we so frequently remind white folk: that we are not one giant, monolithic group of people. There are as many different personalities and politics among us as there are shades of skin color.

But we all share a common origin in this country. We all deal with the same shit. And the sooner we can learn to work together, taking advantage of our differences rather than demonizing them, then the sooner we will make the next great leap in our advancement.

> We've had our first Black president. England had its first Black duke.
> We've recently seen the first predominantly Black movie gross over
> $2 billion. We got a Black Spider-Man and even Black Norse gods. A
> Black teen girl has been Iron Man and the next Captain America will
> be Black. The live-action *Little Mermaid* is gonna be Black. We may
> even get a Black 007. We have Black heroes showing up in shit we
> never thought.

> All these changes in pop culture will have an indelible effect on the
> Black youth of today. Just like TV and movies of the recent past have
> had on my client. Perhaps even more so than any history class will
> ever do. Now, more than ever, we need Black nerds like Mr. Dawson
> to tell these stories and paint the real picture of our people for the
> world to see.

The people in the jury seem to be engaged and even nod in approval.

> **Don:** I'll grant you this. My client *is* definitely one of the "whitest"
> bruthas I know...

With that, Don Cheadle turns around from the jury and looks right at me.

> **Don:** But I'm proud to look at him and call him my *brother*,
> nonetheless.

He turns back to the jury.

> **Don:** And if you got to know him, I know you would too. Nothing
> further, Your Honor.

Don returns to his seat, clasps his fingers and hands together on the
table in front of him, and looks straight ahead.

I sit back in my seat and smile. Ever so slowly, Don raises his fist above
the table to offer me a pound. As our fists bump, Don smiles too.

The verdict is now in the hands of the jury.

Chapter 39:

Revelations

M. Night Shyamalan ain't got sh*t on me!

"Well, that was totally unexpected."

—Line from Baz Luhrmann's *Strictly Ballroom*
(one of my favorite movies)

One by one, the results poured in, and I felt that same knot in the pit of my stomach I felt two years prior when state after state ran red, like so much blood covering this fair nation.

It was the evening of November 6, 2018—arguably the most important midterm election in this country's history (yes, I know they say that every election, but after two years under Trump, by God, did it not feel more real than ever!)

These midterms would be a veritable referendum on the Trump presidency. If there really is a God in heaven, there would be a full-sail rejection of Trump by the Democrats winning the House *and* the Senate. As it turned out, we only won the House.

And that is indeed a big deal. But regardless, on this evening, I'm pissed. I'm pissed because there were three races I wanted to see come out different than they did. Andrew Gillum, the African American running for Florida's governor. Stacey Abrams in Georgia, who could've become the first female African American governor in the country. And Beto O'Rourke for the Texas Senate race against that spineless Ted Cruz. At the time, Beto reminded me of a white Barack Obama. (I'm sure I'm not the first one to think that.) After the Democratic primary debates in the summer of 2019, not so much.

But after tonight, I'm charged. I'm fired up. I'm ready to rain hell and brimstone the likes of which Facebook has never seen. The only thing holding me back from going full-blown season eight Daenerys Targaryen and blowing up social media is a promise I made to my wife to mellow up on the Facebook posts.

I get out my computer and begin to type. I write the following post as a response to the ridiculous situation in Georgia during the gubernatorial race when the Republican candidate, Brian Kemp, was also, as Secretary of State, the guy in charge of managing the very same election in which he was running! This is what I wrote:

"Can someone explain to me how a dude running for governor gets to keep his duties as also the person in charge of overseeing elections? Isn't that kinda like putting the fox in charge of counting the chickens in the chicken coop? WTH! The race in GA is so damn close and given all the crap that Kemp pulled, IMHO, anything but a full-blown, unequivocal victory should be investigated."

And guess who shows up, but my good friend, Mr. Dufus Asshole, proud Confederate Southerner and Atlanta resident. He replies:

"Um... it's the law."

All right. Looks like it's time to lay down another word-based ass-whoopin'. I reply.

"Hey, It's our friendly neighborhood MLK Expert and all around favorite non-racist white dude. I wondered if your bright, sunshiny, Confederate-lovin' face would show up. I'm hopin' as a resident of the good state of Jawja you could enlighten the good folk heeya on how it works down in them pawts. We Yankees aren't too bright about how you good ol' boys do it down south of the good ol' Mason-Dixon. Wanna throw some knowledge on us. We in dire need."

Ron, son, what are you about to do?

Some kind of metaphysical alarm must have gone off because right as I start to let into Mr. Dufus, who shows up, but the Voice of Morgan Freeman.

Me: Morgan? Is that you? It's been a while.

VOMF: Yes, it has. Now, tell me, what are you doing?

Me: Well, I'm about to go to town on all the stupid-ass right-wing, Republican assho—er, I mean people on Facebook.

VOMF: And what exactly is that going to achieve?

Me: It's catharsis, Morgan! Okay. I know very well that these posts do nothing and help no one but me. Who gives a shit? I need to blow off steam. Geeze! Give me a freaking break. I'm getting tired of all your Morgalizing.

VOMF: Morgalizing, huh? That's cute. All right. Enough is enough. I didn't want to do this, not now anyway. But it would appear the time is nigh. Wait right there, son.

A smoky haze fills my room. I hear angels singing in the distance. A color cascade of light flashes around the clouds. And from deep within the smoke and lights, a dark figure emerges. At long last I don't just hear him—I can see him. The one. The only...

Huh? I hate to say it, but my eyes bug out and the hairs on my head stand on end when I see who emerges from the smoke.

A white dude.

Me: Who the hell are you? Where's Morgan Freeman?

Charlie: Allow me to introduce myself. My name is Charlie Hopkinson.

Charlie stands at about five feet, eight inches, has short brown hair, and is *British*, of all things.

> **Me:** Charlie who? What the hell is going on here?
>
> **Charlie:** Well, you see... you know what, it'll be better if I just show you.

The white dude clears his throat then begins to talk. And he sounds *exactly* like Morgan Fucking Freeman.[19]

He quotes a line from *Shawshank Redemption*.

> **Charlie:** For the second time in my life, I am guilty of committing a crime. Parole violation. Of course, I doubt they'll toss up any roadblocks for that. Not for an old crook like me...

I am flabbergasted. I have to take a seat.

> **Me:** Wait one fucking minute. Do you mean to tell me, this whole fucking time when I thought I was hearing Morgan Freeman, it was *you*!?

In his Morgan Freeman voice, he answers.

> **Charlie:** Guilty as charged.
>
> **Me:** This is a joke, right? Oh, I get it. This is a call back to when I was a kid and watched *Candid Camera*. Is Allen Funt going to come out of there and say, "Smile, you're on candid camera"? Or is Ashton Kutcher gonna come out and punk me?
>
> **Charlie:** I'm familiar with Ashton, but who's Allen Funt?
>
> **Me:** Would you stop it with the Morgan Freeman voice already!

---

19 In case you're wondering, Charlie is the real deal. Watch a video of him reading a children's book in his Morgan Freeman voice. Then close your eyes and just listen. It's frakking wild! http://bit.ly/lion-and-fox.

Charlie clears his throat and goes back to his regular voice. His regular, *British* voice.

> **Charlie:** Oh, sorry. Hard to break the habit. But I assure you. This is no prank. I am the voice you've been hearing.
>
> **Me:** This whole time I've been getting advice on how to be a Black man in America, and it has been coming from the voice of some white dude from London?!
>
> **Charlie:** Well, technically, I'm from Leeds.
>
> **Me:** Muthafucker! Shut the fuck up! Who the hell cares? Do you know how bad the optics are on this? I just got out of my trial, now this?! I'm going to lose all kinds of cred! This is really fucking bad, man. This ain't right! You never told me you weren't Morgan Freeman.
>
> **Charlie:** I never told you I *was*, either.
>
> **Me:** Yes, you did!
>
> **Charlie:** No, actually, I didn't, mate.

His British accent continues to throw me for a loop.

> **Me:** What about that whole conversation we had about your Mike Wallace interview?
>
> **Charlie:** I've never been interviewed by Mike Wallace.
>
> **Me:** Not you! Morgan's Mike Wallace interview. You were pretending to be Morgan Freeman?
>
> **Charlie:** I never once claimed to be interviewed by Mike Wallace, nor did I ever give you a first-person perspective answer. Go back and read that chapter.
>
> **Me:** What is this, some kind of *Sixth Sense*, M. Night Shyamalan-level shit where my mind will be blown when I go back and review all my interactions with you in light of this startling revelation?

Charlie: I wouldn't know anything about that. I just know that I never said I was Morgan Freeman. I just never denied it. You were addressing the Voice of Morgan Freeman; it just wasn't Morgan Freeman speaking it. And for the record, not once did I ever give you advice on how to be a Black man in America. Go back. Look at all the places I showed up. All I did was ask you thought-provoking questions. Questions you already knew in your gut were worth asking.

Me: I'm so confused.

Charlie: Look. I was assigned to this case to help make a point.

Me: Oh, and what exactly is that? How the white man continues to trick and deceive the Black man?

Charlie: No. Not at all. All this time you've been listening to me, or engaging with Sam, all hoping to gain guidance on how to be Black. What you needed to do was learn how to be *you*. Didn't you learn anything from the confessions? Your time with Angela Bassett? From the trial? No one can tell you how to be Black. You *are* Black. America won't let you forget it. Nowhere you go will the fact be lost on people.

Me: I don't need a white man from England telling me how to be Black.

Charlie comes over and sits by me.

Charlie: I haven't got a clue what it means to be Black in America. I couldn't even tell you how to be Black in England. I think the reason I was chosen for this job, besides being able to do a pretty dead-on impression of one of the most iconic voices in cinematic history, was to show you that you shouldn't be listening to *any* of us. Not Sam. Not Morgan, if the real Morgan were here, not Snoop, or Don Cheadle, or Angela, or any of the other luminaries you've dreamed about. And least of all me. The point is to just be you. And right now, if being you is an angry man who just happens to be Black, then so be it. I'm sorry you had to find out the truth this way. My supervisor and I argued for days about whether I should reveal myself to you. If I had my druthers, I would have let you go on believing. We all need something to believe in.

Me: Oh yeah? What did he say?

Charlie: He said shut the fuck up and do your job. In the end, I think he was right.

Charlie gets up and starts to leave. He then turns to me and switches back to his Morgan Freeman voice.

Charlie: Ron, some birds aren't meant to be caged. Their feathers are just too bright. And now you know why the caged bird sings. Go and sing, son.

I give him an incredulous look.

Me: Man, that was some corny-ass shit.

Charlie: Welp. You would know, mate.

He chuckles, and with a wink and a smile, perhaps the coolest white man on the planet disappears.

I sit for a moment. Stunned and in silence. I ponder what Morgan, er, I mean, Charlie, shared with me. I wrestle with the idea of a white man from Leeds being the arbiter of my internal conflict and the deliverer of the final bit of wisdom and guidance in this personal play of mine. Why couldn't it have been the *real* Morgan Freeman?

And then, that's when it hits me. None of this has been real. There would never have been a *real* Morgan Freeman. Just like there never was a real Sam Jackson. Or a real Don Cheadle. And that was not the real Charlie Hopkinson. Like I've done for so many years in my life with regards to this subject, I've substituted my voice with the "voices" of others who I think have the market cornered on what it means to talk, walk, or act "Black."

I was worried about the optics of Charlie being the voice of Morgan Freeman that I'd been hearing throughout this book. How would that look? Would I sabotage all I had worked for to gain the respect of the Black folk reading my story if in the end, I made a white dude the quote-unquote, hero?

But in truth, a white man is *not* the hero in this story. And, *the* White Man is not the villain either. Neither are all the bruthas that clowned me when I opened my mouth; or the sistas that gave me the side-eye as they saw me walk down the street, holding hands with my white wife.

This is not like the old *Dungeons & Dragons* campaigns I used to play, where paladins, wizards, and clerics battled orcs, goblins, and the dreaded Drow. There are no real heroes or villains in this story (well, except for Trump. That asshole is most definitely a villain).

No, when it comes to this journey and what it means to be Black in America, I've had the revelation that we all, each one of us, strive to find our place in the world. We all, at some point, feel caught in the in-between. Neither here nor there. Fighting to be heard. To be seen. To be recognized, accepted, and loved for who we are. Each of us is a product of forces over which we had no control. And from those beginnings, from that soil, we each grew and matured into the people we are today. And in that way, we are all alike.

The end?

Chapter 40:

The Verdict

A few more words of wisdom before the "credits" roll

One of the most exciting yet equally exhausting stages of promoting a book is the inevitable book tour. Some tour spots are more exciting than others. Perhaps the most fun and exciting for me was being on the popular syndicated morning radio show *The Breakfast Club* with DJ Envy, Angela Yee, and Charlamagne Tha God.

When I met with them in their New York studio, I was as nervous AF. There is no more terrifying way for a Black man accused of acting "white" most of his life than to be interviewed on one of the hottest urban hip-hop shows in the world! But it was worth it! This is an excerpt from my interview with them.

> **Envy:** Good morning, y'all. Welcome back to The Breakfast Club with me, DJ Envy, Angela Yee, and of course, the one and only Charlamagne Tha God. And today we have something different. We got an author in da house.
>
> **Angela:** Here, here.
>
> **Me:** Thanks, Envy. It's cool to be here. I can tell you this, when I started down the journey of writing this book, this was the last place I expected to be. So I'm really honored to be here.

Envy: Well, we appreciate you coming out. I gotta tell you—I thought this book was funny as hell. But at the same time, you address some serious themes.

Angela: Yeah. I felt the same way. And I especially like the fact that it wasn't just like an all-out attack on white folk. It seems like you have some serious messages in here for people of color, too.

Envy: Well, really, any race could probably hold a mirror up to their face and see themselves in this book.

Charlemagne starts singing "Man in the Mirror" by Michael Jackson, then joins the conversation.

Charlamagne Tha God (CTG): That's all good, but you should have had a character for me in this. I could have easily been one of the confessionals.

Angela: (laughs) Charlemagne, everything don't always have to be about you.

CTG: I'm not saying it does. But how you gonna have "white privilege" as a theme addressed throughout the book and not have the counter theme of "Black privilege"? I literally wrote the book on the topic.

Envy: Yeah, man! How come we didn't get to be in the book?

I smile.

Me: Who said you weren't?

CTG: I did love that court part though. I cracked up when Sam came out as the judge.

Angela: Yes! Oh my god. That was so funny. What a twist. I totally didn't expect that. I like the choice of lawyers. I could totally picture it.

CTG: Yeah, but you know who I woulda had instead of Blair Underwood? You shoulda had Don Cheadle be the prosecutor and had that other Black lawyer on TV be *your* attorney.

Envy: Oh, yeah. Idris Elba from *The Wire*. I totally forgot about him. That would've been dope. *He* shoulda been the prosecuting attorney, though. I liked Don as the defense attorney.

Angela: Oooooh yeah! Idris is so fine! And he's really blowing up right now.

CTG: Nah, not Idris. Besides, he wasn't a lawyer on the show I'm thinking of. I'm talking about the other Black lawyer. You know, on that show with the good lookin' white cat who sleeps around a lot.

Envy: You're gonna have to be more specific, dude. Who you talkin' about? There aren't that many more Black lawyers on TV. Isn't that all of them?

Angela: Sure there is. There's Marcus on *Raising the Bar*.

CTG: Oh yeah. Wasn't he the dude that played Charles Gunn on *Buffy the Vampire Slayer*?

Angela: He was on *Angel*, not *Buffy*. He was great in that show.

CTG: Whatever. But I wasn't talkin' about him. I'm talking about that big, Black, bald dude on that legal show made by that white cat that made all those other legal shows.

Angela: John Grisham?

Envy: Wait. John Grisham ain't no big Black dude.

Angela: No. I was talking about the guy who makes all those legal TV shows. Wasn't that John Grisham?

Envy: John Grisham is the white dude who writes all those legal novels, you know, like *The Firm* and *A Time to Kill*.

Angela: Oh. Was it Michael Crichton then? Oh no. He did *ER*, right?

Envy: Isn't he dead?

Me: The producer Charlemagne is talking about is David E. Kelley. He created *LA Law*, *Picket Fences*, *Ally McBeal*, *The Practice*...

CTG: That's it! *The Practice*. That's the show. With, um what's his face... Dylan McDermott.

Angela: Ooooh. He's fine too. For a white boy and all.

Envy: Oh. Snap. *He* should've been your attorney. That would have turned the whole theme upside down. Have a white lawyer defend you for being on trial for being too white. That would've been bold! Is it too late to change the book? We need a reprint!

Me: I was already nervous enough having a white English dude play the Voice of Morgan Freeman. It would've been pushin' it to have a white attorney too.

CTG: No. You should have had the Black dude from *The Practice*. Eugene! That's his name!

Me: Oh. Yeah. Played by Steve Harris. Yeah. He was good.

Envy: I don't know. If it took us this long to figure out who you were talking about, I'm not so sure. You want someone that people can instantly recognize or picture.

CTG: I know, but he was always like the tough attorney defending the worst criminals. Then he'd do that "Plan B" and <bleep> 'em all up.

Me: So you're saying I could have had him do a "Plan B" on me... Plan B for "Black"?

CTG: Exactly! That's what I'm talkin' about.

Angela: You know what I thought was cool, I really enjoyed the whole meta element of it. How the characters would sort of recognize they were in the book, but at the same time remain autonomous in the story.

CTG: Like I said. I should've been in it. I would've been perfect.

I laugh.

Me: Like *I* said. Who says you weren't?

Envy: While we're on the topic of the trial. Whatever happened to the verdict?

Angela: Yeah. You end on a cliffhanger like you did in the other chapters. I thought for sure you would come back, and we'd find out what they decided.

Envy: Yeah. What's up with that? What's the verdict, Ron?

Angela: What's the verdict, Ron?

CTG: Yeah, Ron. What's the verdict?

At that moment, Envy, Angela, and Charlamagne Tha God freeze as the lights in the studio go dim. They slowly move backward, being absorbed into the darkness. Leaving only me sitting under a spotlight.

So I'm guessing at this point you want to know the answer to that question, too. What was the verdict?

Come on now. Haven't you been paying attention? You didn't really think an indie-film-loving, obscure-pop-culture-reference-making, thematic-element-writing, cinema-phile like myself would serve you up an easy answer and give you the verdict like some alley-oop on a basketball court, did you?

All I know is that this has been one crazy, fantastical journey writing this book, engaging with my inner demons (or angels), and taking a closer look at what has brought me to the place I am today.

The best sci-fi and fantasy stories are the ones that not only ignite the imagination but also offer some allegorical (or metaphorical) commentary on the human condition. Whether it was Tolkien's referendum of the industrial revolution in his depiction of Saruman's rise to power,[20] or C.S. Lewis's "Trojan Horse" strategy to get the Christian message into the homes of millions of skeptics and nonbelievers in the form of a lion, a witch, and a wardrobe. Fantasies that transcend their genre standards are powerful because, like my journey, they allow us to see ourselves—as well as the people and the world around us—in a way we might not otherwise have considered. We're captivated reading about the trials and tribulations of our heroes, never realizing, until the end, that the "hero" was us all along.

They allow us to take a step toward "the other" and hear what they have to say when we might otherwise want to just walk away, or worse, attack. Then, much like the prophet Nathan using the parable of the rich man stealing the poor man's lamb, we, like King David, open our eyes to our own "sins."

In my little *Dungeons & Dragons*-like adventure, I've learned some valuable lessons about myself. Not the least of which is that everything is not always so black and white (pun fully intended). I've learned to slow down and listen; that I know half as much as I think I do and have forgotten twice as much as I wish I hadn't.

And most importantly, I've learned people on social media are stupid (present company included).[21]

I guess what I'm saying is that I accept that I had to spend over a year of my life going through this cathartic exercise for whatever it was I did "wrong" to the Black community. But you're crazy if you think I'm going to definitively tell you whether I think I'm "Black" enough. The truth is, whether you're Republican or Democrat, liberal or conservative, Black, white, brown, red, or yellow—you're going to see me as you want to see me. But in the simplest terms, in the most convenient definitions.

But what I've come to learn in my now fifty years of life is that *each* one of us is...

---

20 For the record, I do know that Tolkien did not consider *Lord of the Rings* allegorical.

21 I wrote this part of the book the week of the *Game of Thrones* series finale. Don't even get me started on the level of sheer insanity I read online trying to defend Daenerys's heel turn. But I digress.

Me: A "Ronald"

Sam: A Sam Jackson

VOMF: A Voice of Morgan Freeman

Charlie: A Charlie Hopkinson

DA: And a Dufus Asshole.

Happy?

Yours truly,

"Ronald"

TOMMIE SMITH-LIKE FIST RAISED.

CUT TO BLACK. CUE MUSIC.

SMASH CUT TO:
END CREDITS

Epilogue:

A Brand-New Day

The "post-credits" scene

*"The very time I thought I was lost, my dungeon shook,
and my chains fell off."*

—James Baldwin, *The Fire Next Time*

It was a harrowing week of waiting. And waiting. And. Waiting. The 2020 US presidential election was by far one of the most contentious in American history. (I'm sure history buffs out there who have a more comprehensive knowledge of American history are no doubt rolling their eyes right now. But cut this political neophyte some slack. No matter how you look at it, that election season was bat-shit insane.)

A pandemic threatened to affect voter turnout. The president started planting seeds of voter fraud and misconduct months before November. Volunteer phone and text bankers were coming out in droves to make sure people voted. For so many of us, it felt like a life-or-death election.

Then November 3 hit, and, as predicted, we did not know the results that night. Or the next day. Or the next. The memes that week were hilarious. As the counting in states like Nevada moved at a glacial pace, we saw all sorts of memes illustrate America's frustration with why it took so damn long! (My favorite was the Brian McKnight song "Back at One" with the caption: "Nevada counting ballots." The photo of Lauryn Hill with the caption "If Nevada was a person" was trending on Black Twitter. That was pretty good, too.)

The electoral vote count seemed to be stuck at 253 for Joe Biden and 213 for Trump (270 is needed to win). For three frakking days! But then, toward the end of the week, as millions of mail-in ballots poured in, the key states we were waiting for—like Arizona, Nevada, Georgia, and Pennsylvania—turned a corner. The numbers tilted toward Biden.

Then, on the morning of November 7, 2020, the major networks called it. Pennsylvania—with its twenty electoral votes—was called for Biden, putting him at 273, and making him the 46th President-elect of the United States! (Naturally, my favorite mail-in ballot meme was the ending fight scene from *Avengers: Endgame*, when a low-morale Captain America was greeted with thousands of warriors magically transported to join the fight. The caption read: "Mail-in ballots be like...")

But long before these cinematic memes flooded social media, I was already thinking about how I would contribute to the online conversation. About three or four years prior, I saved a YouTube clip of the "A Brand New Day" music and dance scene from 1978's *The Wiz*. It's the scene where Diana Ross's Dorothy and everyone else sings and dances in existential jubilation after the death of Evillene (the Wicked Witch of the West). I saved the clip with the hopes that come next election, I could share it on my Facebook wall.

That day was *finally* here, and no set of lyrics seemed more apropos:

> *Everybody look around*
> *'Cause there's a reason to rejoice you see*
> *Everybody come out*
> *And let's commence to singing joyfully*
> *Everybody look up*
> *And feel the hope that we've been waiting for*
> *Everybody's glad*
> *Because our silent fear and dread is gone*
> *Freedom, you see, has got our hearts singing so joyfully*
> *Just look about*

You owe it to yourself to check it out
Can't you feel a brand new day?

I shared the clip, and as the music played, my heart was so overjoyed, I couldn't help but get up and dance and sing along. And just as I started to do my best Michael Jackson "Scarecrow" spin, I heard a knock on my door. I ran over to answer it.

There, in the doorway, doing a slow golf clap, was my old friend Sam Jackson.

> **Me:** Well. I'll be damned. My nigga. I didn't ever expect to see *your* face again.
>
> **Sam:** Apparently. At least you're playing *The Wiz*. Knowing you, I'd half expect you to be singing "This Is Me" from *The Greatest Showman* or some shit.

If this were an episode of *The Office*, I would be giving a mischievous smirk to the camera right now, neither confirming nor denying with that glance that Sam's comment may or may not have been true in some version of this epilogue written before the aforementioned presidential election. But I digress.

> **Me:** Shiiiiit. It's *The Wiz* all the way, my nigga.

Sam gave me that incredulous look like he knows I'm full of shit; and that I still can't pull off saying "my nigga" without sounding ridiculous.

> **Sam:** Uh huh. May I?
>
> **Me:** Sure. Come on in.

Sam walks in.

> **Me:** What can I do you for?
>
> **Sam:** Well, hearing you sing and dance to that terrific number made me think about something.

Me: I wasn't dancing to it. I was just singing.

Sam: Really?

Me: Nevermind. What did it make you think of?

Sam: Well, I hate to rain on your little parade, but I sure as hell hope you don't think life is all roses and daisies just because that orange muthafucka finally gonna be out of the White House. This shit is just getting started. Especially when you look at the record for Black folk that Biden and Harris have.

Me: Wow. You really are a Debbie downer, aren't you? Jesus, Sam. Can't I just enjoy this moment? I don't for one second believe that they're gonna be a magic cure. Besides, their records have both good and bad in them as they relate to policies that affect the Black community. When it comes to issues like this, it's not always so black and white, no pun intended.

Sam: How often are you going to keep going to that "no pun intended" joke?

Me: Until it's not funny anymore.

Sam: Nigga, it wasn't *ever* funny.

Me: Anyway, why you always gotta be messin' up a brutha's enjoyment of shit? After four years of Trump, I deserve this. I just wanna spend a day and let the joy wash over me without making everything so complicated.

Sam: Oh, I'm sorry. Did I interrupt your rose-colored, Hollywood-sedated, brainwashed-induced version of reality? Singing and dancing up in here like it's the end of a fucking movie and shit. You do realize there are still like seventy million muthafuckas out there that voted for that asshole? They didn't just all melt away like Evillene. And a lot of them militia-minded muthafuckas gonna be mad as all holy hell. Pandora's box has been opened, my brutha. No election is gonna put that genie back in the bottle. I bet you in a few months those muthafuckas storm the Capitol or some shit.

Me: First off, I don't think it will ever get *that* bad. And people think *I* have an active imagination. Secondly, you *do* realize that's a mixed metaphor, right?

Sam: Nigga! Do I look like I give a fuck?!

I started cracking up.

Me: I'm *kidding!* Geez. Calm the fuck down.

Sam: Ha, ha! Very funny. But a lot of people are runnin' around here acting like Trump was the problem. Shit. Trump was more like the colonoscopy America needed to reveal the cancer that's been living up there all along. He was a pain in the ass, but at least now you know!

Me: Look, I hear what you're saying. I really do. And I'm down and ready to tackle the next season of this real-life *Game of Thrones* called American politics. But there's a time for everything under the sun. A time to get angry and riled up, and a time to celebrate and dance. And today is time to dance. There is plenty of time to worry about rooting out the cancer. But I need this day, Sam. This nation needs this day. And no cinematic cliché figment of my imagination is gonna change that.

Sam walks over to the chair and takes a seat. He pulls a cig out of his pocket and holds it between his fingers.

Sam: Look, Ronald, I know my methods were a bit, shall we say, unorthodox.

Me: No shit.

Sam: But you gotta admit, there are things I shared with you that made you look at life in a different light.

Reluctantly, I started to nod in the affirmative.

> **Me:** Yes, some of your proselytizing had a generous bit of profundity that did indeed give me pause.
>
> **Sam:** Well, I see your love for alliteration hasn't waned.

He gets up from the chair, walks over to me, then places his hand on my shoulder.

> **Sam:** Hey, man. By the way. Sorry to hear what happened between you and the missus.
>
> **Me:** Oh. Yeah. That. Well, um, yeah. You know. Over 50 percent of marriages end so, you know, it happens. I thought *you'd* be thrilled, her being white and all.
>
> **Sam:** I wouldn't wish that shit on anyone, brutha. You must think I'm one cold-hearted muthafucka.
>
> **Me:** If the shoe fits, as they say.
>
> **Sam:** Shit. Anyway, as white chicks go, she was definitely one of the coolest. I can't help but wonder that things might have gone different for yo ass if I got on this shit a lot sooner.
>
> **Me:** What happened between us had absolutely nothing to do with race. You know that, Sam.
>
> **Sam:** Nigga! Do you think everything we went through…
>
> **Me:** Everything *we* went through?!
>
> **Sam:** Stop interrupting a muthafucka when he's in the middle of a thought! As I was saying: do you think everything we went through was just about you being Black and learning how to code-switch and shit? If so, then you didn't learn a goddamn thing. Don't make me turn this book around, Ronaldo.
>
> **Me:** What did you just say?

Sam: I said, don't make me turn this book around.

Me: No. I mean, you called me Ronaldo.

Sam: Huh? Oh? So I did.

Sam gives me his coy smile and a wink.

Sam: Well, I'm glad you two are staying friends and shit. It coulda gone a whole lot different.

Me: True dat. True dat.

Sam: "True dat"? Awww, shit. I see I *do* still have some work to do.

Me: Get the fuck outta here, you jive turkey.

We look at each other and laugh as he heads over to the door.

Sam: At the end of the day, I gotta say, you one cool muthafucka. You handled yourself pretty well throughout all of this. Gotta give you mighty dap for that.

He gives me a fist bump.

Me: Thanks, Sam. I appreciate that.

As he opens the door, he turns around to say one more thing before leaving.

Sam: Stay frosty, Ronaldo. Oh, and one more thing. Hold onto your butts.

With that he lights his cig, laughs one last hearty laugh, then walks out the door as I close it behind him.

I'm not sure what he meant by that "Hold onto your butts" comment. Maybe it was just one last nostalgic call back to one of his roles. Maybe it was just his way of saying that given my new wokeness and desire to right the wrongs of the world, I can expect more exciting "rides" in life. Or maybe...

As I'm thinking this, the bell rings. I walk back over to the door and open it. There, standing in his long Black overcoat and impenetrable dark shades, is Laurence Fishburne as Morpheus from *The Matrix*.

> **Laurence:** May I come in?
>
> **Me:** Do I have a choice?
>
> **Laurence:** We always have choices, Ronald.
>
> **Me:** What is the deal with all you spirit types getting my name wrong? Anyway, sure. Come on in.

Laurence glides into the room, looks around as if stalking the joint, then points to the chair.

> **Laurence:** May I sit?

I gesture to the chair, inviting him to sit. He smooths his coat behind his legs, sits in the chair, crosses his legs, then puts his fingertips together in that wise mentor sort of way Morpheus does when he's about to drop something heavy.

> **Me:** Look. I appreciate you coming here, and I'm sure there's probably a lot more I can learn about my Blackness. But honestly, right now, I don't want anything to do with anything Black for at least a week.
>
> **Laurence:** Ahhh. I see Sam has helped sharpen your wit. Although my reasons for showing up are indeed to invite you on another quest of self-identity, it has nothing to do with your Blackness. The journey I'm inviting you on is one that will make your journey with Sam look like a stroll through Central Park.
>
> **Me:** Well, depending on what time of day you go, that could be one dangerous stroll.

I started to laugh, but Laurence wasn't havin' it. He puts his right hand into his coat's inner pocket, then pulls out a little black leather-bound book.

He places the book on the side table next to him, then taps it to invite me over to look at it.

Cautiously, I walk over to the table and look at the book. Once I see the title on the cover, I immediately know why he is here and the journey he wants to take me on. And it sends shivers up my spine.

He looks at me, removes his shades, then asks...

Laurence: Are you ready?

I take a deep breath, then look back at the book. On the cover are the words:

"The Holy Bible"

Me: Lord, have mercy.

Acknowledgments

I want to take some time to acknowledge and thank those of you who have in some way contributed to the making of this book.

To Mystère for encouraging me to write my story and for being the NaNoRiMo coach for the family.

To Joshua for being my writing buddy in coffee shops around Europe and the rec room of that WorldMark we stayed at. And for inspiring me with all the books *you* write.

To the many Trump supporters and Facebook trolls whose idiotic, inane, racist, and backward comments lit a fire beneath me and led to so much great book fodder (in particular, "Dufus Asshole," "Clueless Christian," and Pastor "Tom").

To all my friends and supporters on social media who sent me encouraging DMs, liked my provocative posts, supported and encouraged me in the comments, and defended me when the aforementioned TSers and trolls dawned their ridiculous diatribe.

To Chris Spencer for always treating me like fam, and for literally changing my life.

To the friends I made on Medium who read early drafts and gave such praise and encouragement (especially Stephen and Peter).

To Lisa McNamara and Steve Nathans-Kelly for providing early editing and feedback. Your encouragement was more powerful than you can ever know.

And last but certainly not least, to my two Black BFFs and podcast peeps, Joseph DeShawn Cochran and Yolanda T. Cochran. Thank you for clowning me when I needed to be clowned, laughing with me, debating with me, and accepting me for who I am. Thank you for showing and reminding me that I am, and always have been, *Black* (my taste in music, clothing, and my particular vernacular notwithstanding).

About the Author

Ron Dawson is a prolific top writer on Medium who's written for such leading publications as An Injustice!, Better Marketing, SlackJaw, and The Writing Cooperative. He's a filmmaker, cinephile ("cinema-phile"?), blogger, podcaster, and professional content marketer. (If you don't know what "content marketing" is, Google it—which is a pretty meta thing to do and probably a joke only a content marketer would get.)

He was host and creator of *Radio Film School,* a sort of *This American Life*-style podcast for filmmakers, which makes him kind of like the Black Ira Glass. (For a shining moment, it was the #1 visual arts podcast on iTunes.) He is the cohost and coproducer of the *Dungeons 'n' Durags* podcast, part of the Ebony Covering Black America podcast network.

He's a father of two and brother to one and two halves (half-brother from his mom's remarriage and half-sister from his dad's).

He used to dance on a semi-professional Lindy Hop troupe during the swing dance resurgence of the late '90s where his signature move was leapfrogging over his partner's shoulders and landing in the splits.

His favorite Spotify playlist is an eclectic mix of songs that includes Barry Manilow's "I Can't Smile Without You," Neil Diamond's "Song Song Blue," Blue Suede's "Hooked on a Feeling," Modern English's "I Melt With You," Marvin Gaye's "What's Going On," Tupac's "Only God Can Judge Me," and many more songs that in no other universe belong on the same f-ing playlist. (That right there probably tells you all you need to know.)

Mango Publishing, established in 2014, publishes an eclectic list of books by diverse authors—both new and established voices—on topics ranging from business, personal growth, women's empowerment, LGBTQ studies, health, and spirituality to history, popular culture, time management, decluttering, lifestyle, mental wellness, aging, and sustainable living. We were recently named 2019 *and* 2020's #1 fastest-growing independent publisher by *Publishers Weekly*. Our success is driven by our main goal, which is to publish high-quality books that will entertain readers as well as make a positive difference in their lives.

Our readers are our most important resource; we value your input, suggestions, and ideas. We'd love to hear from you—after all, we are publishing books for you!

Please stay in touch with us and follow us at:
Facebook: Mango Publishing
Twitter: @MangoPublishing
Instagram: @MangoPublishing
LinkedIn: Mango Publishing
Pinterest: Mango Publishing
Newsletter: mangopublishinggroup.com/newsletter

Join us on Mango's journey to reinvent publishing, one book at a time.

CPSIA information can be obtained
at www.ICGtesting.com
Printed in the USA
JSHW021606040522
25582JS00001B/2